D1611038

ARCHITECTURE
IN CONTINUITY
BUILDING
IN THE
ISLAMIC WORLD
TODAY

ARCHITECTURE IN CONTINUITY

BUILDING IN THE ISLAMIC WORLD TODAY

THE AGA KHAN ◼ AWARD FOR ARCHITECTURE

EDITED BY
SHERBAN CANTACUZINO
PUBLISHED BY
APERTURE

ARCHITECTURE IN CONTINUITY
BUILDING IN THE ISLAMIC WORLD TODAY

CONTRIBUTORS

Copyright © 1985 Islamic Publications Ltd.
Library of Congress Card Catalogue No. 85-047828.
ISBN: 0-89381-196-3, cloth. ISBN: 0-89381-187-4, paper.
All rights reserved under international and Pan-American copyright conventions.

Published for the Aga Khan Award for Architecture by Aperture, a division of Silver Mountain Foundation, Inc., 20 East 23 Street, New York, NY 10010. Distributed in the United States by Viking Penguin, Inc.; in Italy by Idea Books, Milan; in the United Kingdom and Europe by Phaidon Press Ltd., Oxford; and in Canada by Penguin Books Canada Ltd., Markham, Ontario.

Design by Peter Bradford, Ray Komai, and Joyce Rothschild. Copy editing by Eleanore W. Karsten. Production supervision by Stevan A. Baron. Composition by David E. Seham Associates, Inc., Metuchen, New Jersey. Color separations, printing, and binding by Arnoldo Mondadori Editore, Verona, Italy. Photographs by Stephen Shore, Kamran Adle, Chant Avidissian, Jacques Bétant, Steven B. Cohn, Reha Günay, Ronald B. Lewcock, and Jacques Pérez.

Aperture, a division of Silver Mountain Foundation, Inc., publishes a periodical, books, and portfolios to communicate with serious photographers and creative people everywhere. A complete catalog will be mailed upon request. Address: 20 East 23 Street, New York, NY 10010.

The Aga Khan Award for Architecture was established to encourage an understanding and awareness of the strength and diversity of Muslim cultural traditions, which, when combined with an enlightened use of modern technology for contemporary society, will result in buildings more appropriate for the Islamic world of tomorrow. Address: 32 Chemin des Crêts, 1218 Grand Saconnex, Geneva, Switzerland.

 The Award logo. The name of Allah in Kufic script, reflecting itself, forms the basis of the logo design.

Frontispiece: Sculpture Museum, Ramses Wissa Wassef Arts Center, Giza, Egypt. The brainchild of the architect Ramses Wissa Wassef, the center was founded to promote local arts and crafts. This museum houses the work of Habib Gorgy's students.

Sherban Cantacuzino, editor as well as contributor, is an architect, a former executive editor of *The Architectural Review* and now secretary of the Royal Fine Art Commission, London. He was a member of the master jury of the Aga Khan Award for Architecture in 1980 and a member of the Award steering committee from 1981 to 1983. He is the author of several books, including *Great Modern Architecture, New Uses for Old Buildings*, and (with Susan Brandt) *Saving Old Buildings*.

Nagineh Khaleeli, assistant to the editor, has a degree in international relations and is a researcher for *South* magazine.

Samir Abdulac, an architect and planner, is director of the Conseil d'Architecture, d'Urbanisme et de l'Environnement in Chartres, France. He is also a coordinator for regional seminars at the Aga Khan Program for Islamic Architecture at Harvard and the Massachusetts Institute of Technology and a consultant to UNESCO and other international agencies. He was a member of the techical review team of the Aga Khan Award for Architecture in 1980 and 1983.

Ihsan Fethi is an architect and senior lecturer in the department of architecture at the University of Baghdad. He is the author of *The Architectural Heritage of Baghdad* and (with John Warren) *Traditional Houses in Baghdad*.

Robert Hillenbrand is reader in the department of fine art at the University of Edinburgh. He is the author of *Imperial Images in Persian Painting* and (with Derek Hill and Lucien Golvin) *Islamic Art in North Africa*.

Doğan Kuban is professor and director of the Institute of the History of Architecture and Restoration at Istanbul Technical University, and former director of the International Research Center of Islamic History, Art, and Culture, Istanbul. He was a member of the steering committee of the Aga Khan Award for Architecture from 1978 to 1983 and is the author of many books, including *Problems and Sources of Turkish Anatolian Architecture* and *Influences of European Art on Ottoman Architecture*.

ACKNOWLEDGMENTS

Architecture in Continuity has been produced to present the contemporary architectural projects that were honored in the second cycle (1981–1983) of the Aga Khan Award for Architecture and to make manifest their symbolic, social, and cultural contexts. The introductory chapter, the survey of contemporary Turkish architecture, the essays on the mosque and the diary of a technical reviewer were all specially prepared for this volume. The Awards were presented in September 1983 and the Topkapı Palace in Istanbul at the gracious invitation of President Evren of Turkey.

Many people deserve credit for their contributions. The members of the steering committee for the second cycle were His Highness the Aga Khan, chairman, Professor Mohammed Arkoun, Sherban Cantacuzino, Sir Hugh Casson, Charles Correa, Professor Oleg Grabar, Professor Renata Holod, Hasan-Uddin Khan, Professor Doğan Kuban, Mohamed Makiya, Kamil Khan Mumtaz, and Professor William Porter. The Award office was administered by Dr. Said Zulficar, secretary general, and Dr. Suha Özkan, deputy secretary general. Those serving on the master jury were Dr. Turgut Cansever, Rifat Chadirji, Habib Fida Ali, Professor Mübeccel Kiray, Professor Charles Moore, Professor Parid Wardi bin Sudin, Dr. Ismail Serageldin, Roland Simounet, and James Stirling.

The basic information supporting the visual presentation of the prizewinning projects came first from the architects and clients of each project. Technical reviewers then gathered additional information at each site. These reviewers included Dr. Halim Abdelhalim, Dr. Samir Abdulac, Dr. Yekta Chahrouzi, Bin Haji Abdul Majid Hajeedar, Syed Zaigham Shafiq Jaffery, Darl Rastorfer, Professor Ronald Lewcock, Piers Rodgers, Raoul Snelder, Dorothée Vauzelles, and Dr. Atilla Yücel. Once collected, documents and research were developed for publication by Nagineh Khaleeli, assistant to the editor.

Of the visual material the line drawings were prepared by Walter Conquy from drawings supplied by the architects. Some of the material was supplied by Margaret de Popolo, coordinator of library programs, the Aga Khan Program for Islamic Architecture at Harvard University and the Massachusetts Institute of Technology; Dr. Brian Brace Taylor, associate editor, and Patricia Theseira, manager of production, *Mimar;* and Farrokh Derakhshani, member of the Award office.

The photographs of the Ramses Wissa Wassef Arts Center, near Giza in Egypt, of the restoration in the Darb Qirmiz quarter in Cairo, and of the Hafsia quarter in Tunis were taken by Stephen Shore. The photographs who accompanied the technical reviewers were Kamran Adle, Chant Avidissian, Jacques Bétant, Steven B. Cohn, Reha Günay, and Jacques Pérez.

Photographic credits: *Samir Abdulac: 183 (10). Kamran Adle: 22, 24, 78–79, 146–153, 181–182, 183 (9, 12). Atelier Warmbronn: 10–11. Chant Avidissian: 14. Mustafa Ayaslioğlu: 25. Cengiz Bektaş: 70 (right). Jacques Bétant: 26, 59 (right), 62 (left), 102–109, 170–177. Hadi Abdelrahman Bouchama: 21. Aydin Boysan: 73. Cafer Bozkurt: 64–65. Turgut Cansever: 69 (right). Sherban Cantacuzino: 28, 55 (left), 57 (right), 58 (left), 59 (left). Günay Cilingiroğlu: 68 (left). Behruz Çinici: 67 (left). Steven B. Cohn: 76–77, 138–145. James Cubitt: 20. Dar Al-Handasah: 13. Dar al-Islam: 54. Development Workshop, Toronto: 29. Sedat Hakki Eldem: 66 (right), 69 (left), 71. Muhammad Farra: 55 (right). Ihsan Fethi: 58 (right), 63. Reha Günay: 12, 118–127, 154–169. Robert Hillenbrand: 30–51. Muzharul Islam: 16. Muhammad Anwar Pasha: 8–9. Jacques Pérez: jacket, 110–117. Caudill Rowlett Scott: 62 (right). Stephen Shore: 2, 80–101, 128–137, 178–179, 192. Raoul Snelder: 17. Henk Snoek: 52–53, 61. Mazaffer Sudali: 68 (right). Brian Brace Taylor: 18. Ja'afar Tukan: 57 (left). Şevki Vanli: 74.*

CONTENTS

INTRODUCTION/ESSAYS

10 CONTINUITY AND CHANGE:
    ARCHITECTURE AND
    DEVELOPMENT IN THE
    ISLAMIC WORLD
    —AN INTRODUCTION
    By SHERBAN CANTACUZINO

30 THE MOSQUE IN THE MEDIEVAL
    ISLAMIC WORLD
    By ROBERT HILLENBRAND

52 THE MOSQUE TODAY
    By IHSAN FETHI

64 A SURVEY OF MODERN TURKISH
    ARCHITECTURE
    By DOĞAN KUBAN

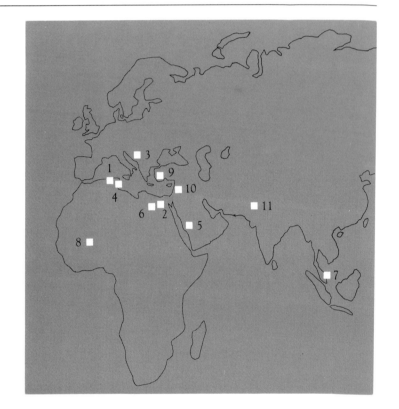

AWARDS

76 RECIPIENTS OF THE SECOND AGA KHAN AWARD FOR ARCHITECTURE 1983

78 STATEMENT OF THE MASTER JURY

82 HAFSIA QUARTER   (1 on map at left)

92 DARB QIRMIZ QUARTER   (2)

102 SHEREFUDIN'S WHITE MOSQUE   (3)

110 ANDALOUS RESIDENCE   (4)

118 HAJJ TERMINAL   (5)

128 RAMSES WISSA WASSEF ARTS CENTER   (6)

138 TANJONG JARA BEACH HOTEL AND RANTAU ABANG VISITORS' CENTER   (7)

146 GREAT MOSQUE OF NIONO   (8)

154 NAIL ÇAKIRHAN HOUSE   (9)

162 AZEM PALACE   (10)

170 TOMB OF SHAH RUKN-I-'ALAM   (11)

APPENDIX

180 TECHNICAL REVIEW By SAMIR ABDULAC

180 INTRODUCTION

180 JOURNAL OF A TECHNICAL REVIEWER

184 NOTES

191 SELECTED BIBLIOGRAPHY

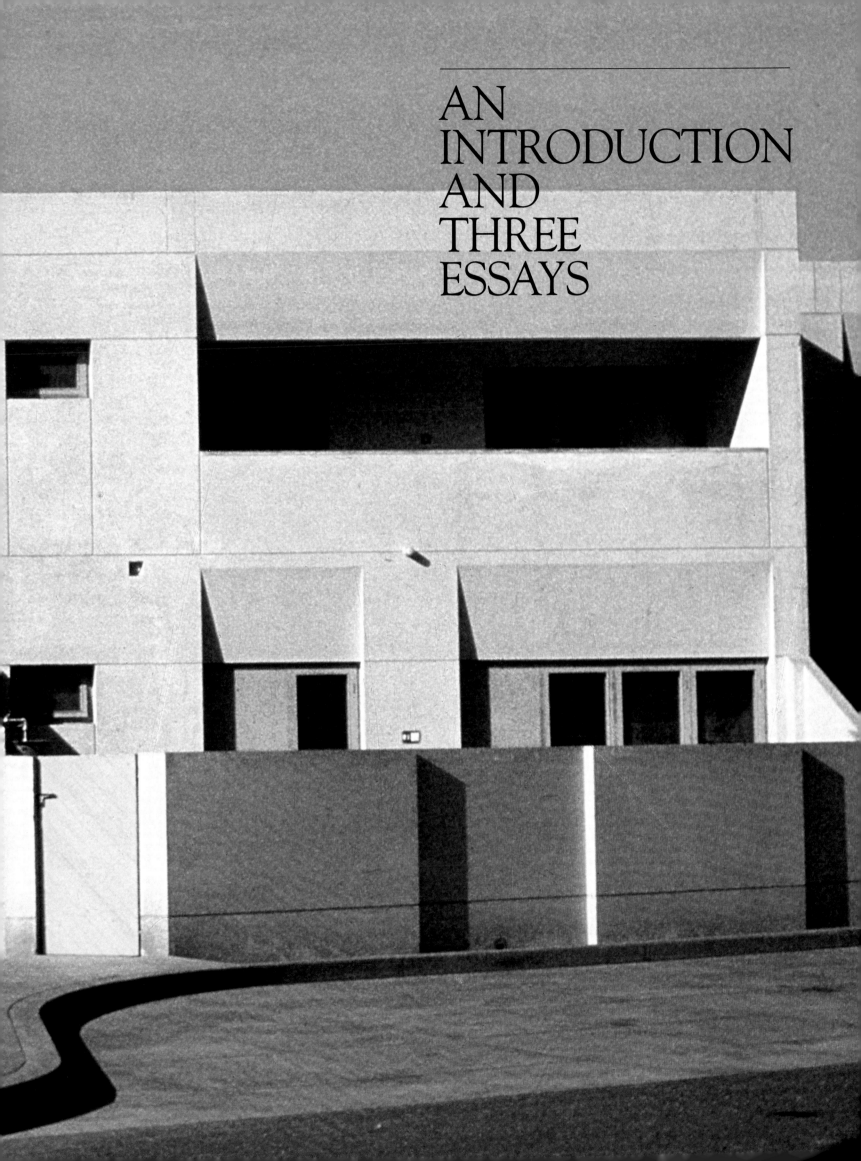

AN
INTRODUCTION
AND
THREE
ESSAYS

CONTINUITY AND CHANGE: ARCHITECTURE AND DEVELOPMENT IN THE ISLAMIC WORLD

AN INTRODUCTION
By SHERBAN CANTACUZINO

This book is not only about the second Aga Khan Award for Architecture. It also makes the three-year cycle, which culminated in the dazzling award ceremony at Istanbul in September 1983, the occasion to address some of the issues facing the Islamic world today. The central part of the book does indeed contain the eleven prizewinning projects, but they are intended to be seen essentially in the context of the other essays and particularly of this introduction. The introduction is intended to place each of the projects in the wider perspective of the 350 or more nominations received by the Award since its inception in 1978 and so of development in the Muslim countries generally. To assist this scene-setting endeavor, the eleven prizewinners have been grouped under headings that will enable the reader to relate each one to some of the major problems that seem to lie at the root of all development in Muslim countries and that will form the substance of this introduction. These problems, which are of course closely interconnected, can best be stated antithetically: the influence of the Western postindustrial world and the aspirations of the receiving country; the conservation of the built environment and new infrastructural needs; and the migration to the towns and depletion of the countryside.

Implicit in these bald propositions are complex ramifications, subsidiary problems, and arguments that extend far beyond planning and architectural considerations to religion, to politics, and to life as a whole. Underlying them all are two questions: how can traditional cultures be maintained or revived without losing the benefits of modern technology, and how can the separate identities of these cultures—the regionalism of Islam—survive in the face of modern views and methods that seek everywhere to standardize and unify? For the strength of Islam has always lain in unity through diversity— the unity of Islam itself through the diversity of its multifarious cultures.

This book is also the occasion to review the aims of the Award, its achievements, and its method of operating. It

Tents near Mecca for hajj *pilgrims, by Atelier Warmbronn. Consisting of a tubular-aluminum frame on extendable legs designed to deal with rough terrain, each tent is lightweight and easy to assemble. It combines traditional form with modern technology. Pages 8–9: Housing for Pakarab Fertilizer Company workers, Multan, Pakistan, by Muhammad Anwar Pasha. Pasha has succeeded in creating a fully landscaped environment in the desert.*

cannot be stressed too strongly that the Award is not merely an institution that gives prizes for good buildings every three years. These prizes are the tip of the iceberg and must be seen both in the immediate context of Award activities as a whole and in the wider context of the Aga Khan's other initiatives related to the built environment. Award activities include seminars, field trips, architectural surveys of countries, and documentation; other initiatives include the Aga Khan Program for Islamic Architecture at Harvard University and the Massachusetts Institute of Technology, and the quarterly architectural periodical, *Mimar* (Arabic for "builder"), which looks beyond the Muslim world to the whole of the Third World. All these activities constitute in Mohammed Arkoun's memorable phrase "a space of freedom"[1] in which ideas can be discussed without any of the restrictions on freedom of thought that the ideologies dictated by political totalitarianism invariably impose.

The eleven prizewinning projects of the 1983 Award are given pride of place and space, not because they are architectural masterpieces or even exemplars, but because they constitute, in the words of the master jury, "accomplishments in a continuing search for relevant forms and designs."[2] Already the jury for the 1980 Award had concluded that the best projects "represented not the ultimate in architectural excellence, but steps in a process of discovery,"[3] and had identified seven categories among the fifteen prizewinners. The 1983 prizewinners are grouped under four headings that incorporate, with one exception, the categories of the previous jury. Thus under "Urban Scale" the Hafsia quarter in Tunis and the Darb Qirmiz restoration project in Cairo can be seen as further steps in developing "Social Premises for Future Architectural Development," which was the jury's category in 1980 for the Kampung Improvement Program in Jakarta and the Pondok Pesantren Pabelan in Central Java. The social implications of upgrading a whole area, whether in the medina of an Arab city or in a self-built settlement in Southeast Asia, are similar, and both can be regarded as a form of urban conservation that improves the quality of life and preserves or makes good the

Lassa tire factory, İzmit, Turkey, by Doğan Tekeli and Sami Sisa (above), and one of the state secretariat buildings, Sokoto, Nigeria, by Dar Al-Handasah (right). The huge complex at İzmit is the only factory nominated for a 1983 award. The plan of the state secretariat building, one of eight housing the needs of various ministries, is developed around courts.

fabric of the city. The restoration of seven monuments in Darb Qirmiz, on the other hand, was seen by the client and consultant as the first step in the eventual rehabilitation of the whole quarter, but emphasizing the social aspect of the project in this way is not intended to diminish its importance as an example of conservative restoration of the kind William Morris, the nineteenth-century English poet, artist, decorator, and printer, among other things, would have approved.

Under "Reinterpretation of Traditional Form," Sherefudin's White Mosque at Visoko in Yugoslavia, one of the Dar el-Andalous apartment hotels at Sousse in Tunisia and the Hajj Terminal in Saudi Arabia also reflect the "Search for Consistency with Historical Context" and the "Search for Innovation," which were both categories identified by the master jury in 1980. The structure of the Hajj Terminal is in a class by itself, highly innovative in its technology and form, yet profoundly traditional in spirit. It carries the attribute of all great classical architecture, in which the beauty of the part gains immeasurably in the whole through repetition and rhythm. In 1980 the innovative projects were either wholly innovative without any reference to history (the water towers at Kuwait City) or personal and romantic in their reinterpretation of traditional form (the Inter-Continental Hotel and Conference Center at Mecca). On the other hand the two prizewinners by Turgut Cansever in 1980, the Ertegün house at Bodrum in Turkey and the Turkish Historical Society at Ankara, remain unrivaled for their architectural brilliance and at the same time are admirably suited to their settings and functions.

The third heading, "Continuing Tradition," includes the Ramses Wissa Wassef Arts Center at Harraniya, near Giza, in Egypt; the Tanjong Jara Beach Hotel and the Rantau Abang

Visitors' Center located respectively sixty-five and fifty-five kilometers south of Kuala Trengannu in Malaysia, the Great Mosque of Niono in Mali, and Nail Çakirhan's own house at Akyaka in Turkey. The equivalent category of the 1980 jury was "Contemporary Use of Traditional Language," and it included two buildings inspired by the noted Egyptian architect, artist, and poet Hassan Fathy, the Halawa house at Agamy in Egypt and the Mopti Medical Center in Mali. All these examples, and particularly the Great Mosque of Niono, should be seen as part of a continuing tradition in areas where the traditional building crafts survive. This continuing tradition, however, is not to be confused with the revival and reproduction architecture now common in the West. The difference is eloquently revealed in the reply of the mosque's master mason, Lassiné Minta, to the question, "How do you do the design?" I try to understand all the requirements of the client," came the answer. "I go to the site and try to understand all the problems of the site. Then I talk to the material."[4]

The last heading, "Restoration," also had its equivalent in two of the 1980 categories, "Restoration" and "Preservation of Traditional Heritage." In 1983 it included the Azem Palace in Damascus, more a re-creation than a restoration and an example of reuse, and the Tomb of Shah Rukn-i-'Alam at Multan in Pakistan. In 1980 it included four projects, among them the conservation of the whole village of Sidi Bou Said near Tunis, and the extensive restoration of Safavid monuments at Isfahan in Iran, the documentation of which, by the Italian Institute for the Middle and Far East (ISMEO), has a parallel in 1983 in the documentation undertaken by the German Archaeological Institute in Cairo of the Darb Qirmiz

monuments. The fact that seven out of the eleven prizewinning projects come under "Restoration" or "Continuing Tradition" is evidence of the importance the Award attaches to forms that derive from the traditional building crafts and to the need for continuity that in the past was sustained by the craftsmen. While this emphasis is understandable at a time when the Award may still need "to nurture within the architectural profession and related disciplines a heightened awareness of the roots and essence of Muslim culture," it is to the other half of the argument, "a deeper commitment to finding meaningful expressions of the spirit of Islam *within the context of modern life and modern technology*"[5] (my italics), that it will sooner or later have to turn.

The category missing in 1983 was the "Search for Appropriate Building Systems," under which the Agricultural Training Center at Nianing in Senegal had received a major prize in 1980 "for developing a labor-intensive building system into a complete architectural language, revitalizing masonry construction and providing a model for a number of projects in Senegal."[6] The structure of the Hajj Terminal could be considered a building system, but it is clearly a unique solution to a unique problem and cannot therefore meet one of the essential criteria, that it provide a model for other projects.

So much for a brief introduction to the prizewinning projects of the 1983 Award and for a broad comparison with those of the 1980 Award. There will be further reference to several of these when the three previously identified problems that lie at the root of nearly all development are discussed. A more general examination of the range of nominations for both Awards, which follows, will provide a background for the prizewinning projects, as well as an argument for some of the remaining contents of the book.

In 1980 the master jury remarked that "certain areas . . . were not fully represented, such as educational buildings, mosques, community centers, and public offices."[7] Conscious also that architecture must become capable of meeting the urgent needs of Islam's impatient masses, it urged that the search for appropriate forms of low-cost housing should be intensified. In a recent statement[8] the Aga Khan identified the following issues for the Award's attention: high-technology building and the way modern construction materials should be used in the future; the conservation of old Islamic cities; institutional buildings such as schools and hospitals; low-cost housing; industrial buildings; and architectural education. Taking the last point first, the fact that there has not yet been an Award seminar on architectural education and training represents a serious gap that should be filled as soon as possible. To anyone who has traveled and lectured in the Muslim world it must be only too evident that many schools of architecture are still teaching design as an outdated Western-imported exercise in aesthetics largely divorced from the realities of time and place.

An analysis by building type of the nominations for the 1983 Award reveals that out of more than 200 projects some thirty were for low-cost housing or basic shelter. The jury selected seventeen of these, more than half, for their initial short list of sixty projects to consider for prizes. That the Hafsia quarter, a scheme that set out but failed ultimately to cater to the needs of the lower-income residents of the medina, was the only urban housing project to receive a prize, is evidence of the difficulty a jury consisting mainly of architects is always likely to face with a building type that is more often than not architecturally flawed. The Hafsia project is in fact being continued with a third phase in which the mistakes made in the earlier phases will be put right by cross subsidies to ensure that some of the housing will go to the poor of the district.

Educational buildings, which were so underrepresented in 1980, numbered thirty in 1983. Eighteen of these were for higher education, including university buildings, training schools, and research centers, while the remaining twelve were for primary and secondary education and included school building programs in Algeria and Libya. The program of twenty-one schools in Benghazi Province, Libya, by the Italian firm Valdadige Spa uses a prefabricated construction of painted concrete panels that is typical of the worst kind of system building in the West and that should never have been exported. It contrasts sharply with the three schools in the M'Zab area of Algeria by Michel Boursay, Gildo Gorza, and F. Dath of the Établissement Regional Saharien d'Architecture, d'Urbanisme, et d'Environnement (ERSAURE, an organization set up by André Ravéreau, a French architect who has worked extensively in Algeria), which have a degree of standardization in their plans but are built of locally made cement blocks (in one case of stone) and with forms that fit in with the local architectural tradition.

There were, on the other hand, only two nominations in 1983 for hospitals and clinics, though a number of housing schemes included health facilities. There was nothing comparable to the Mopti Medical Center, which won a major prize in 1980. One of the 1983 nominations, the Rashid Hospital in Dubai, United Arab Emirates, by the London-based firm of John R. Harris and Partners, with offices in Paris and the Middle East, is an efficient and attractive Western-type hospital in an oil-rich, cosmopolitan city on one of the major international air routes. The other nomination was a small single-story clinic for prenatal and pediatric care in a suburb of Ouagadougou in Burkina Faso by the Association for the Development of African Urbanism and Architecture (ADAUA), built of mud brick with its rooms planned informally around a central courtyard. The two extremes, the uninhibited use of Western technology and the reliance on an age-old local building tradition are again in evidence.

The almost total absence of industrial buildings in the nominations for the Award cycles must be a cause for concern. It cannot be attributed merely to the fact that many Muslim countries as yet have little industry, or refuted by including buildings for agriculture and the crafts. There is after all North Africa and the countries bordering the eastern Mediterranean, where industrialization has been proceeding apace. It is not altogether surprising that the only example of a factory in the 1983 nominations came from Turkey, and it is at least some compensation for the low quantity that the quality of this example is so good. The Lassa tire factory by Doğan Tekeli and Sami Sisa, situated about 50 miles from Istanbul in an industrial area, is impressive by any standards. Rational in plan and appropriate in design language and use of a building technology that has improved existing technology without exceeding local

Private house, Luxor, Egypt, by David Sims and Oliver Seduaoui. The plan is organized around a large central courtyard and four small courts. Domes and vaults are built of mud brick.

needs and capabilities,[9] the vast complex is possessed of an order and a monumentality that raises it well above the level of ordinary building.

Among the 1983 nominations there were seventeen mosques, of which two won prizes, Sherefudin's White Mosque and the Great Mosque of Niono. In 1980 only one mosque was chosen for the short list, the Said Naum Mosque in Jakarta, and none received a prize. The essays on the mosque (pages 33 and 53) are therefore timely. The first, by Robert Hillenbrand, a lecturer in art history at the University of Edinburgh, looks at the mosque in the medieval Islamic world. Having examined the origins of the mosque, its constituent parts, its various functions, and its standard characteristics, Hillenbrand continues with a discussion of the various types of mosque and of the role played by decoration. It is written in such a way that any architect embarking on the design of a mosque today can make use of the information that it contains—and that he will ignore only at his peril.

The second essay, by Ihsan Fethi, looks at the mosque today and at some of the problems faced by an architect designing a new mosque. Two recent architectural competitions, with a total of more than 460 entries, are analyzed. In addition some twenty-five examples of new mosques and mosque designs serve to illustrate the various styles and categories identified by the author. Fethi reveals that whereas in the Madrid Islamic Cultural Center Competition of 1980 the great majority of entries were designed in a contemporary style, in reality today most new mosques are built in a traditional manner. He warns against the dangers of using imported high technology as a form or expression—as an end in itself—and cites Ricardo Bofill's design for the Baghdad State Mosque Competition, in which the columns of a hypostyle hall are also service ducts made of prefabricated hollow sections, as an example of high technology that is used as a legitimate means to an end.

The dichotomy present in Western-imported technology on the one hand and traditional building techniques on the other—in modernism and Islam—is illustrated in a curious but telling example given by Fethi. A mosque in Ankara designed by a Turkish architect, Cengiz Bektaş, has a *mihrab* (prayer niche oriented toward Mecca) with Koranic inscriptions in the Latin alphabet. In Turkey, it was Kemal Atatürk who introduced the Latin alphabet and the European concept of the secular state. To use the Latin alphabet for a Koranic inscription neutralizes to a large extent the symbolic value of the inscription, not only because the Arabic script is traditionally and irrevocably associated with the Koran in people's minds, but also because the Latin alphabet is equally irrevocably associated with European culture.

In the past the mosque made up, as Hillenbrand remarks, for the "lack of formal urban institutions . . . with a corresponding lack of certain types of formal public buildings."[10] As the center of community activities the mosque once served many purposes. That it now serves many fewer is characteristic of a tendency, apparent not only in the Third World but also in Europe and America, to separate functions into specialized buildings and into specialized rooms inside buildings. This tendency, however, does not appear to have improved the architectural quality of such specialized buildings. In fact the former lack of urban institutions continues to be felt in the generally low level of design in public buildings today and in the fact that such buildings tend to be transported Western models, like the Pakistani government secretariat complex in Islamabad by Gio Ponti, Antonio Farnaroli, and Alberto Rosselli, a project nominated for the 1983 Award. Buildings like the state secretariat complex at Sokoto in Nigeria by Dar Al-Handasah Consultants (nominated for the 1983 Award) or British architect Sir Leslie Martin's government offices at Taif in Saudi Arabia (not nominated but presented at the Award seminar held in Amman, Jordan[11]), with their spreading forms and use of courtyards, create shade and control natural light in a traditional way. At the same time they availed themselves of technical advances in structure and services. They remain the exception and constitute a positive step in the search for appropriate forms.

Some of the more remarkable exceptions are in Turkey, as is made clear by Doğan Kuban, a specialist in the history of Islamic architecture and preservation, in his essay on recent Turkish architecture (page 65). The decline of religious architecture and the rise of the public building as an identifiable type can no doubt be attributed to the sixty years of secularism that the country has experienced since Atatürk's revolution. The search for form through a synthesis of modern building technology and traditional principles of design is evident in a number of public buildings, among them Turgut Cansever's Turkish Historical Society and Bektaş's Turkish Language Institute, both in Ankara.

Kuban's essay is based on the first country-wide building survey undertaken by the Award and coincides with the publication of the book *Modern Turkish Architecture*.[12] One reason for including this chapter is the fact that Turkey (perhaps a similar case could be made for Egypt) is some fifty years ahead of most Muslim countries. Westernization began in the nineteenth century, modernization in the 1920s. There have already been two national revivals in architecture, and a third seems to be on its way. For other Muslim countries there are both good and bad lessons to be learned by studying modern Turkish architectural history.

One of the good lessons is Sedat Hakki Eldem's seminar at the Academy of Fine Arts in Istanbul on the Turkish house and his systematic study of traditional architecture, which he began in 1932. Developing a theory of architecture must remain the concern of the architect and one of the Award's primary aims. Theory is impossible without knowledge, and Eldem's research is an important contribution to that knowledge and so to the development of a theory. The need for greater knowledge in fields less directly related to, but nevertheless having an important bearing on, architecture has more recently been identified by Mohammed Arkoun, a professor of Arabic and Arabic literature at the Sorbonne, writing about the Maghrib and its cultural independence.[13] The conditions for this independence, he writes, are the promotion of historical studies that would include the search for, and the editing of, the many important Arabic manuscripts still lying around undiscovered, and to which must be added ethnographic research and a systematic ethnological analysis of the Maghribian space. Elsewhere[14] Arkoun warns that studies of this kind are useless unless they "break . . . with the doctrinal history that glorifies the Golden Age of Islam by restricting itself to the great authors and to the so-called representative works, by despising the age of so-called decadence, by ignoring the vast field of oral culture ('pensée sauvage'), which neither scholarly Islam nor the *charia* (religious law) have ever quite succeeded in taking on board: all of which accounts for the persistence, effervescence, and resurgence of beliefs and practices, and of narrations carried on by the common people."[15]

This argument could well be extended to include the study of both monumental and vernacular architecture. Indeed the architect Nader Ardalan has proposed an inventory of all the major Islamic buildings in the world,[16] while the study of vernacular architecture has become fashionable in academic institutions. The argument could be extended further to include the study of Koranic quotations, especially on minarets, and nonarchitectural visual symbols such as the hand of Fatima and the Crescent, neither of which appears to have been properly investigated.[17] The problem, however, is not one of research only, for it is likely that the research carried out in an academic institution will never reach the practitioner in the field in a way in which it can be of use to him. The problem, therefore, is also one of communication, and that in turn raises the question of the language that makes a communication possible. The reinterpretation of traditional forms and the integration of modern with traditional forms—such as the best of the Turkish examples achieve—need to be analyzed and that analysis disseminated through an organ that transcends the national context, in a language that can be understood but does not yet exist.

The bad lessons to be learned from modern Turkish architectural history come from the period between 1960 and 1980, when the growth of industry and business, stimulated by a market economy, and the migration of the rural population to the towns resulted in the creation of hideous environments and the spoliation of areas of great natural beauty such as the shores of the Bosporus and the environs of Bursa. One of these lessons is the impossibility of pursuing conservation objectives without adequate legislation. Another is the threat to regional distinctions, which become less and less pronounced as development for profit imposes consumer models on what is often little more than a subsistence economy. The ready instrument, architecturally speaking, of both nationalism and the consumer society during those twenty years was the International Style, the continued entrenched strength of which among Turkish architects is represented, according to Kuban, by "the triad image of technology, urbanization, functionalism."[18] The universalism of the International Style is inimical to the diversity and regionalism of Islam, and it is precisely against this universalism that both Turgut Cansever and Nail Çakirhan are fighting with their very different architecture. The renewal of architecture can take place only through a regionalism that transcends national boundaries and first overcomes, as Arkoun has pointed out, the obstacles of nationalist, culturalist, and spiritualist illusions.[19]

Before turning to the three previously identified problems that lie at the root of nearly all development in Muslim countries, it is necessary to say something about the organization, process, and activities of the Award and, in doing so, to introduce the author of the diary contained in the appendix, Samir Abdulac. In his capacity as one of the 1983 technical reviewers, Abdulac has contributed a vivid account of his work "on location" in Tunis. Technical review is the gathering of essential documentation on site of a short-listed project, and is therefore a key step in the Award process, without which the master jury could not function convincingly. The success of a technical review depends on the thoroughness and objectivity of the reviewer and on his ability to communicate the information to the jury both in writing and in an oral presentation. Abdulac's was an exceptionally interesting and successful program. In addition to the project described in the appendix, he reviewed the Lassa tire factory and two projects that won prizes, Nail Çakirhan's house and the Hafsia quarter.

The executive arm of the Award is the office of the secretary general in Geneva, where the documentation of nominations and related information about building development in the Islamic world is collected and put in order and where all other Award activities are organized. The executive is directed by an international steering committee, of which the Aga Khan is chairman; the committee meets twice a year, as well as on the occasion of Award seminars, when most of its members are likely to be present.

The assessment of projects is carried out at three distinct

levels and at different times in the three years of each Award cycle. The first assessment is made by the nominators, of whom there are at least two in every Muslim country and every non-Muslim country with a significant Muslim minority, and who are selected by the office of the secretary general. Nominators are briefed on the concerns and aims of the Award, and are asked to nominate only projects that have been completed and have been in use for at least two years, so that client and, especially, user reaction can be taken into account. Nominators identify the project, its client, and its architect. The material for each nomination is then requested from the client and architect by the office of the secretary general and comes back in the form of drawings, transparencies or prints, and written information filled in on standard Award forms.

The second assessment concerns the short-listed projects only, and is made by the technical reviewer, usually an architect, who is appointed by the steering committee. He or she visits, investigates, and documents the project in depth, with the help of a photographer and an efficient local resident, who makes appointments, organizes entry, and obtains the necessary permits.

The third and final assessment is made by the master jury when it selects the prizewinning projects. Appointed by the steering committee in time to take part in one or two seminars and become acquainted with the aims of the Award, the jury relies largely on the technical reviewer's presentation of each of the short-listed projects to make its choice.

There were some important differences in the Award procedures for the first and second cycles. In the first cycle (1978–1980) the steering committee reviewed all the nominations and compiled the short list. The jury met only once. In the second cycle (1981–1983) the jury met twice, the first time to examine all the nominations and make choices for the short list. In the third cycle (1984–1986) anyone may identify a project to be considered for nomination. These early proposals, which are being submitted to the office of the secretary general, are then vetted by the steering committee, and the projects that pass are sent to the relevant nominators for acceptance or refusal as formal nominations. Finally the steering committee will review all nominations and make selections for the short list, and the jury will probably meet only once as in the

E-type housing for workers at a limestone mining and cement complex at Jaipurhat in northwestern Bangladesh, by Muzharul Islam (left), and a general view of Maader, an experimental village near M'Sila, Algeria, by El-Miniawy architects (above). The village is built of mud bricks made on the site and consists of units of four houses grouped around a shared courtyard, each house having in addition its own private courtyard.

first cycle, having first discussed the main issues with the steering committee, to select the final prizewinners.

These changes have stemmed from two problems: the belief that the master jury ought to see all the nominations (to which the counterargument is that a steering committee with long-serving members is always likely to understand the concerns of the Award better than a one-time jury); and the need to improve the quality of nominations (which is part of a general need for more and better information). It is this that prompted the Award from the beginning to sponsor field trips and, more recently, to commission countrywide building surveys. Field trips are valuable because they can be undertaken quickly and frequently, and regular visits to the same country over a period of time could result in a series of reports providing an invaluable record of development and change. Country-wide building surveys take longer and also need updating. They are more difficult, indeed impossible in some countries, to organize, but they are probably the only way of providing an exhaustive account of building activity and so are the ultimate source of information for the Award.

The nominations, which covered projects completed since 1950 in the first cycle and since 1955 in the second, are beginning to form the basis of a substantial documentation, and one of the questions for the Award is how to make use of this documentation once it has served its immediate purpose of project selection for prize giving. One obvious possibility is to make the documentation available to *bona fide* students. Another is to use it as a source for exhibition material. A traveling exhibition of some thirty projects, selected thematically or by building type, could have considerable impact, especially if it is made the occasion in each place for lectures, articles, and television programs. Yet another possibility would be to use the documentation as the basis for a series of videotapes or a

film. The data could also supply material for a newsletter that would provide regular communication with the large numbers of people who have come in contact with the Award.

Of the related Award activities the most important have been the seminars and the Award ceremonies, which at Lahore in 1980 and at Istanbul in 1983 incorporated a short seminar. Three main purposes have been served by the seminars: to learn from the actual seminar and to develop criteria for the Award; to inform the host country of the Award's aims; for Award personnel to inform themselves about buildings and building activity in the host country. There have so far been eight seminars, the published proceedings of which are listed in the bibliography. The seminar subjects range from building types such as urban and rural housing to conservation and more abstruse subjects such as symbolism in architecture. Recently a program of regional seminars has been introduced, the first of which, on "The Search for Identity in Architecture," was held at Kuala Lumpur, Malaysia, in August 1983.

The problem with all seminars has been the difficulty in developing a coherent follow-up program. The question has been asked whether the Award should remain an observer or develop a program of intervention. After the seminar on "Reading the Contemporary African City" at Dakar, Senegal, in November 1982, it was felt that the Award might consider helping young architects, who would otherwise move to the more lucrative private sector or become bureaucrats, in their efforts to tackle local issues such as prototypical housing or improvements in techniques and materials, the purpose being to help the process rather than the person. It was also felt that the Award should make the seminar an opportunity to publicize and advance the good ideas and projects happening in the host country through the periodical *Mimar* or a newsletter and by recommending technical or financial help.

At the end of the seminar on "Development and Urban Metamorphosis" held at San'a, Yemen Arab Republic, in May 1983, William Porter, who teaches at M.I.T. and is director of the Aga Khan Program for Islamic Architecture, proposed a means of giving "imaginative leadership to the underlying goals of reestablishing Yemen's great building tradition and bringing it into a close relationship with Yemen's contemporary life and cultural values."[20] He recommended for this purpose

Sher-E-Bangla Nagar, the capitol complex, Dacca, Bangladesh, by Louis Kahn. The building contains the great hall of the National Assembly. Its principal axis is established by the entrance hall on one side and a mosque on the other.

the establishment in Yemen of a National Institute of the Building Arts and Sciences. At the same seminar the idea also emerged for a pilot project on urban design in the Islamic world that would involve the support of the country concerned and various international agencies. These are exciting ideas, but they are likely to remain ideas unless the Award, possibly through another organization, develops them into realities.

Among the difficulties that have emerged during the seven years of the Award's existence two in particular need to be singled out and dealt with. The first is the large number of prizewinning projects in each of the the two cycles (a maximum of five prizes was originally proposed) and what some would consider the consequent dilution of the Award's impact. One suggestion made for trying to reduce the numbers was that each cycle be focused on a related set of issues, which would provide the nominators with clearer guidelines on what they should be looking for, thereby improving both the quantity and quality of the nominations. Another suggestion presented was to create categories for each prize—housing, public building, conservation, etc.

The second difficulty is the establishment of criteria. The Award has done well in reorienting attention toward what is appropriate in building. Thus a design must be appropriate to the climate, culture, life-style, and economy of a particular place, and in certain circumstances be replicable to qualify for consideration. But these are negative criteria in the sense that none of them will guarantee a fine building. The Award has therefore tended to fall back on the principle of consensus, or generally recognized quality. It has also tended to avoid a positive definition of Islamic or "in the spirit of Islam" when applied to architecture by denying that the mere application of traditional Islamic forms will make a building Islamic. At best Islamic has been interpreted as an expression of life. "When one talks about Islamic architecture," the Aga Khan said in a recent interview, "one is talking about the way in which people who practice the Faith of Islam around the world express themselves in their buildings and in their environment generally. . . . Islamic buildings have in the past also sought to enhance the unity and sanctity of the family. These elements of the Faith are common to all peoples of Islam. They should

be part of the thinking of building design in the Islamic world."[21] And John Warren, an English architect who has worked extensively in the Middle East and is building in Baghdad, has said much the same but from a practitioner's point of view: "Islam is manifested in a way of life, and if that life is reflected in the way the architecture is used, and if the architecture used is sympathetic to that way of life, then it will become Islamic. But I cannot make it Islamic by sticking things on it."[22]

The question remains, however, is that enough? Should the Award attempt a more specific definition by reference to local life-styles and building traditions as it has already done implicitly by awarding prizes to such projects as Nail Çakirhan's house and the Ramses Wissa Wassef Arts Center? Or should the Award draw attention more to what Doğan Kuban has called the search for "an identity with the past through formal relationships"?[23] Examples of the latter are also to be found in the Awards, namely Turgut Cansever's two prizewinning projects (1980 and 1983), and with a more spectacular input of imported technology, the Hajj Terminal and its microequivalent, the mountain tents for *hajj* pilgrims (a nomination only). The use of mud brick or the provision of privacy in a house are not exclusive to Islam and would not necessarily be recognized as Islamic. Forms that have evolved as a result of local conditions and life-styles on the other hand may be perceived as Islamic in a particular context, because people there may attach a meaning to them. The portal on the street and the courtyard on which the principal rooms of the house are centered remind one of Islam and so assume symbolic value.

But if the courtyard house in, say, Fez, Morocco, is perceived as Islamic, to live in a courtyard house is no longer the aspiration of its owner, the bourgeois of Fez who has moved out to a suburb to live a Western-style life in a Western-style villa and own an automobile. At best the architecture that results may attain some relevance to local conditions, for example, the Alemi apartment block in a residential suburb of Tehran, one of the nominations for the 1983 Award and an accomplished scheme planned around two courtyards and built of local brick. Individual courtyard houses among the bourgeoisie, such as the beautiful house at Luxor designed by David Sims and Oliver Seduaoui and built by local labor with vaults and domes of mud brick, are the exception. Although such a house (the Halawa house at Agamy in Egypt) won a prize in 1980, it must remain a matter of debate whether it is the revival of traditional building crafts and forms or the ability of those forms to adapt to contemporary living requirements that makes a building of this kind Award-worthy. In other words, can the plan and section of the building, with its various spaces and their relationships, have wider application by becoming a model for building development and construction methods other than purely handcrafted ones?

In this context of the influence of the Western postindustrial world and the aspirations of the receiving country, a word is necessary about Nail Çakirhan's house in Anatolia, a 1983 prizewinning project that aroused a great deal of criticism among members of the architectural profession in Turkey. One well-known Turkish architect claimed that a clique had given a prize to a building that was merely a copy of the old and therefore not creative.[24] He derided Çakirhan for indulging in a nostalgia and a sentimentality calculated to have wide popular appeal. In fact Çakirhan's house has a type of plan and a structure that have been used in Anatolia since the time of the Hittites, so that it is no more or less a copy of the old than any of its predecessors. Çakirhan set out to show that there was no need to build concrete boxes in an Anatolian village. His house should not be seen as the *résidence secondaire* of a bourgeois, but rather as a model for the kind of house construction the villagers can afford. Neither should its popularity be seen as a disadvantage at a time when the International Style, especially the cheap "concrete box" aspect of it, is so universally disliked.

If, to quote Kuban again, "the old bourgeois is the motor of the changing ideals of the society,"[25] the rural population, the immigrants, and the great mass of workers become the instrument through which governments can propagate their ideologies. Two examples of factory workers' housing, for a fertilizer company in Pakistan and for a limestone mining and cement works in Bangladesh, are more like Western imports than homegrown specimens, even if they make use of local materials and labor. The fertilizer company is in Multan desert country and reminds one that most Muslim states are in the arid or semiarid parts of the world. "For a long time," Mohammed Arkoun has written about the Maghrib, "the constraints of the environment made sobriety (*qana'*) and frugality (*kafaf*) the most recommendable virtues. The ideology of development increases needs and the push to satisfy these needs; this is contrary to the life-style that is in keeping with the environment."[26] Algeria has experienced industrial development and agrarian reform that have "fostered a dislocation of traditional structures, a marginalization of craft activities, a repression of so-called regional cultures in favor of activities promoted by standardized forms of education, as all-powerful mass media, and a production and exchange system that is typical of production-oriented economies."[27]

In contrast, for the 1983 Award there were several nominations from Algeria, one of which was the experimental village of Maader near M'Sila, one of the thousand new villages of the agrarian revolution. The architects, El-Miniawy, believe that it was the first attempt in Algeria at using only local materials, in the form of earth stabilized with cement, for the housing and public buildings. Since the villagers were nomads, it is difficult to talk about the appropriateness of permanent housing to life-style. The housing is certainly appropriate to

the local climate and economy, and the cluster of four units around an open space for the women, each house also having its own courtyard, allows for social interchange as well as privacy. Typical of a production-oriented attitude, however, the government as client had divided housing into three categories—urban, semiurban, and rural—so that the brief, which at the beginning did not even include the courtyard, failed to relate satisfactorily to people's needs. It was only after the architects had finished building several projects in Algeria that the government came to appreciate the importance of some of the missing elements and agreed to accept them.

Another nomination from Algeria for the 1983 Award, also by the El-Miniawy architects, was a middle school for 800 pupils at El Oued. If this school represents that standardized form of education that poses a threat to regional cultures, it must also be said that as a building it responds to the harsh climate, fits the needs of its users, and establishes a quietly impressive presence in its flat, arid surroundings.

A government, according to Arkoun, "always makes itself greater by supporting all the levels of cultural creation. It diminishes itself by censuring the activity of the mind, even when it puts forward some holy principle, such as national unity."[28] There are many examples of governments' expressing their ideologies through architecture among the nominations for the two Awards. Since the ideologies are mainly of Western origin, it is not surprising that the expression is also mainly Western. Louis Kahn's monumental capitol complex in Dacca is magnificent architecture, but as a group of freestanding buildings expressing national unity and the central power of a secular state it is essentially Western in concept and goes against the notion of Islam's inseparable entities *din* (religion), *dunya* (secular world), and *dawla* (state power). That Kahn succeeded in endowing his buildings with a rich vocabulary of forms, which contains powerful residual references to the monumental tradition in Islamic architecture and is now influencing a whole generation of architects in Bangladesh, may help the buildings be assimilated into the local culture.

Before such assimilation can take place, however, it is necessary for the very purpose of the buildings to be assimilated. This argument applies also to the late English architect James Cubitt's campus-style University of Garyounis at Benghazi (a 1983 nomination), and even to the unfinished University of Qatar by Kamal El-Kafrawi, which is much more obviously Islamic but may in fact be a Western idea of what is Islamic seen through the Western-trained eyes of a Muslim architect. Arkoun has pointed out that secularization, whether of the state or of education, has not yet occurred in Islamic societies, not because Islam has been opposed to this for doctrinal reasons, but because "the social groups in major Muslim countries have experienced neither historical continuity nor the creative tensions that social classes in the West have experienced."[29]

If industrialization is espoused by governments in the belief that it will bring economic independence, Islam is espoused as a political weapon. An example as expressed through architecture is the Hussein Dey Islamic Center and College in Algiers, a university for 2,000 students and part of a program to turn Algeria into an Islamic republic. Its form, a response no doubt to the brief and an apt if disagreeable expression of the ideology, is a vast freestanding symmetrical block, which is more like the Palace of Versailles, than a traditional mosque or *madrasa* (Koranic school), despite the lavish use of minarets and arches.

A different but equally dangerous attempt to control architectural style by decree, which might have provided a lesson to other countries, was the experience of Turkey in the 1930s during the second national revival. Architecture, the state ordained in an attempt to revive regionalism, was to make use of local building materials and construction methods. Historical building elements were to be modernized while modern materials, if used, were to be covered up. Earlier styles of Turkish architecture would be studied to provide inspiration. The state, on the other hand, would adopt one specific style for all pubic buildings, and there would be a jury to determine this style and control its application. The legislation was never fully realized, however, and an admirable idea (to revive regionalism), wrongly carried out, largely failed to materialize.[30]

The architects practicing in the Islamic world have no option but to work within all kinds of constraints, including ideologies that direct the way people think. The Award, on the other hand, is in the unique position of being able to offer these architects and the other specialists involved in development "a space of freedom" in which to express themselves. Much more needs to be known about the forces at work in each society, and the research necessary to acquire this knowledge must be inclusive and comprehensive, and therefore free from control by governments intent on pursuing ideologies that distort the truth by exclusion. The Award with its "space of freedom" could become the catalyst for this research and for an uncensored dissemination of the resulting knowledge.

It is also true that not enough is known about the way traditional systems work, and about the implications of replacing these systems with modern technology. It has taken a long time, and far too much inappropriate and inefficient building, to understand the microclimatic system of the traditional courtyard house in hot, arid zones. Even so there are as yet few examples of the application of this system to new housing and of its integration with modern technology. John Warren has attempted it in his redevelopment of the Kadhimiyeh area in Baghdad. Starting with the assumption that the Iraqi families living in the houses would want television, water coming out of the taps, air-conditioning and an automobile, he has designed two-story courtyard houses with cross ventilation to all the rooms, air-conditioning for use in the heat of the summer, and a basement for vehicular access to private garages, refuse collection, and servicing of shops.

More problematic, however, has been the effect of transferring new technology to an area where buildings, because of their impermanent structure, have been regularly rebuilt. Although in theory there is the freedom to choose the degree of permanence and how one uses the new technology to achieve that degree, Warren remains adamant that in Baghdad only a fully permanent solution is acceptable. "We now have the capacity," he said, "to make permanent buildings where temporary buildings once stood. We can now make our timber resistant to termites; our waterproofing does not have to be renewed every time it rains; and so we are imposing a permanency upon an urban structure that was hitherto always in a transient state."[31]

One of the most illuminating examples of incomprehension and incompetence, as told by Ronald Lewcock,[32] an architect and restoration specialist, is the disastrous result of changing the house drainage system in San'a on the advice of international consultants. The drainage system was part of a complete sewage cycle, which began in a shaft carrying the soil through the house to a masonry box, where it remained until it became odorless. The box was then opened by a man whose hereditary job it was and the contents removed to be dried in the sun and burned as fuel in the public baths, the ash of that human waste becoming fertilizer for the vegetable gardens inside the walls of the city. The international consultants not only failed to understand the beauty of the old system, but substituted for it a water-borne sewerage that leaks and stains the faces of the walls, causing unpleasant odors and eventual disintegration and collapse of the structure.

Wrong advice and the misapplication of technology are so common that Africa, according to an article in the London *Times* has become "a white elephant's graveyard of abandoned factories, unmaintained roads, collapsing bridges, and vast dams producing disastrous side effects."[33] A dam near the Mali–Burkina Faso border, for example, has been sited in the wrong place, with the result that the reservoir is too extended and shallow to prevent rapid evaporation of the water after the rains. The fundamental problem is of course overpopulation, with an increase of 2.7 per cent every year in the Sahelian countries, which has led to overgrazing, soil exhaustion, and deforestation. Tree cutting for fuel has left strips of desert on either side of the main roads leading out of Ouagadougou, the capital of Burkina Faso. In other parts of the Sahel, in Niger for example, there are villages where the roofs of the houses are made of wood and thatch, contributing to desertification. A commendable project by the Development Workshop (Toronto), which was nominated for a 1983 Award, is the Village Literacy Center at Chikal in Niger. The building is for the study of the Hausa dialect, but its importance lies more in the fact that its construction was part of a training program for local masons in the use of mud-brick arches and vaults to provide an alternative to the use of wood and thatch.

A successful example of transferring technology to produce an appropriate building is the Solar Energy Research Center

(ONERSOL) at Niamey in Niger, by Laszlo Mester de Parajd, a French architect attached to the Ministry of Public Works of Niamey. Constructed employing local labor, the building consists of load-bearing walls of mud brick, stabilized with cement, supporting steel trusses of local manufacture. The use of mass and weight in the wall structure deserves attention because one of the most common practices all over the Third World is to erect a steel frame and to infill between the cement blocks. Using steel in compression in this way is a temptation, usually irresistible, to make the infilling wall, which does not have to be load-bearing, too thin to provide the necessary insulation against a harsh climate. The ONERSOL building, which was nominated for the 1983 Award, is intended, as Brian Taylor, an architectural historian and managing editor of *Mimar,* has written, "to serve the objectives of a solar energy program through project conception and experimentation toward practical applications, but it is also a physical structure inspired by traditional local architecture and building materials. Thus it was from the outset designed as a *model* of self-reliance in terms of style, materials, and energy consciousness."[34]

In turning to the second great problem that lies at the root of development in the Muslim world—the conservation of the built environment versus new infrastructural needs—it may help to recall that nations everywhere, in the words of the Aga Khan, "are attempting to reconcile the conflicting demands of maintaining their own cultural identities and yet achieving technological progress."[35] One way of helping to resolve this conflict is by finding new uses for old buildings, thus providing the opportunity not merely to maintain the fabric of the old building but to introduce completely new standards and services. One of the 1980 prizewinning projects, the Rustem Pasha Caravansary at Edirne in Turkey, was an example of such a new use, the disused caravansary being converted into a modest hotel. For the 1983 Award there were several such nominations and one prizewinner, the Azem Palace in Damascus, Syria, which has been converted into a museum. Among the nominations were the Dar Lasram, a nineteenth-century house in the medina of Tunis, converted into a cultural center; the Ksar Haddada at Tatahouine in Tunisia, formerly a communal Berber grain storehouse in the form of multiple vaulted cells, converted into a tourist hotel; the medieval Khan Marjan in Baghdad, converted into a restaurant; and the large sixteenth-century Palace of Ibrahim Pasha in Istanbul, converted and extended into a museum and conference center. More ambitiously in Jidda a number of old houses have been restored by the municipality and are awaiting new uses, while in the UNESCO pilot study for Fez the possibility was examined of using traditional houses for primary schools, dispensaries, and social centers.

While new uses for old buildings is unquestionably an important aspect of conservation, the purpose here is not to discuss the preservation of individual buildings. Many Muslim countries already have organizations that look after the protected monuments and sites, and the 1983 Award included among the prizewinners a magnificent restoration of such a monument—a fourteenth-century tomb in Pakistan—which was also made the opportunity for training craftsmen so that they could continue their restoration work elsewhere. The purpose here is to discuss concepts that hardly exist in Muslim

University of Garyounis, Benghazi, Libya, by James Cubitt (left), and the Hussein Dey Islamic Center and College, Algiers, by Hadi Abdelrahman Bouchama (above). Whereas the Libyan university is planned on the principle of separate buildings linked by covered routes, the Algerian university is a huge symmetrical block.

countries—the concepts of group value in buildings, of spaces between buildings, and of area conservation in cities. One of the reasons why these concepts do not exist is the undivided attention that, under Western influence, has been given for so long to freestanding monuments. This is perhaps the reason why so many Islamic urban monuments, which are traditionally buried in the dense fabric of the city, have been made freestanding in the process of restoration by the demolition of the buildings around them.

But then, why is conservation necessary at all? Oleg Grabar, chairman of the fine-arts department at Harvard and a specialist in Islamic art and architecture, has argued provocatively that "monuments, like peoples and cultures, may best be left to die, that antiquarianism in architecture is a peculiarity of a very limited Western elite and that preservation is a form of congealing a meaningless past, at best useful for flag waving."[36] It is certainly true that in much of the Muslim world, where the traditional architecture no longer receives the regular maintenance required by the transitory nature of the materials it is made of, there is an urge to demolish the past, to redevelop, and to modernize. Yet the answer to the question, "Is conservation necessary?" lies in the paradox, as expressed by Sir Ernst Gombrich, a great historian and philosopher, that it is precisely this "rapidity of change that increases the psychological need for permanence."[37] A second answer is the realization that the old buildings often do their job better than the new ones. It should perhaps be a condition of demolition that the new building must be better than the old one it is replacing. Third, the realization that the earth's fossil fuels are a finite resource has made it clear that no one can any longer afford to demolish buildings that are basically sound. This is not only because old buildings are usually more efficient in energy conservation than new ones, but also because the actual work of rehabilitation or conversion in energy terms costs a mere fraction of constructing a new building. Lastly, and relating to this last point, is the fact that rehabilitation is labor intensive. It creates employment and keeps both the small and the large builder busy, whereas comprehensive re-development and the erection of high-rise buildings rely on factory-made parts and mechanical assembly, which only the few large construction companies can undertake.

The word "conservation" means the act or process of pre-serving something in being, of keeping something alive. And in keeping something alive—in this instance anything from a single building to a whole city quarter—it may be necessary to infuse new activities. Conservation does not exclude either demolition or new construction; it does not, in other words, exclude change. Speaking in the context of the Third World, Hasan-Uddin Khan, editor-in-chief of *Mimar* and a former convenor of the Award, has warned that "in the rapidly mod-ernizing societies . . . so long as *conservation* is equated with *conservatism*, with looking back and not forward, it will be regarded as an impediment to development."[38] There is no need, however, for conservation to be seen as retrogressive if it is treated as an integral part of planning. A conservation policy for a particular area must indeed take into account the wider planning issues. It must take into account social and economic factors; and it must address itself not only to the problems of historic preservation, but also to new development and therefore to the problems of height and density and of the infrastructure.

Before embarking on a planning policy for a particular area, it is essential to find out as much as possible about its buildings. Knowledge of this kind is essential to the planner and con-servationist, because without it he cannot develop a theory; and theory is important because it is the systematic statement of principles concerning, in this instance, the action of keeping a building or group of buildings alive. Bernard Feilden, Eng-land's leading conservationist architect, has said that "in any architectural problem the first task is survey and analysis; with building conservation it is important to understand both the building and the reasons for its preservation; the more im-portant the building, the more painstaking must be the back-ground work, and the more likely it is that individual decisions will have to be justified. The integrity of a building as archi-tecture depends on its design and its fabric, full knowledge of which, in their primary and secondary aspects, may require documentary research besides physical examination and 'opening up.' "[39] Feilden goes on to suggest four stages for this process: a general report, a detailed and meticulous inspection, historical analysis, and an in-depth structural investigation.

Such a survey should not be limited to architectural quality, historical interest, and physical condition. It should include an analysis of the uses to which buildings are put, and of the local economy generally. Even more important it should iden-tify the inherent dynamics of the place, i.e. the mix of people and of uses, as well as movement by people both on foot and in vehicles. Controlling, stimulating, and if necessary changing the inherent dynamics of a place must be a fundamental task of planning if the conservation of individual buildings and groups of buildings to keep them alive is to have any meaning.

Village Literacy Center, Chikal, Niger, by the Development Work-shop, Toronto. The use of mud brick, and consequently of vaulted and domed forms, avoided the use of timber for the roof.

As a result of such a survey the condition of every building would be recorded, and it would become possible to build a maintenance plan into a conservation program. William Morris once said, "Stave off decay by daily care." His advice is par-ticularly relevant to traditional Muslim architecture, and once upon a time it was heeded. Such daily care and maintenance of buildings is a neglected subject today, yet it uses about one-third of the resources of the building industry in the West, and it deserves far more consideration. In fact if maintenance plans were written into the rehabilitation of old buildings, not to mention the construction of new buildings, they would en-sure that the cost of the conservation on the scale that exists in Europe and America today never would be necessary again.

Once an inventory exists, it becomes possible to identify and schedule specific buildings or specific groups of buildings for protection and to identify and declare areas for conser-vation. It is, however, difficult to start protecting historic buildings in a city in which market forces have always deter-mined the pattern of development. A building is threatened when the market value of the site is greater than the market value of the building, and since historic buildings are usually found in historic city centers, there cannot be many that do not fall into this category. In these circumstances it becomes necessary for the planning authority to make a deal with the building owner by offering him another site to develop.

Financing conservation projects is often considered irrel-evant in the Third World. The economic crisis, as the Aga Khan has pointed out, is making it difficult for governments to treat conservation as a priority. So conservation has to make economic sense.[40] This is very much easier if whole areas are designated rather than individual buildings. For Stefano Bian-ca, the author of the UNESCO pilot project for Fez, the major problem was not posed by individual monuments but by the conservation and rehabilitation of the traditional housing stock as a whole;[41] and for Roy Worskett, an English architect and conservationist, housing has been the center of attention in all successful conservation work. In his proposals for Hyderabad, India, the large conservation areas identified were called neighborhood improvement areas and were mainly concerned with the rehabilitation of the existing housing.[42] In the walled Pakistani city of Lahore all essential services have been installed for $72 (U.S.) per person, and most of the money spent is being recovered either through loan repayment or through municipal taxes. Kamil Khan Mumtaz, one of the architects involved in the upgrading of the walled city, has redefined conservation: "Upgrading of the utility services in the streets in order to upgrade a neighborhood, bringing in community services, schools, and community centers is one thing. Conservation of historic buildings or areas is another. . . . Upgrading a city I see as part of the larger conservation effort."[43]

This book is not the proper place for a detailed discussion of the mechanics of project finance. Ismail Serageldin, an architect and planner in charge of the Urban Projects Division of the World Bank and an acknowledged authority in this field, emphasizes the importance of being clear in one's mind what is to be preserved before deciding on ways of financing. In talking about preservation, conservation, and the rejuvenation of the economic base, it is important to ask, what is one trying to preserve? A number of major buildings, as in the Darb Quirmiz project in Cairo? The urban character, as in the Jidda conservation project? Or a way of life, as in the upgrading program in the walled city of Lahore? "Clearly each answer," Serageldin states, "is going to generate a completely different set of solutions."[44] Good projects should pay for themselves, and every country should tailor the kind of project it undertakes to the kind of financing it can afford. There are basically three sources of financing: governmental, institutional, and personal—the people themselves. A public/private partnership works best, and Serageldin cites as an example the Kampung Improvement Program in Indonesia, one scheme of which in Jakarta won a 1980 Award, where the individual house owners invested some of their own resources in the project. To encourage the private sector to invest in this way, it is necessary to create incentives through grants, taxation, and cross subsidies, the last proving particularly effective in the latest phase of the Hafsia-quarter project in Tunis. Encouraging the private sector to take an active interest is also important, because it is the first step in public participation, without which no conservation and rehabilitation effort is likely to succeed.

If the owners of the land and users of the buildings can be persuaded to collaborate in a conservation program, the question of the ownership of the land is not important. What is important is to have a strong planning authority with a sound administrative structure and legislation that works when it is applied. For example, the *awqaf*, the government agency that in most Muslim countries now owns and looks after the old pious-foundation properties, should not be exempt from planning procedures or planning legislation. In a number of countries the setting of a monument is protected by law, but if the local mullah decides to build an extension on his mosque, he cannot usually be stopped or directed to carry out the work

in a particular way, still less to pull down the offending part. Thus it is relatively straightforward to enact legislation that enables a planning authority to schedule buildings, declare conservation areas, and lay down planning-application procedures, but quite another matter to make this legislation part and parcel of punitive measures that must be upheld—but often are not—by the courts.

Most of the formal problems of urban conservation have their roots in the increase in scale resulting from modern needs and modern building techniques. The automobile, which it is everyone's ambition to possess, has imposed roads of a new dimension and in a gridlike pattern alien to the organic pattern of old Islamic cities. These roads have in turn attracted development along them that may be in scale with the new roads but is an offense to the surviving traditional low-rise buildings behind. It infringes on privacy, destroys the microclimate and scars the historic townscape. A conservation policy that looks at whole areas instead of single buildings or sites and that is part of a wider planning policy can help prevent tall buildings from rising in the wrong place by ensuring that developers make up their losses on one site by being offered the opportunity to build on other sites in the area or in the city as a whole. If conservation areas had been correctly identified and officially registered, the modern roads that now cut through the old urban fabric of cities like Aleppo in Syria and Isfahan in Iran would have followed a very different line, or not been built at all. The modern roads exist, however, and the problem is often one of reconciling two scales. One of the most interesting attempts to do this—a kind of prototype—is the Bab al-Sheik project in Baghdad by Arup Associates and Carlfried Mutschler and Partner. It consists of two long blocks lining a boulevard, with commercial activities at street level and housing above. Each block has a five-story vertical face on the street side, but steps down to two stories at the back, where it meets the conglomeration of traditional courtyard houses. From the old quarters, therefore, it looks, not like a wall or barrier, but like a built hill, the stepping also helping to break up the massive form and so relate the new scale to the old.

Either a new road destroys the cohesion of a quarter, or the absence of such a road threatens the viability of the quarter. One of the major objectives of Stefano Bianca's master plan for Fez was to improve accessibility from the periphery without splitting the old city into pieces. This was to be done by a number of radial cul-de-sacs for public transport and servicing. Short feeder roads of this kind, which are not linked so as to discourage through traffic, can be frequent and quite narrow, and can wind their way between existing buildings so that they cause the minimum of destruction. This principle was also adopted by Bagher Shirazi in a proposal, which predated the revolution in Iran and was never realized, to improve service to the languishing but by no means inactive bazaar in Isfahan. The pragmatic way Shirazi intended to carry out his proposal was even more uncharacteristic of the city planner. He proposed to build one feeder road first and to observe its effects before proceeding with the others.

The concepts of conservation areas and area conservation are important because they help to make conservation part of overall planning policies. They are important, too, because they discourage the treatment of buildings as monuments and

direct attention to spaces between buildings. But it is precisely in this space between buildings that a difficulty arises. In the cities of the Third World the great out-of-doors is treated as a rubbish dump. Doğan Kuban has drawn attention to the inability of recently industrialized societies to appreciate the inorganic nature of industrialized objects. "Between the dirt road, which is still ready to absorb the organic waste, and the asphalted surface, which cannot absorb nylon bags, the difference has not been consciously understood by the new city dweller. He still acts as a peasant in a natural environment."[45] This problem is likely to be solved only by education, and certain countries such as India already include environmental training as part of their school curriculum. Also the fact that some Arab countries, notably Saudi Arabia, Kuwait, and Qatar, are building zoological gardens, town parks, and recreation centers may help to persuade a new generation of Muslims that outdoor public spaces deserve as much respect as private indoor ones.

In his essay on recent Turkish architecture Kuban hardly discusses Turkish urban planning, stating bluntly that it was a failure because the dimensions of urban problems were beyond the intellectual, economic, and technical potential of city administrations. Yet some attempt must be made to solve not only the urban problem of immigration but its negative side: the decline of agriculture and the depletion of the countryside. The two sides are inextricably linked, for, as Abdou Diouf, President of Senegal, pointed out at an Aga Khan Award seminar, "There is no solution to the urbanization of cities without development of rural regions."[46] The populations of the Third World have always been predominantly rural (four-fifths, or 800 million, of China's population, for example), but for the last thirty years large numbers have been migrating to the towns. Egypt's rural population, for example, was 67 per cent in 1947 but is only 50 per cent now. The reasons for this are clear: increased population; limited availability of land for cultivation; neglect of the countryside and villages; neglect of

rural housing and the decline of vernacular building; lack of employment opportunities and, conversely, great employment expectations in the towns; and most significantly, the myth of the great city as magnet. A rural economy can be destroyed by importing grain to keep down food prices (as has happened in Mauretania and Burkina Faso), by concentrating resources on industrialization (as has happened in Algeria), or just through insufficient investment in agriculture (as has happened in so fertile and agriculturally developed a country as Iraq).

It follows, therefore, that urban and rural policies together must form an integral part of social, economic, and physical planning. Not that the trend of migration to the towns is ever likely to be reversed. Not only is the myth of the city too powerful, but rural values have themselves been affected by the exposure to city life of immigrants who maintain close connections with those left behind. Nevertheless some way of checking the explosive growth of cities must be found and, to begin with, a hierarchy of settlements from the metropolis to the village, with a clearly defined role for each type of settlement, should be established. Charles Correa, an Indian architect and planner, has suggested that the holding capacity of the villages should be increased, and that market towns and smaller cities should be identified as growth points, with all new investments directed there. More radically, he advocates "a new kind of community which is quasi-urban, quasi-rural, with densities high enough to support an educational system and a bus service, yet low enough for each family to keep a buffalo or a goat—or a banana tree."[47] In China, for example, there is a need for new market towns to gather together remote scattered villages, especially in the northwest and southwest. In Egypt there has been a policy to build both independent new towns and satellite towns specifically to relieve Cairo. In Syria such a policy might have saved the Damascus oasis.

The purpose in every case is to reduce the differences between town and country. To achieve this governments have to promote economic growth and social well-being in the rural sector. In a paper based on the preliminary findings of the research carried out at the Development Planning Unit, University College, London, deputy director Babar Mumtaz and Emma Hooper identify two aspects of rural development policies: socioeconomic and physical.[48] The socioeconomic aspect includes organizational policies for a more effective production control and distribution of goods and services, and for improved education, health, and social services. it also includes agricultural policies such as financial, marketing, and distribution measures, and policies aimed at greater access to land or its more efficient and equitable apportionment. The physical aspect is subdivided into infrastructure, settlement, and shelter. Infrastructure is in turn divided into social infrastructure (land and buildings required for improved education, health, and social services) and physical infrastructure (water supply and disposal, sewerage and sanitation, electricy and power, roads and access).

An example of organizational policies is the encouragement by the government of the Yemen Arab Republic of the use of cooperatives and the development of food-processing industries. An example of agricultural policies is the provision in Saudi Arabia, a country where less then 1 per cent of the land is under cultivation, of generous agricultural loans; and an

Dar Lasram, a nineteenth-century house in the medina of Tunis, converted to a cultural center by Arno Heinz (left), and the Palace of Ibrahim Pasha, Istanbul, Turkey, converted by Mustafa Ayaslioglu to a conference center (above). The conversion of the palace in Istanbul includes modern elements like the windows and staircase in the courtyard.

example of physical infrastructure is the extensive program being undertaken by the Yemen Arab Republic, which includes electrification, the improvement of telecommunications, the development of water resources and water purification, sewage disposal, and road building to link remote areas to the national network. Perhaps the most remarkable and far-reaching achievement is China's way of solving rural energy needs. By 1975 there were seven million biogas tanks, in which human and animal wastes, stems and leaves of every kind, garbage, and other organic matter fermented and produced methane gas, which could be used as fuel, while most of the nutrient component of plants provided high-quality organic fertilizer. This method has the additional advantage of preventing soil erosion and the destruction of farmland that used to result from the old method of collecting fuel—stripping the plant covering from the earth's surface.[49]

Under the heading "Settlement" the paper distinguishes between production-motivated settlements (agricultural) that come about as a result of, say, irrigation projects; production-motivated settlements (nonagricultural) that come about as a result of the construction of dams for the generation of hydroelectric power; consumption-motivated settlements like the *Markaz* centers in Pakistan, which are intended to provide the rural community with better access to education, health care, banks, and communications; and conservation-motivated settlements like the Forest Settlement program in Thailand, a project set up with the Food and Agriculture Organization (FAO) to convert migrant cultivators into settled farmers. Examples of production-motivated settlements as a result of the

construction of dams are the Volta Resettlement Project (begun in 1961), where the government saw an opportunity of establishing a settled and more efficient type of farming; the Aswan Dam in Upper Egypt (begun in 1960), where the resettlement of 70,000 Nubians went hand in hand with the promotion of rural industries and the establishment of social-service centers and agricultural cooperatives;[50] and the Euphrates Dam in northern Syria with its 80-kilometer-long lake (begun in 1968), which provided 70 per cent of the country's electricity and added 600,000 hectares of irrigated land.

Finally "shelter" brings one to housing itself and provides a convenient bridge to urban development, for the problems of building rural and urban housing are much the same. Mumtaz and Hooper suggest six ways in which governments may promote house building.[51] The most obvious way, but also the most expensive, is to provide complete houses, as was done for New Nubia in Egypt and for the Socialist Village Experiment in Algeria.[52] Another way is to provide building elements, as was done in Ghana through the Roof Loans Scheme, which enabled house owners to obtain vouchers through their village housing societies that could be exchanged for roofing sheets, purlins, and hardware. Providing building elements encourages industrialization, whereas providing complete houses or even parts of houses encourages prefabrication, which usually requires government subsidies and cannot compete with traditional building methods.

A third way is to provide finance for building—to subsidize people rather than houses. This has been more successful in towns than in villages. The greater poverty, lower literacy, and small numbers of rural populations have tended to make relatively sophisticated financial transaction unworkable. Yet another way is to provide land either with or without services. "Sites and services" programs are now generally regarded as an effective way of promoting housing in urban areas where development is dense and cost benefit self-evident, even if land speculation by individuals often defeats the objective of housing the poorest sectors of the community. In the more extended rural areas the provision of services is less common, and the size of plot is related to the owner's income and not to the size of his household or to his needs.

A fifth way of promoting house building is to provide improved building materials. Attempts to produce concrete panels to replace conventional wall construction, and asphaltic or reinforced-concrete sheets to replace galvanized iron and asbestos cement corrugated roofing have so far met with little success. As a fairly typical example of building material or component research in the Third World, Mumtaz and Hooper give a low-cost housing program carried out with German technical assistance by Jordan's Royal Scientific Society's Building Materials Section. It embarked on this program without first establishing what people could afford to pay for housing, by what means and methods different households managed to house themselves, what the breakdown of construction costs was between labor and materials, and even more basically what were the needs of the users. "Instead the researchers launched straight into the development of a concrete walling system which is probably too precise, too technical and requires far too fine a tolerance level to ever allow it to be appropriated by the local house-building industry—quite

regardless of whether or not the costs of the houses so produced will be 'low' in terms of the poor in rural areas."[53]

Perhaps the most rewarding and durable way of promoting house building is by providing organization and training. This presupposes self-built housing in the sense of construction initiated and managed by the householder but with the help of professional advice and skilled paid labor, an updated version of the site *mistri,* or mason/carpenter, who helps to this day with the design and construction of the house in the small towns and villages of India. Among the groups that are able to provide this type of organization and training are the Association for the Development of Traditional African Urbanism and Architecture (ADAUA), the Development Workshop, the Intermediate Technology Development Group (I.T.D.G.), and Lauri Baker's group in India. The Development Workshop is based in Toronto and I.T.D.G. in London. ADAUA, on the other hand, operates through bases in Burkina Faso, Mauretania, Senegal, and Geneva. At Rosso in Mauretania ADAUA has built housing for 400 families with the help of the local population, a project that was nominated for a 1983 Aga Khan Award. Plots were given to householders and drinking water was provided. A brick factory was established and workers were trained in the use of local materials and management skills to encourage self-sufficiency. In all its operations ADAUA relies on international financing and the support of local authorities. It runs three workshops with the intention of ultimately handing over their administration to local people. One workshop is for the development of architecture and town planning, and for the implementation of

Anguri Bagh housing, Lahore, Pakistan, by Yasmeen Lari. Built three stories high around terraces and courtyards, the project was intended for low-income families but succumbed to speculation.

mass housing and community building projects. Another is for research into local building materials, including demonstration tests of materials and structures such as mud-brick domes. A third workshop is responsible for sociological surveys and for organizing low-income residents to work for the community.

The Development Workshop has undertaken projects in Iran, Oman, the United Arab Emirates, Egypt, Niger, Indonesia, and Angola. Its Village Literacy Center at Chikal in Niger has already been mentioned in another context. In Lorestan, a rural area in southwest Iran, the workshop initiated a program for the development of indigenous architecture, training ninety youths in local building crafts, developing the technique of vault-and-dome construction and setting up brick and lime kilns. There were three phases of development: planning, design, and construction; research into local building technology and builder training; and the establishment of industries for local building materials. The workshop prepared a regional plan as well as a town plan for Alashtar (the major town of the area) and designed and built three *hammams* (baths), seven schools, two health centers, five centers for cooperatives, five housing projects, and a gasoline station.

A recommendation for organization and training that was not taken up was Hassan Fathy's suggestion for New Nubia that an architect be attached to each cluster of houses in Old Nubia to live with the people so that he could study human needs, living patterns, house plans, and methods of construction. Each architect would then be asked to design the new houses in the resettlment zone for the people of the cluster to which he was attached, the government merely providing the infrastructure. Fathy proposed setting up a training center at which a handful of master masons would train Nubians to build with mud brick. Two masons and four assistants would take forty-five days to build one house.[54] The negative response to these proposals, while understandable in the exceptionally sensitive political climate generated by the project, was symptomatic of the suspicion in which self-build activities were held by officialdom at that time.

Fathy's approach is epitomized in an interview he gave in Beijing in 1983. "Over many centuries," he said, "people in each part of the earth have learned by trial and error how to deal with their housing and environment. They have adapted the rhythm of their life to it, and their habitat and clothes. The solutions they found were not the result of scientific thinking, but grew out of the experience of generations of builders who kept what worked and rejected what did not, and these solutions were handed on in the form of tradition." Today the architect builds *for* people but no longer *with* them, and it is this trend that Fathy wanted to reverse in New Nubia. The possibility must be created and the rights reinstated for the user/owner to make decisions in the planning, design, and construction of his house.

In a developing country the people are its greatest resource. Eighty percent of the populations of the Third World build their own houses, and any housing policy should recognize and define the role of the popular sector as distinct from the public and private sectors, which by themselves cannot satisfy housing needs. The proof of this lies in the vast areas of so-called informal housing—of self-built shantytowns—which now engulf cities such as Cairo, Istanbul, and Karachi. More than 50 per cent of the population of Ankara, Istanbul, and İzmir live in such shanties. In Cairo the population has increased fourfold since 1950 (from 2.4 million to more than 9 million) and the current increase is 350,000 per year, of whom 50,000 are probably migrants. It is the same with the built area of Cairo, which covered 100 square kilometers in 1950 and 220 square kilometers in 1980. Altogether between 10,000 and 12,000 hectares of fertile land are being consumed yearly by the expanding cities of the Third World.[55]

Subsidized housing by government has invariably proved too expensive. Too often, as in the case of the Anguri Bagh housing in Lahore, it has also been taken over by people better off than those for whom it was intended. The result nearly everywhere is an acute shortage of housing for the urban poor and the proliferation of shantytowns, which in Cairo have been estimated to constitute 70 per cent of all new construction. The existing housing stock, moreover, usually cannot help relieve this shortage, because rent control puts maintenance, let alone rehabilitation, out of the reach of most landlords. One way of countering the hurtful effect of rent control on the fabric of old buildings is to bypass the landlord by taxing the tenant who is benefitting from rent control (as is now being proposed in India) and applying this tax to the repair and maintenance of the building, which has suffered as a result of rent control.

While cost, production, and quantity are obviously of fundamental importance in any housing program, such material factors cannot be discussed without considering the quality of design, layout, and environment that results. Thus even the Delhi Development Authority's housing program, one of the most successful in terms of quantity and production, cannot provide a substitute for the variety and liveliness of informal housing. The prescribed form (in Delhi, four-story walk-ups) and the absence of any participation in the planning and design process by the users must inevitably lead to uniformity and sterility. Dakar's self-built satellite, Pikine, which now has a population of 400,000, was originally the result of slum clearance followed by the allocation of building plots to the dispossessed. In an eloquent advocacy of the shantytown Italian architect Giancarlo De Carlo describes "the irrepressible vitality of the place: the streets overflow with activity—men and women dressed in dazzling colors move with astonishing elegance along the paths, which trace their erratic ways in the sand."[56] Public facilities are never concentrated in one place, the various parts of the urban fabric are not "specialized" and, consequently, human life is not compartmented. The simple houses (two rooms divided by a loggia) become complex with use "because the configuration of the compound is constantly changing by the addition or removal of tiny volumes, according to the changing need of the inhabitants, or the different seasons, or the gradual growth of the single tree which spreads its shadow over an ever wider area."[57]

This is not to advocate self-help as a universal panacea for housing. Babar Mumtaz has observed that "nearly every country (rich or poor, east or west) has had some self-help program or other . . . and nearly every one has failed. Failed in the sense that self-help has not proved to be the magic answer to all the housing problems its advocates promised or presumed."[58] What is needed is for government to exercise a degree of control over the informal sector, thereby making the fullest use of its people as a resource in solving the housing problem. Government should control land use and provide infrastructure. It should encourage local people to take initiatives and responsibilities, for "it is most important of all, perhaps culturally essential," as the English architect and planner John F. C. Turner has pointed out, "that people share responsibility for the management, maintenance and modification of their own homes and neighborhoods, where most life-time is spent and which are the greatest material investment people make."[59] Housing must be centrally supported, not centrally supplied. The role of government, which should be redefined, is to guide and channel rather than to control and impose. Architects, says Turner, must now concentrate on developing the tools and procedures for local planning and building design *by* people, and it is noteworthy that the Union of International Architects competition for the UNESCO prize in 1984, which was set by Turner, challenged students of architecture to present themselves as tool-makers and enablers of local planning and design, not as end-product designers.

Architects as well as engineers and small-scale local contractors were involved in the Kampung Improvement Program in Jakarta, begun in 1969 to improve the living conditions of the migrant communities who were living in temporary houses with bamboo roofs and walls, and earthen floors. The program

Terrace houses constructed by the Fenghuo People's Commune in Shaunxi Province, People's Republic of China, near the city of Xian (above), and rural housing in the Lorestan area of Iran, by the Development Workshop (right). Both projects are examples of self-reliance, the Development Workshop improving on indigenous building techniques and setting up kilns to fire brick and lime at the Lorestan site.

has concentrated on the provision of basic services through a policy that accepts, adapts, and improves the existing environment, and makes use of existing community organizations. To the credit of the Jakarta authorities such a policy was preferred to slum clearance and the relocation of displaced families in standard mass-housing apartments. The prizewinning project of the 1980 Aga Khan Award demonstrated how the infrastructure was sensitively designed to fit into the existing layout with minimum disturbance of the existing houses, and how the program succeeded in persuading the residents themselves to upgrade their houses even as improvements were being made to their environment and living conditions as a whole.

Self-built houses are usually single-story structures planned around one or more courtyards where essential activities such as cooking and sleeping can take place. It has been estimated that in much of the Third World the usability coefficient of a courtyard is slightly greater than half that of an enclosed room. The usefulness of private courtyards, however, declines sharply as buildings get taller. Charles Correa has observed that "a courtyard flanked by single-story buildings is for sleeping; with two-story surrounding buildings you can still cook;

five stories and it is suitable only as a children's play area; ten story's relegate it to the role of a parking lot."[60] Municipal authorities and planners tend to equate high densities with height and give the need for high densities as the excuse for not allowing low-rise development, which consumes precious land, extends communications, and increases the cost of the infrastructure. Yet it is a fact that as building heights increase, say, twentyfold, gross neighborhood density increases only about fourfold, and that over the city as a whole, doubling the densities in the residential areas, which occupy only about a third of the total city area, would make very little difference indeed. Correa also points out that the specification for one-five-, and twenty-story buildings vary dramatically, a multistory building (whether of five or twenty floors) having to be built of brick and reinforced concrete, not because the weather demands it (as is the case in Europe), but for structural strength. Low-rise or venacular structures on the other hand, can be made of a wide variety of local materials at a mere fraction of the cost. Multistory housing, moreover, can be produced only by a few builders who can handle the technology and finances involved, whereas "money invested in vernacular housing is pumped into the economy at the bazaar level, just where it generates the greatest amount of tertiary employment."[61]

What then needs to be done for self-help in the housing field to stand a better chance of success? First and foremost the authorities or public sector should recognize the contribution of the popular sector to housebuilding by preserving the existing informal housing areas together with their multifarious commercial and industrial activities. As in the Kampung Improvement Program, infrastructure in the form of essential services should be installed and incentives provided for each person to improve his house. Second, the public sector should maintain an adequate land bank to be able to allocate plots to the urban poor for "sites and services" projects, with or without core house units. Housing programs, as Alfred Van Huyck has pointed out, must have low *per capita* operating and capital costs with the possibility of recovering the cost from the householder. They must provide opportunities for self-help and participation, and they must be capable of change and simple to administer. The public sector must also ensure that there is an adequate housing finance system that provides equity and seed capital to assist housing finance institutions, even if the ultimate burden is on the mobilization of private savings. Housing subsidies, which governments cannot afford and which tend therefore to limit the amount of housing that can be built by the public sector, should be phased out, and viable, self-financing public-sector housing institutions established.[62]

Housing then as continuing process rather than final product, housing built, if not always by, with the participation of, the people—such may help to reinvigorate vernacular architecture throughout the Islamic World. "Vernacular architecture," the Aga Khan recently observed, "has to be rethought, because it fails to cater for contemporary aspirations, either in rural areas or the towns."[63] To rethink and so reinvigorate the vernacular in architecture is a fundamental task, for the vernacular belongs by definition to a region, and it is the separate identities of the many cultures of Islam—the regionalism of Islam—that will benefit and prosper.

THE MOSQUE IN THE MEDIEVAL ISLAMIC WORLD

AN ESSAY
By ROBERT HILLENBRAND

Why study the mosque? For historians of architecture and culture alike, the answer is gratifyingly simple. This is the Islamic building *par excellence*, and as such the key to Islamic architecture. Moreover, the medieval Muslim world, like medieval Europe, was a theocentric society, and the mosque was the natural expression of that society. To examine its functions in detail therefore affords insights into the workings of medieval Islamic culture. For historians attuned to material culture as well as written evidence it is a primary source of the first order.

There are of course other and still more practical reasons for investigating the history of the mosque. This was the building type that by and large produced the finest structures in Islamic architecture; it was built to last, whereas many secular monuments tended to be richly decorated but of flimsy construction. As a result, it has survived in larger quantities than any other type of medieval building. Indeed, the early period of Islamic architecture—from about 700 to about 1000 A.D.—is documented largely by mosques. It was the mosque that embodied the first timid Arab experiments in architecture and it was in the medium of the mosque above all that Muslim builders came to grips with their pre-Islamic architectural heritage. As a result, this is the building type that most faithfully reflects—like the church in the Christian world—the impact of the many distinct local architectural traditions that together shaped Islamic architecture.

It seems appropriate to attempt a definition: The mosque is the principal religious building of Islam, and paramount among its many functions is communal prayer. In its simplest and most widespread form the medieval mosque comprised a courtyard bordered by arcades adjoining a covered hall. Yet this definition, for all its deliberate inclusiveness, gives little idea of the nearly endless variety of forms and uses that characterized this most quintessentially Islamic building. Nor does space permit a reasonably detailed inventory of the significant mosque types and their functions. It is imperative rather to distance oneself from this wealth of detail to better identify the immanent characteristics of the mosque and to appraise its unique role in Islamic culture.

Interior of the musalla *of the Tari Khana Mosque, Damghan, Iran. The* musalla *is the "place of prayer" or "sanctuary," and contains the* mihrab. *Pages 30–31: The interior of the Great Mosque of Córdoba, Spain, is an example of a hypostyle hall and one of the finest of its kind in the world.*

Accordingly this essay will focus less on close analysis of individual mosques than on how the genre expressed the perennial concerns of Islamic religious architecture. These concerns, or underlying principles, governed and are reflected in the choice of component parts of mosque design and their interaction; the functions the mosque was called on to perform; the role of decoration; and finally all that contributes to the visual and aesthetic impact of this building type. Mosque architecture is at base egalitarian, iconoclastic, inward-looking and above all profoundly religious in its intent. The latter aspect deserves particular emphasis because of the much-vaunted identity of the sacred and the secular in medieval Islamic society.

This theory, a favorite construction of some trends in modern scholarship, is ideally as true of Islam as of Christianity. It is, however, only a theory and a glance at common practice is enough to dispose of it. To this day no one walking from the bustle of a bazaar to the serenity of a mosque can seriously doubt that Islam clearly distinguishes between the dues of Caesar and those of God. The architecture proclaims that very distinction. The believer takes his shoes off to enter a mosque, and that simple, homely action symbolizes the transition from the secular to the spiritual realm, just as the same action performed in a domestic context marks the transition from the public world to the private one.

In just the same way, the physical evidence contradicts another fashionable concept: that all parts of the mosque are equally sacred and that its architecture embodies no hierarchy of importance. In mosques provided with a courtyard—and such mosques predominate throughout the Islamic world—a clear visual distinction is drawn between the courtyard with its surrounding arcades and the larger covered space containing the *mihrab*, or prayer niche, which is always oriented toward Mecca. Even the Arabic language singles out this area from the rest of the mosque, calling it the *musalla* ("place of prayer," conventionally rendered into English as "sanctuary"). Similarly, it is in this area that the principal architectural and li-

turgical elements of the mosque are concentrated: the main dome, the largest continuous covered space in the building; the *mihrab*; the *maqsura*, or royal box; and the *minbar*, or pulpit. Finally, it is in the *musalla* that the most lavish ornament that the building can boast is to be found. This is not to say that the mosque as a whole is not sacred. Nevertheless it implies that one part—the *musalla*—was accorded greater visual emphasis and status than the rest of the building.

The origins of the mosque are surprisingly straightforward. Islamic tradition champions the decisive impact of a single building on the evolution of the mosque—the house of the Prophet. Nor is this emphasis misplaced. The briefest acquaintance with Muslim liturgy is enough to explain why the places of worship employed by the other faiths of the time were fundamentally unsuitable for the needs of Islam. Actually many churches and fire temples, and on occasion even portions of Classical temples, were adapted to serve as mosques, but this was only a matter of expedience, never a long-term, deliberate policy. It did, however, have its uses; indeed, several motives could account for these conversions. In newly Islamized territory the pressing need for a place of worship could not always be met as quickly as might be wished. The advantages of using an already existing monument—convenience, low cost, suitable location, the saving of time and effort, and the less easily definable proselytizing, propaganda, and symbolic elements—outweighed the initial disadvantage of using an architectural form not designed to serve as a mosque. Nevertheless, these disadvantages made themselves felt quickly.

Christianity offers an instructive parallel case, except that from the beginning it was less flexible than Islam in its attitude toward places of worship. Pagan temples were not taken over en masse; nor for that matter were the buildings of other cults. Instead the earliest churches were the so-called *tituli*—ordinary private houses that doubled as places of worship. When changed political circumstances allowed large-scale churches to be built, models from other genres of architecture, notably the basilica, or law court, and the mausoleum, were pressed into service.

Islam was able to draw on a much more varied range of models for cultic buildings than was Christianity, which says much for the simplicity of Islamic communal worship and its refusal to be tied down to a narrow range of architectural expression. Its austerely simple liturgy meant that Islam could appropriate almost any kind of building for worship. Even so, there was—at least as far as seventh-century Arabs were concerned—an optimum design for mosques, and it is revealing that its roots should be in domestic rather than public architecture. This is not to say that the mosque is simply the Arab house writ large, for both Christian and Zoroastrian places of worship left their mark upon its design, as did the aulic architecture of late antiquity. These external influences, however, took time to make an impact on mosque architecture, and even at their strongest they were only rarely the determining factor.

Mature Ottoman mosques, which cannot be understood without reference to Byzantine churches of the sixth century, notably Hagia Sophia, are the exception that proves the rule. Muslim architects happily plundered, both literally and metaphorically, the religious architecture they encountered in the

Minarets of the Masjid-i 'Ali, Isfahan, Iran (opposite), and the Qutb Minar, Delhi, India (above). Both are monumental—the Qutb Minar is 238 feet high—and could not have served their purpose of calling the faithful to prayer satisfactorily. They were symbolic of power and so effective propaganda.

Mediterranean, Arabian, Persian, and—nearly six centuries later—Indian worlds. Yet the materials and ideas they quarried from these buildings were not enough to make the mosque an Islamized church, fire sanctuary, or temple.

The places of worship used by the adherents of religions that Islam supplanted were basically ill-suited to Muslim needs. Churches emphasized depth rather than breadth if they were basilical in form and centrality if they were variations of the martyrium type. The sanctuaries of fire worship in the Persian Empire were built for ceremonies involving a few priests, not large congregations—indeed, the congregation gathered in the open air—while the temples of Arabia and India also put no premium on housing great numbers of worshipers within a covered hall, let alone ensuring easy visibility among them. For these practical reasons the cultic centers of other religions were of limited value to early Muslim architects, who accordingly looked elsewhere for inspiration.

It was Muhammad's house at Medina from which the mosque developed in its crucial formative stage, and it is therefore sensible to examine this building in some detail. The house was demolished within a century of its erection to make room for the Mosque of the Prophet, intended by the caliph Walid I to be one of the principal sanctuaries of Islam. The characteristics of the original building are, however, preserved in the numerous accounts of the Prophet's life, and the details of the structure given in these sources agree tolerably well. It was roughly square, measuring some 56 by 53 meters, and by far its most prominent feature was the great empty courtyard, which took up well over 80 per cent of the surface area. Thus both austerity and ample open space were embedded into mosque design from the very beginning. On the south side was a double row of columns, eighteen to a row, with a roof of mud and palm leaves to give shade; here the early believers worshiped. Along the southern flank of the east side was a row of nine huts that housed Muhammad's wives; this was the sole concession to domesticity.

The vast courtyard sufficed to proclaim the essentially public nature of the building. It quickly became the nerve center of the burgeoning Muslim community, where worship was conducted, public announcements made, meetings held, parades reviewed, cases tried, the treasury housed, and councils of war convened. Like the religion of which it quickly became a potent symbol, it encompassed both the spiritual and the secular domain. Later mosques in theory maintained this dual allegiance, and the lack of formal urban institutions in the Muslim world, with a corresponding lack of certain types of formal public buildings such as town halls or law courts, put a premium on this double role. Thus by a natural process it became the community center of the new faith. Larger mosques in particular continued throughout the medieval period to offer a more or less wide range of facilities unconnected with worship. Smaller mosques on the whole did not. This functional distinction reflects a difference in status and purpose that became established within a century of the Prophet's death and was formalized by the adoption of two quite separate terms, both meaning mosque: *masjid* and *jami.*

Masjid, derived from the root *sajada,* "to prostrate oneself," is used in the Koran itself, though in rather a broad sense, to denote a place of worship. Its meaning was quickly refined to indicate more specifically a mosque for daily private prayer. The simplest architecture, right down to a single unadorned room, sufficed for such oratories, though it was not rare for splendidly embellished *masjids* to be erected at the behest of some wealthy patron. No Muslim community was without a *masjid,* even if it was no more than a small space set aside in some larger building. In towns it was common practice for each individual quarter to have its own *masjid,* and yet other *masjids* were built specifically for members of a certain tribe, sect, profession, or other exclusively defined community. Finally, the growing popularity of joint foundations from the tenth century on meant that *masjids* were built in association with a wide range of buildings whose prime emphasis was secular, such as caravansaries, mausoleums, and palaces, as well as buildings with an overtly religious significance, such as *ribats,* castle-like structures that housed warriors for the faith, and *madrasas,* or Koranic schools. This association of the *masjid* with secondary places of worship ensured that the physical form of the *masjid* would become more and more varied.

The *jami* was an altogether more ambitious kind of building, which was entirely in keeping with its much grander function. The religious obligation imposed on every adult Muslim, male and female, to meet for communal worship every Friday for the *salat,* or public service, created a need for a building conceived on a much larger scale than the *masjid.* The very word *jami,* which derives from the Arabic root "to assemble," recalls and perpetuates this crucial function of the building. It had to accommodate thousands instead of scores or a couple of hundred. It had in addition a public role, with undertones of symbol and propaganda perforce denied to the *masjid.* It was in some sense a showpiece for the faith and often for the person, dynasty, or area most closely associated with it. Not surprisingly, the crucial experiments in the evolution of the mosque as well as the first realizations of it, have been reserved for the *jami*. The Western term "cathedral mosque," though obviously a solecism, is thus an appropriate transference of ideas. The building of a *jami* was no more to be undertaken lightly than was that of a cathedral. Indeed until the tenth century the express approval of the caliph was required before a *jami* could be erected, and for centuries only one such building per city was permitted. Gradually, however, the population pressure in the major cities forced a relaxation of this·rule.

Despite the clear functional distinction between *masjid* and *jami*, there was not necessarily any corresponding distinction between the two building types so far as their basic layout was concerned. The generalizations at the beginning of this chapter therefore hold good for both genres of mosque. True, the *jami* normally had an extra dimension not only literally, by virtue of sheer size, but also metaphorically, because of its extra degree of embellishment. Yet often enough *masjids* were built that yielded nothing in decorative splendor to the finest *jamis* of the same style.

Certain types of *jami*, however, especially in the early centuries of Islam, did develop certain distinctive features not encountered in *masjids*, though it must be emphasized that these features represent only minor modifications to the basic schema of open courtyard and covered sanctuary common to both *masjid* and *jami*. Their introduction is of key importance to the history of the mosque, for it heralds an influx of foreign ideas, techniques, and materials that decisively transformed the primitive Arabian simplicity of the mosque. Henceforward mosque architecture evolved against a backdrop of Classical, Byzantine, and Persian influences. As a result, from the later Ommiad period on the physical form of the mosque was unmistakably rooted, at least in part, in the millennial traditions of the Near East and the Mediterranean world. The *masjid* in its original form was well able to do without these addenda, but there is no doubt that their incorporation into mosque design substantially enriched the whole subsequent development of the genre.

These new features were five in number: the *mihrab*, the *minbar*, the *maqsura*, the raised gabled transept, and the dome over the *mihrab* bay. Not all of them were to be of equal importance, nor were all to be encountered often in the same building. In the context of the present general discussion it is less their individual evolution than the motive behind their introduction that is relevant. Their origins are unmistakably Classical, filtered and in some measure distorted through the medium of Byzantine art. Significantly this latter connection is both religious and secular, whereas in Classical art proper it was the secular milieu in which these features were most at home. Their final incarnation in a Muslim religious building is therefore simply the logical fulfillment of a process begun many centuries before. The readiness with which Islam adopted these five features, and the natural way in which they acquired a liturgical *raison d'être*, speaks volumes for the powers of assimilation possessed by the new religion.

The choice of these particular alien features is interesting on other grounds too. All have a close connection with palace architecture and court ceremonial, an element that was overlaid by an ecclesiastical veneer in the Byzantine period but still retained its original potency. The evocative power of these

Dome over the musalla *of the Qarawiyyin Mosque, Fez, Morocco (top), and an exterior view of the mosque at ʿAbdallahbad, Iran (above). The dome was often used to visually emphasize the* musalla. Opposite: Mihrab *and* minbar *of the Tari Khana Mosque. The* mihrab *is a recessed arcuated niche indicating the direction of prayer. The* minbar *is in this instance unusually built in.*

architectural symbols was thus virtually undimmed when Islam adopted them.

The *mihrab* is perhaps the clearest case of all. The deeply recessed arcuated niche could hold a cult statue in a Greco-Roman temple or the emperor in person in a late-antique palace. Writ large, it contained the altar of a Christian church; correspondingly reduced in size, it did duty as a *mihrab*, though even in the context of a mosque some vestigial memory of its original function lingers, in that at the Friday *salat* the imam, or prayer leader, stands within the *mihrab* to lead the worshipers. The fact that it was part of the caliph's duties to act as imam vividly illustrates the capacity of the new faith to reconcile in a new synthesis the hitherto conflicting demands of church and state. The innate interchangeability of this feature is perhaps most revealingly illustrated in the late-Ommiad palace of Mshatta. The triconch form of the throne room, which terminates the main processional axis, finds its closest counterparts in a sixth-century cathedral and bishop's palace in Busra, in southern Syria. The architectural form is the same in all three cases, even though the great central niche is put to different uses in each: to hold the altar, the bishop's throne, and the caliph's throne, respectively. In due course the same form entered the vocabulary of mosque design, with a *mihrab* set within the central niche.

The *mihrab* was not an absolute requirement of any functioning mosque, and it should be remembered that the earliest example dates from as late as 705, when the rebuilt Mosque of the Prophet at Medina was furnished with one. There is no question, however, of the earlier mosques, which lacked *mihrabs*, being regarded as somehow deficient for that reason. In a properly oriented mosque the entire wall that faces the Ka'ba, the holy Black Stone at Mecca—the so-called *qibla* wall—serves as a directional indicator. It thereby makes the *mihrab* superfluous. Thus it was no liturgical necessity that called the *mihrab* into being. The evidence suggests rather that a growing desire to secularize the mosque, or at any rate to bring it more into line with the highly developed architecture of the ancient Near East and of the Classical and Byzantine world, was the decisive factor. Once "invented," the *mihrab* was so obviously a signal success as a symbol and as the cynosure of worship that its future was assured. The various types of *mihrab* that were ultimately developed—flat, concave, or recessed so as to form a separate chamber—are so varied as to demand a study beyond the scope of this account.

The *minbar* never attained the nearly universal popularity of the *mihrab* in Islamic architecture. To begin with, its function is much more specifically concentrated in the Friday *salat* and thus in the *jami*, whereas the *mihrab* quickly became an essential component of even the humblest *masjid* and is frequently to be found also in *madrasas*, mausoleums, caravansaries, and other kinds of buildings. An integral part of the Friday service was the *khutba*, part bidding prayer, part sermon, and part formal address. This element of the service had a strong political flavor. Indeed, a ruler's claim to legitimacy depended, *inter alia*, on the formal mention of his name in the *khutba*. Like the diptych in Byzantium, the *khutba* thus became an instrument for affirming allegiance. Clearly it was important for the *khatib*, or preacher, who delivered the *khutba* to be easily visible and audible; hence the development of the *minbar*, which was customarily placed immediately to the right of the *mihrab*.

The obvious analogy to the *minbar* in Christian practice is of course the pulpit, and in fact the closest known prototype to the *minbar* is the ambo, the lectern and pulpit found in early medieval churches as well as the bishop's throne in Byzantine ones. Coptic churches in particular had ambos with the same striking simplicity of form found in *minbars*: a primitively stepped right-angled triangle set against a wall. No *minbars* securely datable before the early ninth century have survived, however, so that the precise relationship between the Muslim form and its presumed Christian prototype is hard to determine.

This problem is compounded by the existence of alternative hypotheses on the origin of the *minbar*. One of these holds

that the later *minbar* is simply a monumental version of the raised chair from which Muhammad addressed his followers. No trace of this has survived, which makes it impossible to follow up the proposed connection in any detail. The other theory associates the *minbar* with the raised throne from which the Sassanian commander-in-chief reviewed the Persian army. Here again, the lack of physical evidence scotches any extended discussion. The irritating gap of two centuries or more between pre-Islamic Christian ambos and the earliest precisely datable *minbar*, generally held to be the teakwood specimen in the Great Mosque at Kairouan in Tunisia, may not, however, be quite the obstacle it seems. A comparison of the example at Kairouan with the ambo of a typical Coptic monastery, like that of Apa Jeremias at Saqqara in Lower Egypt, reveals sufficient basic similarity of form to justify the analogy. The built-in *minbar* in the Tari Khana Mosque at Damghan in Iran, perhaps as early as the eighth century and scarcely likely to be any later than the year 900, provides an even closer parallel to the Coptic ambo and is moreover of mud brick rather than wood. Since mud brick is a traditional Persian substitute for stone, the stepped triangular form used at Damghan can most conveniently be interpreted as a translation of the Coptic stone ambo into the most closely related material available.

Perhaps the simple stone, brick, or mud *minbar* coexisted with a more elaborately developed version executed in wood. The latter type was sometimes wheeled, and could therefore be brought out into the courtyard when a particularly large congregation had gathered. The link with princely life had already been established in the early-Ommiad period, for it is recorded that the caliph Mu'awiya I took his *minbar* with him on his travels. It is tempting to assume that it was a *minbar* of this type that Muhammad himself had used. Certainly the *minbar* served in early Islamic times as a kind of throne from which the ruler could address his subjects or receive their allegiance, often in the form of a *bay'a*, or oath.

The example at Kairouan is typical of the subsequent development of the *minbar*, though minor modifications and improvements were introduced over the centuries. In order to boost the acoustic properties required by the very nature of the *minbar*, for example, a canopy, often polyhedral in shape, capped the upper platform or landing, performing much the same function as a tester in European pulpits. A hinged gate often gave access to the steps, again in somewhat European

fashion, though there is no need to postulate any direct influence in either direction. Supplementary *minbars*—and for
that matter supplementary *mihrabs*—were sometimes placed
elsewhere in a *jami*, for example in the courtyard, perhaps
carved out of rock in an open-air mosque, or in an *'idgah* (a
mosque for extraordinary intercessory prayer at the time of the
two great *'ids*, or festivals), or in times of drought, famine,
and the like.

   The decoration of *minbars* was by some quirk of tradition
remarkably stereotyped. Their wooden construction laid a
premium on the use of many small modular units that on being
fitted together created the overall pattern, which was nearly
always geometric, though some of the early surviving *minbars*,
such as those at Fez and Marrakesh, favor floral designs. From
the fourteenth century on more varied types of *minbar* appeared. Examples sheathed in tilework were erected in Persia
and increasingly in Ottoman Turkey. The latter area also favored stone or marble *minbars* with banisters of elaborately
fretted openwork tracery. *Minbars* of iron and baked brick also
exist. In general the use of durable materials brought in its
train a markedly simplified design; as late as the seventeenth
century, in Safavid Isfahan, a *minbar* could be built that exactly
repeated the shape of the Damghan example of a millennium
earlier, but with costly marble instead of mud brick.

   Far fewer examples of the *maqsura* survive, and it is likely
that this situation reflects their relative scarcity in medieval
times. The reason is not far to seek. Much more explicitly
than either the *mihrab* or the *minbar*, the *maqsura* implies the
presence of a ruler. By contrast, every *jami* requires an imam
and a *khatib*. In form, the *maqsura* is a separate, usually square,
enclosure within the mosque and close to the *mihrab*. Its walls

Musalla *interior of the Mosque of Arhai-ka-din-Jhonpra, Ajmir,
India. The twelfth-century mosque consists of an open hypostyle
hall preceded by a massive screen of seven arches.*

may be of masonry, but wood or metal latticework is more
common. This sufficed to screen the occupant from the other
worshipers but allowed him to see and participate in the *salat*.

   Several reasons may account for this seclusion. One could
have been a desire straightforwardly to adapt the Byzantine
practice of housing the emperor in a royal box, the *kathisma*,
and thereby to emphasize his high rank and his essential apart-
ness. Another, related motive might have been to secure privacy of worship for the ruler. This might explain the frequent
provision, as at Damascus, of a door beside the *mihrab* com-
municating both with the royal palace and with the *maqsura*.
Thus the ruler would have been absolved of the need to mingle
with other worshipers. Such exclusiveness would have been
of a piece with the growing emphasis in the Ommiad period
on the remoteness of the caliph, a far cry from the unpretentious democracy of Arabian practice. A third reason might
well have been a naked fear of assassination. Two of the first
four caliphs, Omar and Ali, were murdered in the mosque,
and a third, Othman, was killed while reading the Koran.
Behind the *maqsura* screen the caliph was visible but not vul-
nerable. The emphasis on openwork screens in the typical
maqsura opens up the possibility of a formal connection with
the choir screens that were a marked feature of Byzantine architecture. These too were located close to the liturgical focus
of the building.

   Whatever the origins of the *maqsura*, its symbolic function
can scarcely be in doubt. It was a visible exaltation of the

ruler's rank and therefore an integral part of the strong secular element in the early Islamic *jami* and of its intimate connection with royal pomp and ceremony. The subsequent history of the *maqsura* betrays a weakening of these associations. The word came to mean the detached part of a mosque set aside for communal as distinct from private prayer. As such, naturally, its form underwent a major change. From the eleventh century on *maqsuras* in the form of large domed chambers incorporated into the sanctuary of a mosque began to proliferate, especially in the eastern Islamic world. The example of the mosque of Baybars in Cairo shows that this fashion penetrated to western Islam too. As with the *minbar,* the *maqsura* appears in a variety of forms and contexts, among them mobile examples in wood (as at Kairouan) and others in multipurpose foundations such as the complex of Sultan Qala'un in Cairo.

For all its symbolic importance and the physical impact its sheer size guarantees, the *maqsura* could not claim to have any significant liturgical role even when it came to connote the domed sanctuary itself. This is even true of the two remaining features of foreign origin that were incorporated more and more often into large urban *jamis*: the raised gabled transept and the dome over the *mihrab.* The transept never attained any great popularity, if only because it was not a form that could be imposed on all kinds of mosque. Far from it; to make its desired effect the transept called for a sanctuary whose roofing system extended parallel to the *qibla,* not perpendicular to it. The whole purpose of the transept was to assert an axis at variance with the preponderant one in the sanctuary and thereby to emphasize the *mihrab,* which terminated the axis thus highlighted. The extra height of the gabled transept, towering above the sanctuary and driving at right angles across its roofline, was the outward visual embodiment of this processional way.

By a fortunate chance the mosque that first expressed this idea was one of the supreme generative buildings of Islamic architecture, the Great Mosque of Damascus. The transept was recognized at once as an integral part of the Damascus schema, and in one form or another it is reproduced in all mosques that depend upon that prototype. However, it has no locus in mosques that derive from other sources, and these constitute the vast majority. Clearly, then, it is in no sense an obligatory or even a customary part of a mosque.

Accordingly the obvious question is why was it introduced in the first place? It must suffice to outline the two most likely possibilities. First, the wholesale transposition of the west front of a typical Syrian church to serve as the centerpiece for an interior mosque facade must have overtones of triumph in political and religious terms if indeed it is not to be interpreted as outright parody. Such a deliberate reformulation of the components of an established style is a typically Ommiad proceeding. Even so, the second possibility—a connection with princely ceremonies—seems more likely. By that reckoning the key parallel would lie not in religious architecture at all but in palaces, whether gubernatorial as at Ravenna, episcopal as at Busra, or imperial as at Constantinople. In all these contexts the gabled facade encloses an arched entrance that gives onto a processional way. The latter customarily leads to a throne room. There is of course no throne room in a mosque, nor is there any provision in the Koran or in earliest Islamic

practice for formal royal receptions in the mosque. Nevertheless the processional entry of the caliph or sultan into the *jami* for the Friday *salat* was a long-established tradition in the medieval Islamic world. The gabled raised transept, the dome over the *mihrab,* and eventually the *maqsura, minbar,* and *mihrab* would together create an architectural *mise en scène* that would be the natural corollary to such pomp and circumstance. A comparable and much better documented process may be observed in Western medieval architecture.

The significant progeny of the transept in the Great Mosque at Damascus is to be traced almost exclusively in the western Islamic world. The easternmost limit of its influence is probably the Great Mosque at Diyarbakir in Anatolia. Interestingly enough, the mosques in Egypt that repeat the transept motif, though relatively few in number, include some of the finest mosques of their time, those of Al-Azhar, Hakam, and Baybars. This suggests that when the transept motif traveled outside the confines of Syria it retained its royal associations. In time its form became simplified so as to allow a smoother integration into the courtyard facade, of which it was the cynosure. This is particularly noticeable in the major Maghribi mosques, where the greater breadth of the transept vis-à-vis the flanking aisles is maintained intact, but its external silhouette rises much less markedly above the rest of the roofline. Most significantly, the basic notion of the conflicting axes crucial to the transept form is lost. In these Maghribi mosques the aisles are all perpendicular to the *qibla,* and it is only by its greater width, height, and vaulting that the central one stands out. In the long run, therefore, the concept of a transept proved to be an aberration within the context of Islamic architecture as a whole.

Finally, what of the dome over the *mihrab?* Roman architecture had decisively established the honorific character of the dome by giving it pride of place in palatial architecture. It is no accident that the greatest of all Roman religious edifices, the Pantheon, makes the dome its focal point. These lofty associations did not prevent the Romans from using the dome in humbler contexts, but a pattern had been set and was confirmed in Byzantine architecture by the large-scale use of the dome in churches and monasteries. It was therefore a natural transition to employ it in mosques, and incidentally in key locations within Islamic palaces.

Within the mosque the obvious place for the dome was near the *mihrab,* as part of an intricate nexus of royal associations established by that feature, the *minbar,* the *maqsura,* and the transept. Each of these elements derives added impact from the nearness of the others. In a mosque with principally flat or pitched roofs or at most shallow vaulting, the presence of a full-scale dome is obviously intended to emphasize some liturgical focus if not to express some religious or political symbolism. Given the fact that the *mihrab,* even when it projects slightly beyond the rest of the external *qibla* wall, is essentially part of the interior formulation of the mosque and that its position is therefore not readily identifiable from the outside, the value of the dome as an outward sign of that spot is obvious. More than that, its form, with its rich inbuilt secular associations, emphasises the princely role of the *mihrab.* Finally, it marks the location of the *qibla,* an important consideration in an urban setting otherwise devoid of fixed directional points.

The dome over the *mihrab* proved to be one of the most durable and versatile aspects of medieval Islamic architecture. By degrees its usefulness as a distinguishing mark won such recognition that the idea was applied on a more extensive scale. Pairs or trios of domes over the *mihrab, maqsura,* and transept area or along the center stretch of the *qibla* wall multiplied the effect. A favorite combination for Islamic architects was to mark the erstwhile transept, now reduced to simply a larger central aisle, by a dome at each extremity or to assert the *qibla* wall by a dome at each end and one in the middle. These architects composed their buildings with an eye to the overall design, using domes like grace notes to punctuate the regular beat of an articulated wall or a peristyle. This specialized architectural context did not, however, entirely divest the dome of its traditionally weighty secular and religious associations, even when the popularity of domical architecture was at its zenith. As late as the high-Ottoman period a clear hierarchy based on gradations of size ensured that the principal domes were suitably highlighted by the diminutive scale of the surrounding ones.

As mentioned earlier, none of the five features of the *jami* for which a foreign origin of at least partially royal character may be claimed are to be regarded as vital to the proper functioning of a mosque. However, since both *mihrab* and *minbar* have the sanction of an unbroken tradition stretching back some thirteen-hundred years, they might well be considered an indissoluble part of the *jami;* the force of custom cannot be discounted in these two cases, whatever a strict interpretation of Muslim liturgy might suggest. The other three features obviously lacked this direct appeal to Muslim taste and by degrees fell into disuse or at best maintained their popularity in a few areas only. This decline from their earlier importance is almost certainly attributable to the gradual divorce of the

Mihrab of the Friday Mosque, Nain, Iran (left). This superb early example shows plaster decoration at its richest. Above: North facade of the Friday Mosque courtyard, Isfahan, Iran, with one of the four iwans placed axially on the domed chamber of the musalla. Right: Gable and musalla (seen from the north), of the Great Mosque, Damascus, Syria. The gabled facade encloses an arched entrance that leads to the "transept" and to the mihrab at the far end. Far right: Interior of the Khirki Mosque, Delhi, India. The plan of the mosque is unusual in that its hypostyle hall is arranged around four courtyards.

caliph from the conduct of the Friday *salat.* As the caliph delegated those of his functions that bore directly on the Friday service to the imam and the *khatib,* the motive for singling out those parts of the mosque especially connected with the royal presence disappeared.

The five princely components of the mosque are far from exhausting the tally of its constituent parts, some of which are of equal or even greater importance. The minaret, the courtyard, the covered sanctuary, facilities for ablutions all play a significant role in the overall design of a mosque, to say nothing of such lesser facilities as a *dakka* (raised platform), carpets or other floor coverings, and latrines. These various aspects of mosque design must be given due emphasis in the context of the present discussion.

Perhaps the most strikingly Islamic of them is the minaret. Like the *mihrab,* the minaret was a somewhat late arrival in Islamic architecture, not called into being by any strict liturgical imperative. Indeed, in some parts of the Islamic world it has never fully established itself, for example, Saudi Arabia. There, as in the most ancient Islamic practice, the call to prayer may still be given from the roof of the mosque, as was done in the time of the Prophet by Bilal, an Abyssinian slave

notable for his stentorian voice. The Persian *guldasta*, a diminutive kiosk perched on the roof of a mosque, usually over the crown of an *iwan* (deep vaulted hall), perpetuates this custom in monumental form, although nowadays the kiosk is more likely to contain a loudspeaker than a muezzin.

Two distinct origins have been proposed for the minaret, and it is quite possible that both theories have a solid foundation of fact. Both derive strong support from etymological arguments. According to one hypothesis, the form derives from the towers of Syrian churches, which served as campaniles. The fact that a popular early term for minaret was *sauma'a* (monk's cell) strengthens this supposition. Even today the minarets of the Maghrib, which alone in the Islamic world have continuously preserved the form of these early minarets in Syria, are known by this name. Given the central role of Syria in the formation of Islamic architecture, it might well be concluded that church towers are the best parallel, both functionally and geographically, for the minaret in the initial stages of its development.

The second theory turns on the standard word used for minaret in Islam: *manara* and its variants. The word means "place of fire" or "place of light," and while this could be taken in a purely metaphorical way—i.e., a tower spreading the light of Islam—it is surely more straightforward to assume that some reference to a signal tower is intended. In that case the obvious parallel would be the great lighthouse at Alex-

andria, the Pharos, which was still functioning at the time of the Arab conquest. The distinctive stepped silhouette of that Wonder of the World does in fact recur in some minarets, such as that of the Great Mosque at Kairouan, but it is far from certain whether any such minarets were built in the crucial first century of Islam. The custom of putting lights in minarets is, however, recorded in Persia and elsewhere in the medieval Islamic world, not only for purposes of signaling— for example, in the desert or on the seashore—but also to celebrate the *'ids* or other special occasions.

Technically redundant though it was for the purposes of Islamic worship, the minaret had a symbolic and propaganda function that was quickly recognized. Indeed, among the very first minarets were those of the Damascus mosque, where the corner towers of the ancient temenos, or sacred precinct, served to proclaim the victorious new faith to the conquered Christian town. Soon the message was driven home, for these square corner towers were heightened dramatically. It is a moot point whether the intention behind this was indeed to harp on the theme of victory, but it must be conceded that no imaginable liturgical need would call for a quartet of minarets. Occasionally in later centuries tall minarets situated in remote or commanding locations and raised by rulers in the wake of some great victory might again invite the suspicion that the motive behind their erection was political rather than religious, especially when they were so high that a call to prayer made from their crown would be inaudible.

These examples are exceptions. The standard formula of a slender minaret towering over a relatively low mosque has long been accepted as emblematic of Islamic architecture, as a symbol of Islam itself. This is not to deny that in larger settlements the minaret is a much more practical way of making heard the *adhan* (call to prayer) than is a rooftop. Continuity with the past, religious symbolism, and functional appropriateness are therefore combined in a single, architecturally elegant form. There is no standard location for a minaret. At first a favored position was at the far end of the courtyard,

Minaret of the Wazir Khan Mosque, Lahore, Pakistan (above), and the minaret of the Yivli Mosque, Antalya, Turkey (right). The brick walls of the seventeenth-century Wazir Khan Mosque are covered with glazed-tile mosaic. The fluted fourteenth-century minaret of the Yivli Mosque is atypical of Turkish minarets, which generally are slender and pencil-shaped.

opposite the sanctuary on the axis of the *mihrab;* later minarets were often placed in a corner of the courtyard or even outside the mosque. In time the possible options were extended still further by increasing their number. Paired minarets often soaring higher than a hundred feet at the main entrance to the mosque proved popular throughout the eastern Islamic lands. In India, and occasionally elsewhere, the idea tentatively expressed in the Damascus mosque was taken much further by heavily buttressed corner towers that gave the whole mosque an embattled air. In Ottoman Turkey, however, minarets were used most freely to articulate the mosque. Sometimes they serve to mark out the perimeter of the building as a whole; at others they cluster more closely to identify and exalt the sanctuary. Four are common and six occur occasionally in this tradition. In the nineteenth century such careful propriety was lost in a welter of attenuated minarets that festooned, for example, the larger Shi'ite shrines in Iraq and Persia. In these buildings the minaret is reduced to one motif among many, its religious and architectural character alike debased.

The minaret experienced a remarkably varied formal development over the centuries. Square minarets remained the norm in the Maghrib; Egypt developed multistory minarets, each with a different elevation and ground plan; Iraq and Persia preferred tall cylindrical brick minarets, often on an octagonal or flanged plinth, whereas those of Ottoman Turkey were slender, pencil-shaped, and girdled with tiers of balconies. In ninth-century Iraq an aberrant type based on ancient Mesopotamian ziggurats, of cylindrical form with an external spiral ramp, enjoyed a brief vogue. In Saharan Africa the minaret took the form of a pylon, and examples with external staircases were also popular there and on the Persian Gulf. Predictably, minarets in the Far East and Southeast Asia were free adaptations of the pagoda. Virtually throughout the Islamic world it was the practice to give the minaret lavish applied ornamentation, whether of brick, tile, stone, or other materials.

There is much less to be said about the courtyard, although paradoxically this is in some ways the most striking aspect of mosque design for the casual observer. Its impact is due largely to its size: the huge empty space gives the visitor pause and serves notice that he has left the workaday world behind him. Like the atrium of early Christian churches, the courtyard heralds the sanctuary proper and defines an area that is holy even if not used regularly for worship. There was no set form for the courtyard, but the rectangle dominates, whether the emphasis is on depth or width. Arcades or a flat-roofed portico customarily articulates the courtyard's inner facades, while the open space itself may be punctuated by a small domed treasury, shrine, or other edicule and perhaps a *minbar,* pool, or *dakka.* These additional elements, however, are not allowed to impinge too strongly on, or to detract from, the sense of unbroken space the courtyard creates. In the larger towns the courtyard held the overflow of worshipers from the sanctuary at the Friday *salat,* and even in smaller centers its capacity might be required on the occasion of the 'ids or extraordinary prayers. It was never a dead space.

Islamic worship demanded *mid'a* (ritual ablution) as a necessary preliminary to prayer. Facilities for washing are therefore standard in most mosques. They take various forms. Sometimes they comprise a domed or open fountain within the mosque, intended for washing only. Alternatively, ritual ablution may be carried out near the latrines outside the mosque, in which case drinking water may be provided by a fountain in the courtyard. The influence of the Classical house with its impluvium in the atrium may perhaps be detected in those mosques (such as those of Ottoman date at Bursa in Turkey) where the ablutions facility is placed below a skylight in the sanctuary itself. In Iran and India especially, much of the courtyard is taken up by a large pool, which acts also as a landscaping feature, alleviating the bare expanse of the courtyard and introducing a broad band of contrasting color. Elsewhere, in areas where the dominant *madhhab,* or school of law, was Hanbali, this was not permitted on the grounds that ablutions had to be performed with running water. Water in Hanbali mosques is therefore provided by taps. None of these practices, incidentally, excludes the possibility of performing ablutions with sand where water is scarce.

In the larger mosques the burgeoning size of congregations gradually highlighted a problem not previously encountered: the press of people tended to make it hard to see the imam

Apart from mosque lamps the only other furnishing commonly found in mosques was some kind of floor covering. Mats of woven reeds were the most popular solution in much of the Arab world; the particular type of matting varied from sect to sect. The custom no doubt evolved from the religious requirement that all must enter the mosque unshod. Muhammad sometimes used a carpet when praying, and it is therefore not surprising that in Iran and Turkey especially—countries with a millennial tradition of carpet weaving—mosque floors were bedecked with rugs, either pile or flat-weave (*kilims* or *zilus*). Luxury carpets were reserved for the great feasts, which ensured that they suffered much less wear. This helps to explain why some of the finest and oldest carpets have been found in mosques. The more puritanical Muslims rejected such luxury as being un-Islamic.

These, then, are the component parts of a typical mosque in medieval times. Most bear on the essential raison d'être of the building, namely communal worship, but they allow for other uses too. Still other features were sometimes added to serve purposes of a less explicitly religious nature. In the great urban *jamis* a host of satellite functions had to be provided for, thereby greatly extending the surface area of the complex. The necessary ancillary buildings themselves sometimes served dual or even multiple functions.

Education was perhaps the principal secondary function of the mosque, especially in the first four centuries of Islam. Education comprised a wide range of religious activities: the study of Islamic law and of the so-called "religious sciences" such as *tafsir* and *fiqh;* the memorization of the Koran, often carried out in a building known as *dar al-qur'an* or *dar al-huffaz;* and the study of the Hadith, or Traditions of the Prophet, for which a *dar al-hadith*—a school was sometimes provided. A *kuttab*—a school with a very strong emphasis on religious teaching—was also sometimes sited within the precincts of the mosque. Teaching customarily took place in the sanctuary; the lecturer would seat himself against a pillar and the class would squat around him. In time, purpose-built *madrasas* took over the role of teaching institutions that mosques had formerly discharged, though even these *madrasas* might on occasion be located next to or within a mosque. To this day certain outstanding mosques are more famous for their roles as universities than as places of worship: Al-Azhar in Cairo, founded in 970 and beyond doubt the oldest continuously functioning university in the world; the Qarawiyyin Mosque in Fez, an educational institution without peer in the western Maghrib; and the Zaituniya in Tunis, its equivalent in the eastern Maghrib.

The mosque maintained, throughout the Middle Ages and in some cases right up to modern times, close links with a particular facet of education: the world of scholars, scholarship, and books. It was in the mosque above all that scholars gathered for discussion, lectures, and to hear the latest works being read. Publication before the advent of the printing press meant a public reading of the work in question, validated by the presence of the author himself or by someone authorized by him in writing. Everyone thus authorized could in turn authorize others by the same process, for which the mosque was the obvious public forum. Wandering scholars, who were as much a feature of medieval Islam as of medieval Western Christianity, were accustomed to seeking shelter in mosques.

leading the worship. The solution adopted in such mosques, from about the ninth century, was to build a raised platform, or *dakka,* on which groups of muezzins would perform the movements of prayer in time with the imam and in full view of the worshipers farther back. Not surprisingly, this became distracting and the practice was largely discontinued except in mosques whose layout made it imperative.

This tally of items constitutes a typical mosque. Islamic tradition had no place for the furnishings that are so regular a feature of Christian churches—pews, fonts, monuments, altars, and various kinds of ecclesiastical sculpture such as retables, reredoses, testers, choir screens and the like. Stained glass—abstract rather than figural—seems to have been used in mosques more frequently than is generally supposed, but virtually the only objects to break the puritanically bare expanse of the average sanctuary are *qandils* (mosque lamps). In the larger mosques these *qandils,* in form like a triangular candelabra, were hung by the hundreds or even thousands, suspended on long chains to just above the height of a man. The symbolic value of such lighting as a metaphor for spiritual illumination is made explicit by the practice of depicting such a lamp on *mihrabs* and enclosing it by a quotation from the Sura of Light (Koran 24:35): "God is the light of the heavens and the earth, the likeness of his light is as a niche wherein is a lamp, the lamp in a glass, the glass, as it were, a glittering star." On special occasions *mihrabs* and minarets were decked with lights.

These effectively took over the functions of hostelries, and some had additional features such as soup kitchens, hospitals, and even morgues. That inveterate scholar-traveler Ibn-Batuta traveled the length and breadth of the Muslim world in the fourteenth century expecting—and finding—free board and lodging at a wide range of religious institutions, foremost among them being mosques. By a natural extension of usage the mosque was an obvious early port of call for foreigners—that is, Muslims from other parts of the Islamic world.

While worship was the primary function of the mosque, it was the natural setting for a series of related activities. These included sermons or theological lectures; retreats (especially popular during the last third of Ramadan and taking the form of nocturnal vigils; the systematic teaching of recitation of the Koran; the practice of *dhikr,* namely the ritual repetition of stock formulas, especially of praise and adoration of God; and finally the offering of special prayers, (in cases of barrenness, for instance), the sealing of oaths or covenants, and the celebration of rites of passage (birth, circumcision, marriage, divorce, and burial). Foremost among these "lesser" religious or semireligious purposes was the use of the mosque as a place of pilgrimage. This special distinction applied only to certain mosques, usually those associated in some particular way with Muhammad or with some notable saint. Naturally such mosques are more numerous in the Levant and Saudi Arabia than in the rest of the Muslim world; the most important are those at Mecca, Medina, and Jerusalem. The Hadith averred that prayers offered in such mosques were much more meritorious than those offered in other mosques, while prayer offered in an ordinary mosque was itself worth twenty times as

much as that offered elsewhere. By degrees such special sanctity was extended to mosques somewhat farther removed from the heartlands of Islam, such as those of Kairouan in Tunisia and Konya in Turkey. To this day many Shi'ites from Iran, Iraq, and the Arabian peninsula make pilgrimages to the Great Mosque at Damascus.

There is a long and honorable connection between the mosque and the administration of justice; Muhammad himself used the mosque for this purpose. The use of the mosque as a venue for taking and registering oaths and for notarial acts is only one aspect of this association. Much more important in the medieval period was the custom of turning over a part of the mosque for use as a law court on set days, with the *qadi* (lesser judge or magistrate) presiding. In early Muslim times this was the duty of the caliph, and the fact that caliph and *qadi* alike used a *minbar* like that of the *khatib* is an eloquent testimony, as indeed is the use of the mosque for so many different purposes, of the underlying unity of so much of Islamic civilization. Equally revealing is the fact that while cases concerning Muslims were heard in the mosque, those concerning Christians were held on the steps leading up to it.

Finally, the political dimension within which the mosque evolved and functioned needs to be emphasized. This aspect finds manifold expression in the mosque: the five alien elements mentioned earlier as being incorporated into its schema far from exhaust the range of relevant connections. Many early mosques, for example, were located in the middle of camps where the Arab soldiery lodged, and right next to the dwelling place, and ultimately the palace, of the ruler. The *khutba* was one of several ways in which this close relationship was expressed. It functioned as a mark of legitimacy, and participation in it was equivalent to a collective oath of allegiance. In times of civil strife or other kinds of political instability there was no quicker way of informing the populace of who the true ruler and his accredited deputy might be than the *khutba.*

Hence the high feelings that, despite the sanctity of the mosque, vented themselves on occasion in the stoning or even

Lateral hall (far left) and detail of vault decoration (left), Friday Mosque, Yazd, Iran. Detail of the exterior of the dome, Lutfallah Mosque, Isfahan, Iran (above), and muqarnas *in the ruins of the Masjid-i-Malik, Zuzan, Iran (right). These examples of Islamic ornament, whether in plaster or tiles, demonstrate its abstract nature. The purpose of ornament is to dissolve matter, to deny substantial masses and substitute for them a less palpable reality.*

murder of the *khatib,* or conversely in the ritual cursing from the pulpit of enemies of the regime. Just as in later times the captain of a British warship had to read himself in before his authority had official confirmation, so too in medieval Islam a governor's first task on taking office was to mount the *minbar,* glorify God, and read out the caliph's letter of appointment or simply announce the fact that he had been invested with that dignity.

The *minbar* was also the scene for political announcements and harangues of all kinds. The tradition that the mosque was a place of political asylum, like the church in Western Europe, was deeply ingrained in Islam. In some cases provision was even made to employ the mosque as a military building, with fortifications behind which the faithful could take refuge in times of uprising or war. Such bastions became a traditional feature of some mosque architecture even when Muslim society had long outgrown the need for them.

These wider and in large part secular functions could in theory be discharged by *masjids* and *jamis* alike, though in practice they tended to bulk larger in the latter. There was, however, another category of mosques (usually *masjids),* which responded to the needs of particular groups of people. Among these were mosques reserved for certain tribes, which flourished especially in Arabia in the first century of Islam and were a potent force for disunity, and mosques for separate quarters in a town or, as a logical extension of this, for certain crafts or occupations. Sometimes mosques reflected theological differences, not only the obvious schism between Sunni and Shi'ite, but also the relatively minor distinctions between the various

madhhabs. These mosques, like the tribal ones, also fostered dissension, and their legality was open to question on these grounds.

There was also a category of mosque that could broadly be termed memorial. It included mosques built on sites sanctified by certain events in the life of the Prophet, including places where he had prayed as well as locations where some seminal event had taken place, like the Aqsa Mosque in Jerusalem, which commemorated his *mi'raj,* or night journey to hell and the seven heavens; also in this category were mosques with specific Biblical associations, such as the mosque of Abraham at Hebron. Both types recall the Christian martyrium. With them may be classed funerary mosques, which were denounced a number of times in the Hadith but drew vitality from pre-Islamic tradition in which the graves of ancestors often became sanctuaries. Muhammad's tomb at Medina, around which developed the Mosque of the Prophet, is an example of this. By a natural transition mosques were built over the tombs of some of the great men of early Islam such as the Companions of the Prophet, and pilgrimages—admittedly unorthodox—were made to them. In time a whole complex of buildings sometimes evolved around the tomb of the notable in question.

Thus a variety of functions characterized the medieval mosque, which explains the popularity of a nuclear plan onto which extra elements could easily be grafted. This innate flexibility can be traced to the origins of the mosque, which—and this cannot be emphasized too strongly—did not begin life as a primarily religious center. Muhammad's house was more a political headquarters than a place of worship; people camped, argued, and even fought there. An early viceroy of Iraq decreed that the gravel floor of the Al-Kufa Mosque should be paved because people were habitually scooping up pebbles to throw at the *khatib* when they disagreed with his preaching. It was only by degrees that the sanctity of the mosque asserted itself. Under the Ommiads, for example, it was still permissible for Christians to enter mosques. For a long time only specified parts of the mosque were held to be fully sacred: the *mihrab,*

the *minbar*, and the tomb of a saint who might be buried there, which would be venerated for the *baraka* (holiness) emanating from it. Rules of behavior gradually imposed themselves. The removal of shoes became obligatory, and worshipers were enjoined not to spit (or to spit only to the left). They were required to preserve silence and decent conduct (a provision aimed at the unruly Bedouin), to ensure their ritual cleanliness, to wear their best clothes on Friday, and to observe a host of similar prescriptions. The role of women in the mosque became more sharply defined. They were to sit apart from the men, to leave before them, not to wear perfume, and not to enter the mosque during menstruation. Often a specific part of the mosque, such as the upper galleries around the courtyard or an area at the back of the sanctuary, was reserved for them.

This discussion cannot proceed without some account of the major schools of medieval mosque architecture: Arab, Turkish, and Persian. Unfortunately this involves such enormous simplifications as treating the mosques of the Indo-Pakistani subcontinent, which account for perhaps half of those preserved from medieval times in the entire Muslim world, as offshoots of the Arab or Persian types. It also ignores the many vigorous if quasi-vernacular subschools of Islamic architecture such as those of China, Southeast Asia, and Africa south of the Maghrib. However, what follows is nevertheless intended to encompass the significant basic types of medieval mosque.

There can be little doubt that the determining factor in the evolution of the mosque as a whole was Arab influence. Here the example of Muhammad's house was of paramount importance. It is worth noting that even this structure involved some degree of modification before it could serve as a mosque, since worship was not its original function; small wonder then that many early mosques, like that at Damascus, were conversions of existing though usually religious buildings and thereby exploited the ready-made sanctity of the site.

Within the first generation after Muhammad's death the mosque of so-called "Arab plan" had established itself as a type. It comprised an open courtyard—the warm climate of the Middle East encouraged worship in the open air—with shallow, flat-roofed arcades on three of its four sides to give shade. The fourth side faced Mecca and contained a relatively deeper sanctuary, often marked by a raised transept or domes. Much of the architectural detailing was borrowed from the Classical tradition or, more rarely, from ancient Near Eastern models, and the depiction of spolia was widespread. As very early mosques at Al-Kufa and Basra in Iraq and at Al-Fustat (Old Cairo) show, the visual impact of this type of mosque could be transformed by adjustments to the depth, breadth, or absolute size of the courtyard and sanctuary; even slight variations in the depth of peripheral arcades could be telling.

It was not long before further articulating devices made their appearance. At the mainly ninth-century mosque at Kairouan in Tunisia the sanctuary arcades ran perpendicular to the *qibla*, with the bays adjoining the *mihrab* wall built higher and wider than the norm. This, when combined with an extra-wide central aisle, created a T-shaped transept that became a standard motif in North African mosques. The contemporary

Musalla (left, seen from the minaret) and the window above a gateway (above) of the Great Mosque, Córdoba. The mosque was built between the eighth and tenth centuries, the Christian choir in the background in the sixteenth century. The decoration around the window is a fine example of arabesque.

mosque at Samarra in Iraq and the Ahmet ibn-Tulun Mosque in Cairo, on the other hand, opted for a greatly expanded surface area, with huge outer enclosures (*ziyadas*) containing the minaret. At Córdoba in Spain it was the sanctuary itself that was continuously enlarged in four major successive building campaigns without any resultant loss of direction. Vistas of seemingly infinite space unfold in all directions, with fixed intercolumniations used in modular form to create rows of identical units. These naturally evoke the long files of worshipers at prayer, much as Byzantine mosaics of saints in procession mirror the liturgy and basilical architecture to which they belong. The Córdoban use of parallel gabled roofs was enthusiastically adopted elsewhere, though the system of supports—two superposed tiers of columns—was too bold to have significant progeny. In Fatimid Egypt (969–1171) monumental projecting entrances, domes at the angles of the *qibla* wall, huge minarets terminating the main facade, and a plethora of lateral entrances all served to enliven the standard plan. Mamluk mosques in Egypt and Syria (1250–1517) adopted much of the vocabulary of *madrasas*, and their generally small scale forbade any radical rethinking of the Arab plan.

The second major tradition in mosque architecture is that of the Persian world, whose influence radiated west into Iraq and Turkey, north into the Caucasus and Central Asia, and eastward as far as India. Individual features of Persian inspiration sometimes traveled even farther afield. According to literary sources, the centuries immediately following the Arab conquest saw the frequent conversion of Zoroastrian fire tem-

ples into mosques. In form these temples typically comprised square, domed chambers with four axial entrances. Placed as they were in the center of large open enclosures, they were admirably suited to the liturgical requirements of Islam and it seems likely that at least on occasion such a domed chamber itself served as the *musalla* of a mosque. In the mosque at Neyriz in Iran (tenth century or earlier) the aisled sanctuary is replaced by yet another feature deeply rooted in pre-Islamic Persian tradition, the *iwan*, a deep, vaulted hall open at one or both ends and encased in a rectangular frame. The form had been widely used in Sassanian palace architecture, and its royal associations dovetailed quite naturally with those of the *mihrab*, the *minbar*, and the other borrowed features discussed previously. The future of mosque architecture in the Persian world was to lie in the varied combinations of domed chamber, *iwan*, aisled sanctuary, and courtyard, and it is possible that originally each of these features was itself used in isolation as a mosque. Subsequently, however, it was only the domed chamber that established itself as a mosque type.

There are numerous simple mosques of broadly Arab plan from the period ending about 1100. Thereafter a new synthesis may be observed, in which the influence of the *madrasa*, itself in origin a Persian institution, is perhaps detectable. In this arrangement, which was developed most intensively in a series of twelfth-century mosques in the orbit of Isfahan, an *iwan* is placed at each of the main axes of the courtyard, a domed chamber is made the focus of the sanctuary, and the arcades enclosing the courtyard are disposed along two tiers. This is the classic formulation of the so-called four-*iwan* plan, and it held continuous though not exclusive sway in Persia from then on. It was susceptible to various mutations: the number of *iwans*, for example, could be reduced to two or their size could be altered. Thus it was standard practice for the *qibla iwan* at the center of the sanctuary facade to be the largest of the four,

a direct transposition, incidentally, of the formulaic use of a great *iwan* preceding the domed or vaulted throne room of a Sassanian monarch.

In subsequent centuries architects by and large were content to tinker with the forms and combinations they had inherited rather than engage in any fundamental rethinking. Thus Mongol architects refined and attenuated Seljuk forms, often greatly increasing their scale, while in Timurid and Safavid times the emphasis shifted from structure to decoration. Safavid Isfahan, however, is of interest in that it reveals the response of mosque architects to urban planning on a vast scale. The Lutfallah Mosque and the Masjid-i Shah, both of the early seventeenth century, follow ancient schemas—namely the domed square chamber and the four-*iwan* plan. Both open onto the great *maidan* (square) intended as the nerve center of the new city and are therefore integrated into a larger design. Nevertheless, both have bent entrances so that their sanctuaries are correctly orientated to the *qibla*, which is an ingenious resolution of potentially discordant objectives.

The Turkish tradition of mosque architecture is a somewhat late starter in comparison with its Arab and Persian counterparts, for the Islamization of the country began only in the eleventh century and took four hundred years to complete. The early mosques had a pronounced experimental character. A few were of hypostyle form, omitting the courtyard altogether; but their low, multicolumned naves were afflicted by such dim lighting and cramped space that the scope for development along these lines was limited. Others were simple domed structures, sometimes provided with a courtyard and *iwans* but nearly always with a monumental portal. By degrees the courtyard was relegated to a secondary feature by a growing emphasis on the dome. The severe Anatolian winter is often cited as the reason why the covered mosque took root in Turkey; whatever the reason, this type encouraged the development of a highly integrated style. As with the dispositions of *iwans* in Persian mosques, so the number and grouping of domes allowed Turkish architects ample scope. Sanctuaries might have one, two, or three domes; a series of triple-domed aisles; a domed central transept; and many other variations on this theme, all of which displayed their own handling of interior space. Multidomed porticoes reminiscent of the narthex in Byzantine churches also gradually became standard features. Sometimes the courtyard was reintroduced in a curiously attenuated form by the device of opening up the central bay of the sanctuary and giving it a skylight with a fountain beneath.

By the early fifteenth century Turkish architects at Bursa and Dimetoka had evolved the concept of the sanctuary as a fully integrated interior dominated by a dome, and at the Üç Şerefeli Mosque (1437–1442) in Edirne a courtyard enclosed by twenty-two adjoining domed bays has been tacked on to the impressively domed sanctuary. To all intents and purposes, the nucleus of the Ottoman style, and with it such additional features as pencil-shaped minarets, semidomes, flying buttresses, and multiple lesser domes, was established before the capture of Constantinople in 1453. Thereafter, the influence of Hagia Sophia and Justinianian architecture must be reckoned with; but in all fairness it must be conceded that the various stages of the mounting Ottoman obsession with the dome can be traced for at least two centuries earlier.

Mature Ottoman mosques of the sixteenth century display a pronounced centrality of plan, with multiple domes and vaults grouped around the great central dome so as to create an inner space as extensive and unified as possible. Massive piers and spherical pendentives support the dome but hardly impair the spatial subtleties thus created. All this area is lit by windows arranged in obedience to a carefully calculated diffusion of light. Billowing niches suggest the expansion of space into the farther recesses of the mosque. Where clusters of subsidiary buildings need to be accommodated, they are placed so as to harmonize with the main axes of the mosque as defined by the principal dome, courtyard, and minarets.

Externally, these Ottoman mosques—such as the Selimiye at Edirne and the Suleimaniye and Sultan Ahmed Mosques at Istanbul—are perhaps the most dramatically sited and eye-catching religious structures in the Islamic world, with their orderly stacking of units to form a rippling but tightly interlocked silhouette cascading downward from the central dome, and guarded by minarets placed at the angles of this concentrated mass. These mosques reflect not only an empire at the height of its wealth and political power but also a gigantic state-financed program of public works, of which the presiding executive genius was the court architect Sinan. In the course of his long life (1489?–1587) he built, by his own reckoning, some 334 structures and may be said, with only a little exaggeration, to have created single-handedly this highly developed architecture. The decoration applied to these exteriors is parsimonious, but the exquisite stereotomy, the matchless sense of interval, and the unfailing grasp of the overall design is ample compensation. This mature Ottoman style maintained its impetus until the mid-seventeenth century but thereafter petered out in repetition and pastiche.

It is now time to relinquish the specific in favor of the general and try to pinpoint the abiding characteristics of mosque design throughout the Islamic world over almost a millennium. Four trends can perhaps be singled out: an innate flexibility; an indifference to exterior facades; a corresponding emphasis on the interior; and a natural bent for applied ornament.

Mosque architecture owes its flexibility, which is so pronounced a feature that it is not always possible to recognize the building as a mosque at first glance, to several distinct factors. Perhaps the most important of these is the lack of

Arcade of the Great Mosque, Raqqa, Syria (left), and the lateral aisle of the Tari Khana Mosque, Damghan, Iran (above). Two early examples of Muslim architecture are the eighth-century Abbasid mosque at Raqqa, where the front wall and later minaret are all that remain, and the ninth-century remains at Damghan.

sacramental and other formal ceremonies in Muslim worship, which means that there are few ritual requirements to be met. This has made it possible for a very wide variety of buildings to serve as mosques. The lack of a well-developed architectural tradition in Arabia meant that Muslims encountered the cultic buildings of other faiths with remarkably open minds, if only in the sense that they had no clearly defined notion of what constituted an appropriate kind of sanctuary. From this sprang a willingness to adopt alien architectural traditions and to adapt them freely, indeed ruthlessly, to suit Muslim needs. This was equally true whether the mosque was a free variation on themes borrowed from pre-Islamic tradition, or whether its structure was that of a pre-Islamic place of worship taken over by the Muslims for use as a mosque and subsequently modified. The net result of all this was to present Islamic architects, at least in theory, with a remarkably wide range of options in designing a mosque. In practice, of course, they tended to work within the limits of their own local schools.

Several reasons might be cited for the indifference Muslim architects customarily displayed to the notion of a highly articulated exterior facade in mosque design. They might, for example, have been influenced by the stubborn insistence of orthodox opinion that the Prophet would have disallowed

elaborate display in architecture. This attitude found expression in numerous *hadiths*. Alternatively there is the ingrained custom in Islamic lands whereby domestic and much public architecture presents an unyieldingly blank face to the world and thus preserves the privacy of those within. An even more practical consideration is the layout of most towns in the Islamic world. The absence of wheeled traffic meant that most streets were narrow, while Islamic law safeguarded private property rights; and this, together with the absence of municipal corporations of the European type, discouraged town planning on a spacious scale.

The operation of these various factors ensured that the layout of the average medieval Islamic city was too labyrinthine to contain much in the way of long, straight avenues, crescents, piazzas, or other similar features that might foster the development of elaborate facades. Thus the concept of the mosque as a major feature of the cityscape never took root. Despite a few major exceptions, which include mosques built in open country, it was standard practice for medieval mosques to present unpretentious exteriors. Very often they were located in the thick of bazaars and domestic housing, literally and metaphorically at the level of everyday life. So modest might the various entrances be that it would be quite possible to enter a mosque without immediately realizing it. In addition to all this the exterior perimeter of a mosque might well have grafted onto it, by a process of gradual accretion, whole clusters of subsidiary buildings—treasuries, latrines, mausoleums, halls for prayer in winter, *madrasas,* and even palaces. All would conspire to block any integrated exterior view of the mosque.

The relative neglect of the exterior facade brought in its train, by a pleasingly exact reciprocity, a consistent emphasis on the symmetrical planning of the interior. The facade, in short, moved inside the mosque. The role of the courtyard was crucial in all this, and significantly it is nearly always large enough to permit a full view of the sanctuary facade. *Iwans*, arcades, gables, and domes were the most popular methods of articulation, while the use of alternately projecting and recessed masses was also known. Islamic architects knew how to manipulate the masses of a building on the grand scale. The interaction of courtyard, *riwaqs* (covered arcades or cloisters), and enclosed sanctuary allowed them to experiment with various combinations of open, half-covered, and enclosed space, and to exploit multiple contrasts between light and shade. Broad, uncluttered surfaces helped to instill a peaceful atmosphere and prepared the worshiper to enter the cool, dark ambience of the sanctuary. The device of turning the mosque outside in, as it were, had an appealing simplicity; but more than that, it allowed the architect a freedom of maneuver that would be denied to him in the world outside the mosque. He could plan every detail of the facade, including the vital aspect of its interaction with its immediate surroundings, liberated from the constraints imposed by the secular architecture engulfing the exterior of the mosque on all sides.

No account of mosque architecture would be complete without reference to the decoration that embellishes it. The unwavering Muslim hostility to figural decoration with its accompanying overtones of idolatry encouraged an intense focus on abstract ornament. This soon came to be valued in its own right as an aid to contemplation, which is why such care is lavished on panels just above floor level and therefore at just the right height to be comfortably taken in by someone sitting on the floor. Whether the ornament is architectural or applied, its purpose is the same: to dissolve matter, to deny substantial masses and substitute for them a less palpable reality whose forms change even as they are examined. This is done by repeating individual units indefinitely—columns, arcades,

Exterior (left), interior (above), and interior of dome (right), Suleimaniye Mosque, Istanbul, Turkey. Sinan's masterpiece, which was built in the middle of the sixteenth century, displays the pronounced centrality of plan that is a common characteristic of mature Ottoman mosques.

muqarnas (cells of a honeycomb vault), and especially the various forms of applied decoration, whether floral, geometric, or epigraphic.

That the craftsmen who produced this ornamentation experienced a sensuous delight in the mingling of colors, materials, textures, and design motifs is scarcely to be questioned. But there is much more to Islamic decoration than this. Each of the three categories—floral, geometric, and epigraphic—has a deeper dimension. The endless variations that Islamic craftsmen were able to conjure forth on the theme of floral motifs, and which brought the word "arabesque" into European languages, of themselves suggest the inexhaustible richness of God's creation, and they are frequently interpreted in a symbolic religious sense as references to paradise and Allah himself. Geometrical ornament makes much play of multiple superimposed levels and of patterns that continue beyond the frame that encloses them; in both there are obvious suggestions of infinity. Finally, the epigraphic mode encountered in mosques is overwhelmingly and explicitly religious in content, comprising quotations from the Koran and the Hadith, with historical matter coming a poor third. These inscriptions are, quite simply, the Muslim answer to (not the equivalent of) icons. Their text, whether the mosque is in Spain or China, is in Arabic, a tribute to the potent unifying force of that language in the Muslim world.

Such then are the basic principles of medieval Islamic architecture. So faithfully were they observed across vast gulfs of space and time that almost any medieval mosque is instantly recognizable as such, whether it be in seventh-century Iraq, tenth-century Córdoba or seventeenth-century Delhi. Here if anywhere is the ocular proof that Islam is one.

THE MOSQUE
TODAY

AN ESSAY
By IHSAN FETHI

"Islamic culture has only recently begun to emerge from a past whose aesthetic values were based on craft toward a future whose aesthetic values will surely be based on machine production."[1]

This statement by the master jury of the Aga Khan Award for Architecture concerning the prizewinning Niono Mosque in Mali, is both profound and committed. Purely traditional or vernacular architectural solutions today should perhaps be regarded as the exception rather than the rule. They tend to be isolated examples of a rapidly disappearing culture and, at their best, an appropriate response to the conditions in the rural areas of Islam where traditional ways of building have never died. Such solutions, however, do not seem appropriate in the context of expanding urban centers, which have been fundamentally affected by Western culture and technology and where the widespread economic benefits from development would preclude any major reversal of the trend.

Islam, unlike most other religions, is an all-embracing faith that defines not only man's spiritual context in relation to the cosmos through the act of submission to Allah, but also regulates in great detail his daily life in the context of a disciplined social coexistence. It is on the latter that the influence of Western culture has been most profound.

Whereas in the past Islamic architecture was clearly the product of manual aesthetics, based on the subtle interaction of devoted builders and craftsmen and regulated by tradition, today it has become the product of machine aesthetics, based on a universal system of clients, architects, and contractors. The difference between the two systems is enormous: the first produces works of art slowly, which are highly distinctive and regionally identifiable; the second produces standardized or stereotyped buildings quickly, which tend to be anonymous and devoid of any valid symbolism. In some of the wealthy Muslim countries most major buildings are designed and executed by foreigners using largely imported materials. The difference between the Western import and the traditional method is well put by Bernard Huet, a French architect who has lived and worked periodically in Tunisia. "Whereas in our society," he writes, "there is a separation between intellectual

Conference Center Mosque, Riyadh, Saudi Arabia, by Trevor Dannatt and Partners. The view of this contemporary/modern example of mosque architecture is from the musalla, *looking into the courtyard. Its simple form follows local tradition.*

and material work, with specific and autonomous conceptual and methodological tools for creation and execution, in traditional cultures the person who actually conceives and he who executes (if there are two different persons) operate in exactly the same way and within the same conceptual framework—even though the knowledge of one may be more vast than that of the other."[2]

In the last few decades the method of building in most Muslim countries has had to keep pace with the rate of development. Hence the widespread adoption of Western methodology and technology, both of which have made for speed and efficiency. Not surprisingly even the architecture of mosques, which tends to be conservative, has succumbed to this procedure.

In absolute terms, the Muslim act of prayer can be performed in any clean place. Early mosques in Islam were very simple, austere structures—each basically an open space enclosed by a wall, with a small shaded area for prayers, the plan for which the prototype, as we have already seen, was the Prophet's house at Medina.

The orientation of all mosques toward the holy Ka'ba, or Black Stone, at Mecca, and the preference of worshipers to pray as close as possible to the *qibla*, necessitated an oblong plan for the prayer hall, with the *mihrab* marking its central axis. The spread of Islam, however, over a vast area with different cultural and ethnic characteristics brought about many changes and variations in mosque typology and style.

In terms of overall plan, most *masjids* and *jamis* fall into one of the four types described in the preceding essay—the Arab hypostyle, the Persian cruciform, the Seljuk pillar and dome, and the Ottoman centralized dome.[3] Similarly, there was a further development in the liturgical-functional typology of mosques. From the simple daily mosque (*masjid*) developed the congregational Friday mosque (*jami*), the monastic mosque (*takya, ribat*), the collegiate mosque (*madrasa*), and the memorial mosque (*mazar, mashad, marqad*). Certain plan types were found to be more suitable than others; in the case of *madrasas*, for example, the cruciform type was almost universally adopted throughout Islam.

The development of the volumetric, formalistic, and structural elements, however, was related more to the section of the mosque and its stylistic regional influences than to the type of mosque. It is in these elements that we find almost limitless variations. The Arab hypostyle Friday mosque was monumentalized horizontally by enlarging its area. The mosque at Samarra, for example is 156 by 240 meters. The Ottoman centralized-dome mosque was kept relatively compact in area but monumentalized mainly vertically through its height. The dome was often stretched to its maximum structural limits and reached a diameter of as much as 30 meters and a height of more than 50 meters. Similarly Ottoman minarets were raised as high as 85 meters, as in the Suleimaniye Mosque at Istanbul.

Stylistic variations and the production of hybrids arising from local architectural traditions are obviously more visible and tangible than the usually slight, subtle typological changes. Thus symbolic elements such as the minaret, structural elements such as vaults, arches, and domes, and decorative and other finishing techniques took different forms, depending not only on their historical chronological context but also on their

geopolitical and regional context. For example, square minarets became associated largely with Syrian and Moorish architecture, while slender pencil minarets became almost exclusively Turkish. Consequently it is in the stylistic rather than in the typological development of mosque architecture in Islam that the local identity and important symbolic association are more strongly in evidence.

The arrival of modern technology and the general liberalization in architectural design have resulted in the breakdown of tradition and in a new permissiveness that has been the cause of some sound innovation but also of much misguided experimentation, resulting in stylistic transplants and strange hybrids. It has become more difficult, therefore, to define the typology of mosque design. Of the four basic mosque types only two seem to persist today—the Arab hypostyle and the Ottoman centralized dome, although in modernized or adapted forms. In addition there are other, more profound changes: in the urban context of the mosque, in the role of the Waqf Administration as a major client, in the stylistic and symbolic associations of the mosque, and in the quality of architectural design generally. Consequently it is perhaps more relevant today to attempt to identify and analyze stylistic design trends in the context of the contemporary factors that may have caused these trends.

Studying new mosques, built or designed within the last four or five decades, has proved difficult because of the obvious lack of good documentation in the Islamic world generally. The data obtained, however, from various published competitions, articles, books, and the documentation of the Aga Khan Award has provided enough information to identify recent design trends in mosque architecture. Five broad trends seem to have emerged: 1) traditional/vernacular; 2) conservative/conventional; 3) new classic Islamic; 4) contemporary/modern; 5) eclectic/Arabian Nights. The classification of new mosques into such categories is risky and perhaps too simple, but it may help to clarify some of the confusion in mosque architecture today and encourage further argument.

The inclusion of some mosque examples under a particular category may be disputed by some readers, or indeed by the designers themselves. This difficulty, implicit in any attempt at classification, may be modified if it is assumed that there are no sharp boundaries separating the five categories. In most cases, in fact, putting an example into a particular category was a question of degree, and in some cases there was even an overlap between two or more categories.

Dar al-Islam Mosque, Abiquiun, New Mexico, by Hassan Fathi (left). The first of a group of buildings to be built for an Islamic community in the United States that are to include a school, a clinic, a shopping center, and other public buildings, the mosque can be classified as traditional/vernacular. The Tauheed Mosque, Aleppo, Syria (above), and the Othman Mosque, Damascus (right), belong to the conservative/conventional category.

The following examples have been included because the documentation in every case was sufficient to make classification possible. The list is therefore highly selective.

1. Traditional/Vernacular. These mosques have distinctive regional characteristics and are essentially continuations of traditional building techniques. They are built mainly by local masons using locally available materials. The majority are in rural areas and unmodernized regions of Islam.

Algeria: Mosque, Timimoun New Town (1930).

Burkina Faso: Great Mosque, Bobo-Dioulasso.

Egypt: Mosque, New Gourna, by architect Hassan Fathy (1945).

Kenya: Riadha New Mosque, Lamu (1970).

Mali: Great Mosque, Niono, by master mason Lassiné Minta (completed 1973, Aga Khan Award 1983). Great Mosque, Mopti (1935).

Philippines: Molundo New Mosque (late 1970s).

Tunisia: New mosque, Jara. Sidi Salim Mosque, Harusi (1963). Zamzamia Mosque, Gabès (1963). Shanini Mosque, Médenine. Mosque, Tatahouine (1958). Sidi Makhluf Mosque, Le Kef (1966).

2. Conservative/Conventional. The following mosques largely adhere to existing regional building characteristics, using fa-

miliar and stereotyped forms, with some modern architectural materials and services. Though modern structural systems such as reinforced-concrete roofs, beams, and columns were largely used, the mosques were still heavily dependent on local masons and craftsmen for finishing techniques, decorative work, and calligraphy. In other words, they tend to be quite modern in their structure, but conservative in their architecture and liturgical imagery.

Egypt: Abi Abbas al-Mursi Mosque, Alexandria, by architect Mario Rossi (designed 1928, completed 1945). Zamalik Mosque, Omar Mukarram Mosque, and Muhammad Karim Mosque, Cairo, by architect Mario Rossi. Salah al-Din Mosque, Cairo, by architect Ali Khairat. Sayida Safiya Mosque, Nasr City, Cairo, by architect M. A. Eissa (designed 1977, completed 1980). Fooli Mosque, Al-Minya (1946). Sports Club Mosque, Heliopolis (1953).

India: Nakhoda Mosque, Calcutta (1942).

Iraq: Ramadan Mosque (Al-Shaheed), Baghdad, by architect Fawzi Itani (designed 1940, completed 1957). Assafi Mosque, Baghdad, by architect A. Saghir (completed 1957). Qazaza Mosque, Baghdad, designed by *awqaf* (completed 1966). Adila Khatun Mosque, Baghdad, designed by *awqaf* (completed 1962).

Nigeria: Central Mosque, Ilorin (1978).

Pakistan: Maiman Mosque, Karachi (under construction 1984). Buhra Sect Mosque (three-story prayer hall), Karachi.

Senegal: Mouride Mosque, Touba (Moorish style). Great Mosque, Kaolack (Turkish style) (1983). Great Mosque, Dakar (Moorish style).

Syria: Othman Mosque, Damascus, by architect Muhammad Farra (designed 1961, completed 1974). Tauheed Mosque, Aleppo, by architect Hickmat Yasji.

Tunisia: Habibiya Mosque, Tunis (1961). Sidi Daoud Mosque, Tunis (1964). Bourguiba Mosque, Monastir (1963). Bourguiba Mosque, Qafsa (1967).

United Arab Emirates: Great Mosque, Abu Dhabi.

3. New Classic Islamic. In these mosques an adapted classic Islamic architectural vocabulary has been used, especially in forms, patterns, and signs. The mosques have mostly modern structures, often incorporating sophisticated and innovative construction techniques and architectural services. In other words they are essentially modern, but an attempt has been made to make them fit in with the locality by the use of a traditional vocabulary and symbolism. They cannot be called

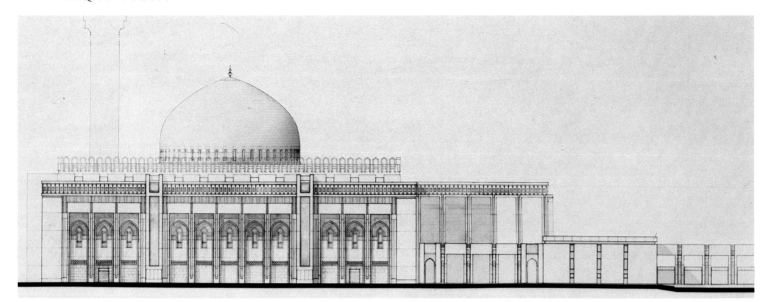

conservative, because they are adaptive and innovative; and they cannot be called contemporary, because they clearly depart from the usual internationalist architectural idiom.

Iraq: State Mosque Competition, Baghdad (1983, designs only): by Ricardo Bofill, Taller de Arquitectura (Barcelona), and Iraq Consult (Baghdad); Venturi, Rauch and Scott Brown (Philadelphia); Minoru Takeyama (Tokyo). Khulafa Mosque, Baghdad, by architect Makiya Associates (designed 1962, completed 1964).

Italy: Mosque and Islamic Cultural Center, Rome (1975, design only): by architects Paolo Portoghesi, Vittorio Gigliotti (Rome), and Sami Mousawi (Iraq).

Kuwait: State Mosque, Kuwait City, by architect Makiya Associates (designed 1978, under construction).

4. *Contemporary/Modern.* In the following mosques a contemporary International Style vocabulary predominates in usually abstracted forms and streamlined geometry, using modern structural construction techniques, services, and materials. Consequently they do not necessarily attempt to attain a specific local identity architecturally. They are perhaps more innovative than the previous categories and some show a remarkable degree of originality and purist simplicity.

Bangladesh: Bait al-Mukarram Mosque, Dacca, by architects Thariani and Co. (designed 1960, completed 1963).

Indonesia: Salman Campus Mosque, Bandung, by architect Achmad Nae'man (designed 1960, completed 1972).

Iraq: University of Baghdad Mosque, by architects Walter Gropius and T.A.C. (United States) (designed 1956, under construction). Dauodiya Mosque, Rashdiya, Baghdad, by architect Abdulla Ihsan Kamil (designed 1962, completed 1963). Buniya Mosque, Baghdad, by architect Qahtan Madfai (designed 1967, completed 1971).

Iran: Mosque for University of Jondishahpour, Ahvaz, by architects D.A.Z. (Kamran Diba) (designed 1971, completed 1974).

Jordan: King Abdullah Mosque, Amman, by architect Rasem Badran (1979, design only); alternative design by architects Ribhi Sobeh, Hasan Nouri, and Jan Cejka (1979, design only).

Kuwait: Fatima Mosque, Abdulla Salem District.

Lebanon: Aysha Bakkar Mosque, Beirut, by architect Ja'afar Tukan (designed 1970, completed 1973).

Malaysia: Negara Great Mosque, by architect Eriche Baharuddin (designed 1957, completed 1965).

Oman: Sultan Mosque, Ruwi District, by architects Maath Alusi and T.E.S.T. (Baghdad) (1975).

Pakistan: King Faisal Mosque, Islamabad, by architect Vedat Dalokay (designed 1968, nearing completion). Ahle Hadith Mosque, Islamabad, by architect Anwar Said (designed 1970, completed 1973). Al-Tooba Mosque (Defense Society mosque), Karachi, by architect Babet Hamid (1969). Shuhada Mosque, Lahore, by architect Babet Hamid. Clifton Mosque, Karachi.

Qatar: Osman ibn-Affan Mosque, Doha, by architect Halim Abdel Halim in collaboration with Arab Bureau for Design, Egypt (award-winning design 1981).

Saudi Arabia: Mosque in conference center, Riyadh, by architects Trevor Dannatt and Partners (designed 1966, completed 1976). Mosque in conference center, Mecca, by architects Rolf Gutbrod and Frei Otto (designed 1966, completed 1973). Mosque for Youth Welfare Development, Dammam (designed 1980). Mosque for University of Petroleum, Dahran, by architects Caudill Rowlett Scott (designed 1966, completed 1974). Mosque for Riyadh Railway Station, by architect L. Barbera (1978, design only). King Khalid Airport Mosque, by architects Vesti Corporation (Boston) (completed 1984).

Singapore: Majlis Ugama Islam Mosque, by architects of Housing and Development Board (1980). Al-Muttagin Mosque, Ang Mo Kio, by architects of H.D.B. (completed 1980).

Sudan: Safia Mosque, Khartoum North, by architect M. Hamdi (designed 1972, completed 1974).

Tunisia: Hammam Sousse Mosque, Sousse (1965); Sidi Abdul Salam Mosque, Gabès (1965). Bin-Bashir Mosque, Jandouba, (1967).

Turkey: Mosque for Etimesgüt Armed Units, Ankara, by architect Cengiz Bektaş (designed 1965, completed 1967).

Yugoslavia: Sherefudin White Mosque, Visoko (Aga Khan Award 1983), by architects Zlatko Ugljen and D. Malkin (completed 1980).

5. *Eclectic/Arabian Nights.* These are mosques in which whimsical and often bizarre combinations of Islamic forms and

Plan of State Mosque, Kuwait City, Kuwait (left). The design is for a new classic Islamic type of mosque. Aysha Bakkar Mosque, Beirut, Lebanon (above), and a mosque in Abu Dhabi (right). The first is representative of the contemporary/modern trend, while the second is a clear-cut example of the eclectic/Arabian Nights tendency in mosque design.

symbols have been used. The eclectic use of symbolic elements from various regional architectural styles, such as multifarious onion domes and frilly minarets, curious arches, and the excessive use of decoration, evoke Hollywood images of the Arabian Nights. As such, they tend to be imaginative but often clumsy in proportion and lacking in overall discipline. They seem to be popular in Pakistan and the Muslim Far East but also in some parts of the Arabian Gulf.

Brunei: Great Mosque, Bandar Seri Begawan.

Jordan: Queen Aliya Mosque, Amman, by architect Edward Mansfield (designed 1977, completed 1980).

Malaysia: Aboudiya Mosque, Kuala Kingisar. Zahir Mosque, Alor Setar, Kedah.

Oman: Omar Bin al-Khattab Mosque, Sur, by architects Ayoub Oghanna Associates (Masqat) (designed 1980).

Pakistan: Jeem Mosque, Chitral.

Although the mosque—both *masjid* and *jami*—is fundamentally a place for worship, it has traditionally played a much

wider role in the life of the Muslim community. Its traditional functions of school, library, hostelry, law court, sociopolitical center, and much more have already been noted in the preceding essay. The *jami,* because of its relatively large size and close association with the Islamic state, was traditionally the biggest and highest building in the city. This tendency to monumentalize mosque architecture, first fully evident in Iraq under the Abbasids, did not result in the physical isolation of the mosque from the rest of the city, as was the case with some shrine mosques. Despite its size, the *jami* remained an introverted building, closely integrated with the dense urban fabric. It nearly always occupied a central location and was usually contiguous with the *suqs* (markets), *hammams* (baths), *khans* (caravansaries), and houses of the area.

Since the late-nineteenth century Western influence on the urban fabric of Islamic cities, transmitted indirectly by European colonists, has caused an almost total change in the urban context of both *masjid* and *jami.* The arrival of the car led to the destruction of significant parts of the historic fabric to provide for the easy movement of vehicular traffic. As a result many mosques were demolished, while the more historic examples frequently were severed from their former urban context and pedestrian linkages by wide roads.

Furthermore, within the last fifty years, as a result of rapid urban growth combined with the importation of Western ideas in city planning, the new suburban mosque has been conceived as a freestanding extrovert monument, occupying a whole city block as defined by the four roads of a gridiron plan. This new context of the mosque has had as profound an effect on its function as a religious and social center as on its architecture.

The notion of the mosque as an isolated monument, depending on vehicular accessibility for a congregation that no longer lives in its shadow, has become widespread. Thus the

Exteriors of the seventeenth-century Shah Mosque, Isfahan, Iran (above), and the 1969 Al-Tooba Mosque, Karachi, Pakistan (right), compared. Domes, arches, and minarets are used in both, but it is the minaret only that signals the identity of the Karachi mosque. The change of axis in the Shah Mosque absent in the freestanding Al-Tooba Mosque also shows the change from the orientation to Mecca to the axes of the city plan.

mosque, even if its catchment area is a well-defined suburb, no longer appears to belong to a specific locality, because it is no longer physically connected to the surrounding urban fabric. One of the consequences of conceiving the mosque as a freestanding structure surrounded by large open spaces rather than as an inward-looking structure hugging the perimeter of the site has been the obsolescence of the great courtyard, which has either shrunk in size or been omitted altogether. The mosque is therefore designed as an enclosed building, which cannot function properly without the active support of such modern services as artificial lighting and cooling, a tendency that is particularly evident in the wealthier Muslim countries where energy consumption and cost factors are often not considered to be of any major consequence.

Two outstanding examples may help illustrate the negative effect of this new urban context. The Um al-Tubool Mosque in Baghdad, built in 1964 as a major Friday mosque, has become so isolated from the surrounding residential districts, because of an elaborate multilevel traffic intersection, that it fails to attract even a modest number of worshipers on Fridays, let alone other days.[4] The Hilali Mosque in Kuwait is in a worse predicament, because it is situated in the center of a large traffic circle.

The dismemberment of the mosque from its traditional urban setting and the reorientation of its traditional introverted form to an extroverted one has also resulted in the disappearance of the outer wall and its gateways. This wall, which represented the physical demarcation between the profanity of the street and the sanctity of the mosque, is now replaced by a low, often see-through parapet, which represents a major break with tradition. Similarly, the main gate, traditionally facing the *qibla*, has tended to become artistically unimportant and visually insignificant.

Westernization and political nationalism have helped to bring about a *de facto* secularization in many Islamic states. The *awqaf*, the guardian of mosques, has lost its independence and become an official governmental organization. In most Islamic states it has acquired a large share of the real-estate market and is heavily involved in property development. As a result it has often become too busy, with its heavy investment program, to give proper attention to the care and maintenance of its large stock of historic mosques or to the building of well-designed new ones.

The available evidence suggests that most private mosques are built by local contractors with permission from the municipal planning authorities and not the *awqaf*, which does not appear to give much architectural guidance or exercise design quality control in most Muslim countries. Because good, experienced masons and craftsmen are now hard to find and in any case prohibitively expensive, hundreds of badly executed and strangely hybrid mosques are built every year all over the Islamic world. Some examples in Pakistan, Southeast Asia, and the Gulf countries—the eclectic/Arabian Nights category—are difficult to accept as serious contributions to religious architecture. It would be tempting to dismiss them and to regard their proliferation as a degenerative trend in Islamic architecture if it were not for their genuinely popular appeal. Indeed the same ostentatious love of color and gaudy decoration can be found in Hindu temples and in houses and extends in Pakistan and Afghanistan even to motorized vehicles. This suggests that the trend is perhaps a genuine manifestation of folk art. But whereas this manifestation may be acceptable in the design of small rural and urban *masjids*, it cannot be considered appropriate for the large-scale *jamis*, which are architect-designed and officially sponsored and which must therefore display a degree of dignity and *gravitas*.

The influence of some European engineers and architects has also helped to give credence to the concept of the mosque as freestanding monument. Mario Rossi, an Italian architect (1897–1961), for example, was influential in the development in Egypt of a new, but still basically conservative, style of mosque design. His mosques in Cairo and Alexandria are an

Interior of the fourteenth-century Friday Mosque, Isfahan, Iran (above), and the 1973 Ahle Hadith Mosque, Islamabad, Pakistan (right), compared. The vaulting in the contemporary mosque is insubstantial and seems to float in comparison with that in the medieval hypostyle hall.

attempt to create a synthesis of the Ottoman and Mamluk styles, with some innovations of his own. Rossi came to Egypt while in his twenties and was first employed by the Ministry of Works, which assigned him duties in the Royal Palaces. Later, in 1928, he was commissioned to design the Abi al-Abbas al-Mursi Mosque in Alexandria, which took sixteen years to complete. During this period Rossi was converted to Islam and began his systematic study of mosque architecture in Egypt. He compiled an impressive atlas of Islamic architecture and decoration, which remains unpublished and is kept by the *awqaf*.

With the exception of certain innovations, Rossi's mosque designs show a basic adherence to tradition, especially in his repeated use of the Ottoman centralized dome type. His experiments were mostly stylistic, in the decoration of the mosque and in the shape of the minaret, dome, etc. Of particular interest are his mosques of Zamalik and Omar Mukarram in Cairo, and the Mahatat al-Raml, Muhammad Karim, and Abi Abbas al-Mursi Mosques in Alexandria. In most of his designs he did away with the open courtyard altogether, and raised the mosque well above street level, thereby treating it as a totally enclosed monument. The mosque was reached by ascending a flight of steps that led to a colonnaded portico instead of the usual *iwan* gateway. The omission of the open courtyard, in particular, became popular, because it was difficult to find large enough plots in town centers.

Rossi's notable stylistic innovations include new forms of arabesque (*tawrique*) decoration, especially for filigree masonry screens, which he used extensively and which became very popular in Egyptian mosques; carved stone domes in the corners

of mosques in addition to the main central dome; and his treatment of the minaret, whose form and height he sometimes exaggerated as at the Mahat al-Raml Mosque (1948–1951), which soars to 73 meters above ground level.

Rossi's mosques, together with those of several Egyptian architects, notably Ali Thabit and Ali Khairat, established a style that became popular in Egypt and spread as far as Saudi Arabia, the Gulf countries and even Iraq, which has a strong building tradition of its own.[5]

The current approach to mosque design by architects all over the world seems to favor a modern style, though the majority of mosques actually realized are in fact conservative. The Madrid Islamic Cultural Center Competition of 1980, which included a mosque as a major component of a larger complex, attracted 455 entries from more than 2,000 architects. Of the forty-five different countries represented, sixteen were Muslim. The Union of International Architects (U.I.A.), the organizers of the competition, published a monograph that reproduced all the entries. It is a document of exceptional interest, because of the wide variety of types and styles it covers, which makes it a major source for anyone thinking about mosque design today.

A detailed analysis I did of all the submissions revealed several interesting and some startling results (table, p. 60). As far as design approach is concerned, the overwhelming majority of architects (76 per cent) opted for an unconventional modern solution, while only 13 per cent opted for a low-key conservative one. Yet today, barely five years later, few new mosques are being built in a truly contemporary style. The evidence shows a remarkable attachment to familiar and stereotyped forms, due perhaps to the resistance of the Islamic clergy and *awqaf* to formal innovation. Because there seems to be no religious objection, on the other hand, to the use of advanced technology, traditional forms often disguise modern structures as well as imported materials and technical services.

Why is it, then, that unconventional styles—modern or

eclectic—are encouraged in certain Muslim countries and not in others? The reasons are complex and are to be found in the particular religious, geopolitical, and cultural circumstances of each country. In general, a conservative approach is more likely in a country that possesses a strong building tradition than in one that does not, or where there are other building traditions besides the Islamic. This may explain why the eclectic/Arabian Nights type is abundant in certain oil-rich Arab Gulf countries, in Pakistan, and in the fringe regions of Islam such as Malaysia, Singapore, and the Philippines, but hardly found at all in such countries as Iraq, Egypt, Tunisia, Morocco, Iran, and Turkey, all of which have a strong Islamic building tradition. It may be of interest to note that the type is often architect-designed and that, in the Madrid competition, twenty-four entries fell into this category, two of which were by Muslim architects.[6]

Only thirteen entries (3 per cent) that could be classified broadly as "high tech" were identified, though some may also be described as "postmodern".[7] This is hardly surprising since it is difficult to imagine a mosque designed in an exposed steel frame with clips and gaskets ever being acceptable to the Muslim clergy, let alone the people. The problem, however, is one of distinguishing between means and ends. If an architect were able to use high tech as a means to an end that fulfilled the cultural aspirations of a people rather than as an end in itself—as the style that it has become—the possibility of such a mosque being built becomes plausible. A design like Ludovico Quaroni's for the Rome Mosque,[8] or Toyokazu Watanabi's for the Madrid Mosque[9] might then do for mosque architecture what Philip Johnson/Burgee's Crystal Cathedral in California (1980)[10] has done for church architecture.

The fundamental difficulty in mosque design arises from the fact that it is not always possible to draw clean lines between what is feasible or acceptable and what is not, when there are only a few rules governing mosque architecture. The Koran refers to the word *masjid* twenty-eight times, but in none of these references is there any relevance to mosque architecture. Equally, the Hadith, the Traditions of the Prophet, do not specifically refer to mosque design and, surprisingly, there is no major historical account of architecture by Muslim scholars. The only rules that qualify a building as a mosque are that it should be a clean enclosure or sheltered space, with a *mihrab* oriented toward Mecca.

Indeed there are thousands of small mosques in the Muslim world that contain only a small *musalla* with a *mihrab* and ablution facilities. They have no minarets, domes, arches, or decoration, but perhaps some Koranic inscriptions painted simply on the *mihrab* and the entrance gate. The only condition of making a *masjid* into a *jami* is the addition of a *minbar* (pulpit), essentially a piece of furniture to facilitate Friday *khutba* (sermons).

There are on the other hand many unwritten rules and traditions (*urf*), which the architect cannot afford to ignore, especially when the mosque is of significant size and of urban and townscape importance. These rules are the accumulated traditions, norms, associated symbols, and signs of a particular culture in a particular region.

The history of the mosque itself shows a slow but definite evolution from the simple utilitarian models of early Islam to

The Madrid Islamic Cultural Center Competition, 1980—Selected Analysis

Style	number	per cent
Traditional/vernacular	0	0.0
Conservative/conventional	58	13.0
New classic Islamic	14	3.0
Contemporary/modern	346	76.0
Eclectic/Arabian Nights	24	5.0
High tech	13	3.0
Total	455	100.0
Musalla plan		
Square	176	38.8
Rectangular (oblong)	175	38.6
Rectangular (deep)	51	11.3
Polygonal	40	8.6
Circular	7	1.5
T-shaped	3	0.6
Diagonal (*mihrab in corner*)	2	0.4
Triangular	1	0.2
Total	455	100.0
Musalla columns		
Hypostyle	265	58.2
Minimum number of columns or none	190	41.8
Total	455	100.0
Symbolic elements		
With one minaret	423	93.0
With more than one minaret	8	1.8
Without minarets	22	4.8
With leaning minaret	2	0.4
With dome(s)	136	30.0
With arches	204	45.0

Sources: *Madrid Islamic Cultural Center Competition;* U.I.A. monograph, Paris, 1980.

the unsurpassed monumentality and magnificence of Ommiad, Abbasid, Fatimid, Seljuk, Safavid, Mogul, and Ottoman models. The history also shows a continuous evolution in mosque architecture, even within one region. It is beyond doubt that the designers and builders of those historic periods employed the most sophisticated building technology available at the time and were willing to experiment with new materials and techniques. In fact Islamic architecture as we know it today is the result of a long synthesis of a number of cultural interactions and adaptations, and what gives Islamic architecture its vitality comes from the great variety of regional contexts that together form an overall unity.

The minaret, for example, has become functionally obsolete, because for the last forty years loudspeakers have commonly been used in town mosques. But the minaret, irrespective of its shape, is now so deeply established as an important sign of the Islamic faith, that it is difficult to think of a mosque of any architectural significance without one. It is not surprising, therefore, that minarets continue to be used despite their obsolescence as functional elements. In the Madrid competition the overwhelming majority of mosque designs (93 per cent) had at least one minaret. It is my opinion that, in terms of external formal symbolism and recognition, the minaret and not the dome is the most important single architectural element in mosque design. Without it the form will not easily be recognized as a mosque. Domes alone can be taken for a shrine, a *hammam* (bath), or indeed any other public building. So important was the minaret to Makiya's design for the Baghdad State Mosque Competition, that he elevated it to a height of 240 meters, "forming a monument with a powerful vertical axis. As such it becomes a spiritual, visual and cultural symbol expressed on the skyline of the city."[11]

Another architectural problem associated with mosque symbolism and not functionality is the special ambience of the *musalla*. While it is a well-known fact that in Islam a rectangular plan with its long axis parallel to the *qibla* is preferable, there is no specific religious objection to other shapes. It follows, however, that to emphasize the sense of direction toward the Ka'ba, the Black Stone, the volume of the *musalla* should be designed to achieve and preferably enhance this essential symbolic requirement. Consequently any nondirectional shape that has equal sides, such as a square or an octagon, should be avoided because of its tendency to emphasize the centrality of the space rather than the axiality of the *qibla*.

Circular or triangular shapes are unacceptable.[12] The Al-Tooba Mosque in Karachi (built in 1969), which is virtually an enlarged copy of Walter Gropius's design for the University of Baghdad, is not only symbolically disconcerting, but with its circular domed space it creates acute acoustical problems. Similarly, the frequent examples of square and octagonal plans today suggest that the symbolic meaning of the interior space of the mosque is misunderstood by many architects. In the Madrid competition there was an unexpected fifty-fifty split between oblong and square *musalla* plans (38 per cent for each).

Equally important in the plan of a large *musalla* in a *jami* is the question of the modular and structural punctuation of its space. In traditional Arab hypostyle mosques the *musalla* had to be subdivided by columns or arcades in spans determined by the structural properties of the materials in current use. Besides the obvious economic advantages of such a method, the frequent supports also acted as physical reference points that helped worshipers to align themselves in parallel rows. The division of space into smaller, equal bays gave the hypostyle hall its characteristic ambience and sense of equipoise. Furthermore, when the dome became common in mosques, it was placed nearer the *mihrab* area and away from the center of the *musalla*. In this sense the dome, which symbolizes the sky and the cosmic turtle, emphasizes the shift in the space toward Mecca. Ottoman centralized-dome mosques, therefore, represent a major break with this important symbolic tradition.

Unlike the Gothic church, whose volume is essentially vertical, the volume of the hypostyle mosque is strongly horizontal. The meaning of this horizontality must be properly understood by architects and clergy alike, for it constitutes one of the basic requirements of mosque design. Yet it is a requirement that seems to be widely ignored. One needs to

Conference Center Mosque, Riyadh, by Trevor Dannatt and Partners. The minaret and entrance area of this contemporary/modern mosque are given weight by clean lines, plain surfaces, and harmonious geometric shapes.

look no further than one of the 1983 Aga Khan Awards, Sherefudin's White Mosque in Visoko, Yugoslavia, to find a *musalla* with a top-lit vertical space, whose source is more easily found in the work of certain modern European masters than in traditional mosque design.

Modern technology offers the designer virtually limitless possibilities in the choice of structure. It is quite possible, for example, to have a very large *musalla* without any supports other than the outside walls—an advantage for worshipers who prefer to see the *mihrab* and the *khatib* on the *minbar* during Friday sermons. The symbolism associated with the "palm forest" of columns, however, remains irresistible, to judge from the Madrid competition, in which nearly 60 per cent of all entries employed the hypostyle plan. In the Baghdad competition all seven competitors opted for a hypostyle plan, despite their widely divergent design ideologies. Interestingly the Ricardo Bofill and Iraq Consult entry for this competition was based on the principle of standardization and prefabrication, with hollow columns for the distribution of air-conditioning in an integration of symbolism, services, and structure.

Symbolic elements in mosques—the minaret, dome, pointed arch, decoration, calligraphy, crenellations, and finials, which incidentally are often used as standards to mark the particular sect to which a mosque belongs—are not absolute requirements but nevertheless offer great potential for stylistic elaboration. The associated symbols have evolved in the past and may do so in the future, but whereas in the past it took many generations for an established symbolic element to be changed, today such changes are fast and frequent.

The compression in the time scale of modern development

has offered new horizons but has also meant the disruption of tradition. This is especially pertinent to mosque architecture where the religio-functional requirements and constraints are minimal but the psychosymbolism is extremely demanding. The resultant cultural discontinuity and the loss of identity, created by the dramatic intervention of Westernization and global technology, are manifested in the present confusion in Islamic architecture generally.

In the somewhat desperate search for reassuring symbols many architects, both Muslim and non-Muslim, have made choices in their mosque designs that must be called into doubt, and the following examples are cited in a questioning rather than condemnatory spirit. The use of metaphorical analogy can be seen in the Bait al-Mukarram Mosque at Dacca (built in 1963), which imitates the cubic form of the Black Stone.[13] The mosque, according to the architects, has become a special attraction for non-Muslim tourists who otherwise cannot visit Mecca. Its height of 99 feet from *mihrab* level, moreover, is supposed to correspond to the ninety-nine names of Allah, a conceit that is obscure enough but would become meaningless if the height was measured in meters.

Similarly a mosque in Amman, Jordan,[14] designed by the British architect Edward Mansfield has four domes to signify the four years of marriage of the notable commemorated by the monument. In Saudi Arabia a mosque designed by the Iraqi architect Basil Bayati takes the form of an open book (the Koran), complete with open leaves and inscription, and contains five shafts, which are to be understood as the Five Pillars of Islam.[15] A mosque built in Ankara in 1967, described by the architect as the first really modern mosque in Turkey, has Koranic inscriptions in the Latin alphabet on its *mihrab*.[16] Paolo Portoghesi in his design for the Rome mosque (1975) compares the elaborate shafts of the *musalla* to "hands during the act of prayer," which prompted Charles Jencks's comment that the "flying exuberance of these structural members, a modernist conceit . . . are like a Nervi structure on a holiday."[17] Among the Madrid competition entries there were a Greek temple,[18] a Black Stone,[19] a hypostyle hall with real palm trees,[20] two designs with inclined minarets,[21] and a minaret incorporating residential appartments, which was given fifth mention despite strong objections from several members of the jury.[22]

At the same time the Madrid competition included many sober entries that deserve full credit for the way in which the

Said Naum Mosque, Jakarta, Indonesia, by Atelier Enam (left). The building is contemporary in spirit, with distinctly traditional characteristics of the region. Above: University of Petroleum Mosque, Dahran, Saudi Arabia. The mosque falls uncompromisingly into the contemporary/modern category. Right: Um al-Tubool Mosque, Baghdad, Iraq. The isolation of the mosque by a multilevel traffic intersection is indicative of an increasingly common characteristic of modern Islamic cities. Instead of an intimate part of the urban fabric and daily life of the people, mosques are often accessible only by automobile.

architects tried to create a truly contemporary mosque. The winning design, for example, by the Polish architects Jan Czarny, Jolanta Singer, J. Zemla, and M. Zemla[23] shows a courageous approach that makes use of modern technology, attempting a subtle fusion of traditional architecture and to-day's needs.

In conclusion it must be said that the architecture of the mosque is generally in a stagnant state, due in no small measure to the erosion of its regional vitality. The unquestioning acceptance by the clergy of modern planning requirements has severed the mosque from its lifeblood and made it a detached monument, whose importance as sculptural form is essentially untraditional. The resistance of the clergy, on the other hand, to all design innovation has made most architects today adopt the conventional approach and the use of familiar imagery as the safest path to client satisfaction. Despite its shortcomings, the contemporary approach—seen in Sherefudin's White Mosque, the Aysha Bakkar Mosque in Beirut, the Conference Center Mosque in Riyadh, the Sultan Mosque in Sur, Oman, and the Hamman Sousse Mosque in Sousse, Tunisia—can produce bold and original results. Similarly, Makiya's mosque in Kuwait and the designs for the Baghdad competition by Bofill and Iraq Consult and by Venturi, Rauch and Scott Brown are equally bold attempts at a reinterpretation of traditional elements and the way these are put together.

A truly contemporary approach must take into account the needs and aspirations of the people for whom the mosque is built. The technology is the means by which it is built, and the choice of technology, to be appropriate, must depend on the conditions of a particular place. It is through an honest response to such considerations rather than through a literal expression of past styles that the mosques of the future will retain their differences and remain close to the spirit of Islam.

A SURVEY OF MODERN TURKISH ARCHITECTURE[1]

AN ESSAY By DOĞAN KUBAN

The nature of Westernization has a different character in Turkish history from that in other Islamic countries. The Turkish presence in Europe dates from the mid-fourteenth century, and European artistic forms were introduced in Turkey in the early-eighteenth century. Furthermore Turkey has never become a colony. This long historical accommodation in, as well as confrontation with, Europe makes Turkish/Western, i.e. national/international, relationships a long experience peculiar to Turkish history.

Ideological Basis. Two conflicting attitudes shaped the thinking of non-Western intelligentsia in the nineteenth century: modernization, industrialization, and civil liberties were necessary items for survival; at the same time these demands coincided with the awakening and consolidation of nationalism and a strong sense of resistance against Western imperialism. The former was based on Western ideologies and know-how, the latter was inherently anti-Western. This dilemma between the wholehearted adoption of Western science, technology, and education on the one hand and the assertion of a national cultural identity on the other created highly complex problems of interpretation, which are still being felt in every field of activity throughout the Islamic world and in the other so-called Third World countries. The problem of identity was further complicated by the dichotomy between Islamic *umma* (religious community) and nationalism in its Western sense.

Until the second half of the nineteenth century, the question of historical heritage or identity posed no problems for the sultans and the ruling elite. Selim III, Mahmud II, Abdul-Mejid, and Abdul-Aziz had single-mindedly followed Western examples. The architects, if not Westerners, were mostly from non-Muslim minorities and better prepared to adopt and introduce Western ideas. Even the problem of revival, so fashionable in Europe, was introduced with a bizarre eclecticism as European "Saracenic."[2]

At the turn of the century a more genuine attempt at the creation of a neo-Ottoman style was made by Turkish architects Ahmet Kemalettin and Mehmet Vedat, which lasted for the

Interior of an office building at Yalova, Istanbul, by Cafer Bozkurt (1974). Now a well-known name, Bozkurt is one of the architects who started practice in the late 1960s and became prolific. Like much of the work of his contemporaries Bozkurt's lacks any pronounced individual style.

first decade of the Republic.[3] After the revolution and the proclamation of the Turkish Republic, national identity was sought in the depths of national history. The response of the early republicans to this historical question was peculiar to Turkey.

Kemal Atatürk's basic ideas on the history of modern Turkish people is of considerable originality and anthropological depth: for him, Turkish history was neither the history of the Ottoman dynasty and its immediate predecessors nor of early Islam. Nor was it only the history of the Turks, which could be traced to the pre-Islamic history of the vast Asian steppes. It should also include the history of the land itself, of Anatolia, which Atatürk introduced as an inseparable part of Turkish history.[4]

The historical framework of the modern Turkish Republic was the integration of the histories of the land and the people. This universal and humanitarian vision encompasses and appropriates the historical experiences of the Turkish people, nomadic, settled, the history of Islam and the history of Turkey, pre-Turkish and Turkish. Atatürk's vision united historical space and time, and defined the man in his multidimensional and contemporary complexity.

His ideas were strongly implemented in a vigorous political framework of secularism. This was not the refusal of Islam in the life of a people, but the replacement of Islamic ecumenism by a larger perspective of human history, in which each cultural component would allow the existence of its antinomies: Turkish and non-Turkish, Muslim and non-Muslim, traditional and modern. Obviously with a clear sense of direction and historical mission, the goal was a unified modern universal civilization without ambiguity of reference except for the self-identity that was necessary for the sake of internal coherence.

Thus the dichotomy of the past and present, modernism and Islam or tradition did not exist in the minds of Atatürk and his followers. This sets the basis for the modernization in which the creation of the physical environment cannot but reflect a single reality: modern life and modern technology. As a general direction this goal cannot be refuted. Nowhere in today's world are the amenities of modern life and the use of modern technology refuted. There is a nuance, however, in the interpretation of the term "modern technology." It does not mean, and cannot mean, the same thing for different societies. Neither can it be bought or taken wholesale from a universal market. For the period following the First World War, the problem for Atatürk and for the political leaders was

Traditional wooden houses in the Suleimaniye quarter of Istanbul that survived the process of rapid urbanization in the '50s and '60s (left). Above: Apartment house, Ortaköy, Istanbul, by Sedat Hakki Eldem. Its geometrical division of facades, characteristic of this architect's work, provides a noteworthy example of contemporary Turkish architecture. Right: Faculty housing, Middle East Technical University, Ankara, by Behruz Çinici, an architect of experiment and phantasy. Far right: Apartment blocks, Istanbul, an example of the kind of speculative private-sector housing that has replaced historic quarters.

to point out the main goal as a pure image. It set in motion a whole political system geared toward modernization. But in its realization there was the necessity of deeper understanding, more detailed definition of circumstances, and more studied analyses of implementation techniques.

Today the questioning of the earlier radicalism in the straightforward use of Western vocabulary and techniques comes from the realization that the political and philosophical goals represented basic attitudes and not definitions for everyday practical use. We should also recall the fact that the acceptance of the Western image prevailed in all non-Western countries, independently of political or ideological biases.

Education and the Role of Foreign Architects before the Second World War. A short review of the education of architects will explain the orientation of the new architecture.[5] The only school of architecture at the beginning of the Republic was at the Academy of Fine Arts in Istanbul, founded during the Empire. Its teachers and graduates were responsible for the early-Republican architecture, which was a simple continuation of the neo-Ottoman style.[6] The first buildings in the capital, Ankara, were built in it. In 1929, at the School of En-

gineering in Istanbul, an architectural curriculum was introduced, with particular emphasis on engineering and technology. And for three decades these two schools produced the bulk of Turkish architects, who created the physiognomy of modern Turkey. In both schools the philosophy of design was dictated by European architects who were also engaged in the building of the capital. The most eminent among them were Ernst Egli, who taught at the Academy of Fine Arts, and Clemens Holzmeister, the architect of the government quarter at Ankara, who taught at the School of Engineering.[7] They were followed by Turkish architects Sedat Hakki Eldem at the Academy of Fine Arts and Onat at the School of Engineering, the most eminent among the early Republican architects and educators. Onat had completed his education at Zurich with Otto Salvisberg; Eldem had his experience of modern architecture with Auguste Perret in Paris, and later in Berlin.

Both Egli and Holzmeister were representatives of modern functionalism, though Holzmeister had a certain classic attitude. The Academy of Fine Arts also had as a teacher another eminent German architect and representative of modern architecture in Bruno Taut. These three architects introduced modern European functionalism both in theory and in practice. For the students of that period their authority and their example were followed without question. Thus "Turkish modern" was set up on the Central European, namely German, model. The Bauhaus had its influence on design. Corbusier had a lesser influence, though he was invited to prepare a master plan for İzmir.[8]

Nevertheless after the death of Atatürk, Turkish modernism, following the examples of European countries, fell into the grip of a new classicism and monumentalism, which was again formulated with the use of classic Turkish themes and motives. Yet, even if the representatives of the modern style, such as Onat and Eldem, accepted the new fashion with its political overtones, functionalism was not suppressed. For about a decade it survived under the slogan of "national style." The fashion of this national style was short-lived. Its fate was sealed with the advent of the political and economic supremacy of the postwar United States, and of the new Western cultural trends. After 1950 Turkish schools had their Turkish teachers, and eagerly and simultaneously followed all the trends offered by the international scene. Since the early 1930s, therefore, except for the intermezzo of the '40s, Turkish architects strongly adhered to Western ideas and practice, and more probably to practice than to its intellectual background.

Here, however, a little excursion is necessary to point out an intellectual and emotional trend that also survived as an undercurrent: in 1932 Sedat Hakki Eldem started a seminar on the Turkish house at the Academy of Fine Arts. "Turkish house" is a generic term applied to a house type that appeared in a developed form after the sixteenth century in large areas of the Ottoman Empire, stretching from east-central Anatolia to the Balkans. It is based on a wooden framework, with highly standardized plans and architectural elements.[9]

Its beautiful examples still survive in numerous localities in Turkey and in the Balkan countries. The motivation behind the seminar was the creation of a modern architecture, based on the analysis and interpretation of traditional forms. The creation of a national style was consonant with the nationalism of the '30s. But if the secular character of the regime could not allow forms connected with the religious image of the past, the vernacular tradition as a basic expression of the Turkish people was permissible. The intention, moreover, was not to imitate but to interpret. Thus the seminar took place, partly in response to nationalistic trends, partly to that deeper urge to create a national architectural style. The impact of the seminar was not immediate, but it served the totalitarian trends of the 1940s, being remembered subsequently as an academic performance. For the man who conceived it, it became the source of a personal style that has lasted to our own day, and to which further reference will be made.

Organization of the Building Field. A few observations on the organization of the building field, especially during the first decade of a multiparty system, need to be noted. The enthusiasm for a rapid postwar development and the efforts to transform the country from an agricultural to an industrialized one started with the bold economic liberalization of the Democratic Party. The years between 1950 and 1960 were years of total surrender to Western ideas, forms, and technology. Yet they were also years in which the Turkish professional architect strongly emphasized his role in the reconstruction of the country and organized the professional field.[10]

The Chamber of Architects (before there was an Architect's Union) was founded in 1954 by law, and every architect was required to be a member. The relationship with international organizations such as the Union of International Architects (U.I.A.) was developed. The employment of foreign architects was restricted. Private architectural offices proliferated. In 1954 the Institute of Standardization was created. New regulations for modern construction techniques, for steel, concrete, and wood, were prepared.

Since the 1940s governments had adopted a policy of holding national and international competitions for important

projects. The '50s were glorious years of national competitions, which became a means of earning money for many talented young architects. Not always for the good, however, for this was also a period of hectic activity to modernize the cities. The process of rapid urbanization was well and truly started, while vehicular transportation became a priority for politicians and planners.

In architectural schools Corbusier, Mies Van Der Rohe, Walter Gropius, and later Frank Lloyd Wright and Alvar Aalto were idolized. It was a period of architectural blossoming without restraint. Obviously the economic and technical potential of the country never corresponded to the exuberance of the ideas and grandiose schemes of the politicians. And because of the dichotomy between the desires and the means of attaining them, there were good intentions with bad results, which defaced many cities. The level of architectural design was always above the technical realities. The image of an architecture and a city brought in from the West, and the enthusiastic spirit of reconstruction of the postwar world spread also to Turkey; it helped Turkish architects to develop a sense of modern professionalism and introduced modern methodologies of design. But the end result as architecture and as city was neither satisfactory nor convincing. Urban chaos set in and architects could not control the development that they so fervently advocated.

Architecture since 1960. [11]   In my observations and evaluations of Turkish architecture I do not intend to give much information on the specific development of urban planning and its implementation. It can be defined simply as a failure. City plans started with good intentions, were rarely completed, and were never implemented. The data and prognostic bases were insufficient and urban politics disorderly. The dimensions of urban problems were beyond the intellectual, economic, and technical potential of city administrations and the country. Even if Istanbul, with its population rising from one million in the 1940s to six million in the '80s, was able to survive, it became, in professional jargon, "ruralized," like many other cities. What we call urbanization is in reality ruralization. Yet our cities are not villages. There is no corresponding historical model for such agglomerations.

Thus there was a need for new concepts to define these rural cities. The absence of historical precedents and the impossibility of applying Western methodologies, because they

were not created for this purpose, have remained the basic problem until the present day. However, the image of modern architecture and the city has also been part of the intellectual baggage of the politicians, and decision making has been directly related to this image. Forced to produce acceptable solutions in the framework set by politicians and faced with its chaotic results, architects have continued to the present day to search for a definition of a professionally acceptable or correct modern idiom.

Since the modern idiom established itself in contradiction to the traditional one, the question of a relationship between good modern and the traditional left no agenda for architectural discussion. A recent series of interviews with architects showed that they did not generally consider establishing any kind of relationship with the past. Their education, the image of modern architecture, economic and technological necessities, and a taste for the modern have been too strong to encourage intimate relations with the past. That would be considered borrowing by most Turkish architects. Most of the middle-aged architects have been indoctrinated against any kind of historicism; an architecture in the spirit of tradition or in a spiritual kinship with Islam, even in harmony with tradition, might trap them into another period of reaction against modern design. The exception is Eldem.

This survey shows the entrenched strength of the International Style among Turkish architects, a style that still influences their design. Today they accept intercourse with tradition in a positive but not in a postmodern sense. The survey also confirms once again that, despite the growth of discontent with today's ills in the cities and despite the debased quality of average architecture, architects are not much concerned with a new evaluation of architectural theory or practice, and their attitude toward the application of a standardized modern style is not seriously questioned. Writers in the architectural journals, teachers at the universities, and groups of architects are aware of the recent developments in the field of architectural theory and postmodern experiences, but there seems no serious challenge to the established authority of the modern commercialized International Style. Since this undisturbed trend of the wholesale acceptance of the triad image of tech-

Pensoy house, Yeniköy, Istanbul, by Günay Çilingiroğlu (far left). Built between 1974 and 1976 and situated on the slopes of the Bosporus, the house attracts attention with its daring overhangs and represents a kind of New Brutalism. Left: Lav house at Rumelihisari, Istanbul, by Mazaffer Sudali (1962).[12] This bold design expresses the structure of the house in a straightforward manner. Above: Kiraç house on the Bosporus at Vaniköy, by Sedat Hakki Eldem. Right: Nadaroğlu house, Burgaz, Istanbul, by Turgut Cansever (1971–1972). Cansever's approach is evident in the houses he built on Princes Island, like this one.

nology, urbanization, functionalism has not created a single decent urban and architectural environment, its shortcomings need to be critically and seriously reevaluated.

The period from 1950 to 1960, in both social content and formal variety, was a period of maturation at the end of which architects felt equal to the modern world and were eager to experience the most advanced ideas, at least theoretically. There was no problem of cultural identity, but a stronger move toward integration with the modern International Style.[13] All the great names of modern architecture, Alvar Aalto, Kenzo Tange, Louis Kahn, Eero Saarinen, Paul Rudolph, Pier Luigi Nervi, and lesser stars filling the architectural journals somehow shared the enthusiasms of the young Turkish architects, who were eager to follow their example.

Theoretical discussion, on the other hand, concentrated more on the social issues. After the overthrow of the government by a new regime, new governmental agencies for housing, rural development, and the growing problems of industrialization and urbanization attracted architects' attention. New forms for new problems, never before discussed in such detail, were raised in most cases with political vehemence.

The main building tasks with the exception of housing were still carried out by the government. The practice of holding national competitions for government buildings, schools, hospitals, university campuses, already established in the 1950s, continued to be the basic mechanism by which talented architects could obtain significant job experience of new forms. There was a dichotomy between the liberalism of styles and the restraint proposed by social-minded architects. A compromise, dictated by the limitations of the building technology and the economy of the country, determined the direction of architectural design.

The limitations of technology are readily observable in the use of the steel frame and ready-made elements. The cost of steel restricted the number of tall buildings and large covered structures. Except for industrial buildings, reinforced concrete became the only structural material. Until the late '70s building technology did not produce ready-made elements, and construction remained a painstaking, semi-industrialized activity carried out by artisans. Building regulations, prepared by governmental agencies (mostly by the Ministry of Public Works) on the basis of a country-wide analysis of building practice, were designed to suit the underdeveloped building technology that was available in the country. This was again a severe restriction on the freedom of architectural expression. Possibly the most significant building form that exemplifies this restriction is the tall building. New buildings today are much taller than the buildings of former periods, yet the skyscraper does not exist in Turkey.

The earliest tall building in Ankara was a twenty-one-story office building designed by Enver Tokay at Kizilay (1957–1964). It was followed by the Stad Hotel, by Metin Hepgüler, Doğan Tekeli, and Sami Sisa; and by the Ankara Hotel, by Saugey, a Swiss architect (1960). The Istanbul landscape today offers only five, the Sheraton Hotel,[14] two other hotels, and an office building at Odakule by Kaya Tecimen and A. Kemal Taner (begun in 1970).[15]

Approaches to Design. It is possibly correct to say that the attitude of the major architects toward design tends to be consonant with the social and economic realities of the country. The two poles of design philosophy remained as Western/international and national/traditional, the former constituting the main tendency. But the latter remained as a latent soul-searching attitude that sporadically rose to the surface. So while the majority in architecture subscribed to the International Style, experiments with the traditional vocabulary were not lacking. The upsurge in the last decade of buildings with reminiscences of the past is based on these earlier experiments and is also due to the influence of postmodernist trends. The idea of spiritual continuity with the past is no longer rejected.

After 1960 the earliest champion of this idea, Sedat Hakki Eldem, followed his earlier experiments with increased sophistication.[16] His Social Insurance Agency Building at Zeyrek, Istanbul, was praised for the sensitive composition of articulated volumes, which harmonizes exceedingly well with the traditional background and the complex topography of the site.

But the architectural expression is mechanical and dull. The highly debated Atatürk Library at Taksim, Istanbul, is an elegant building composed of interlocked polygons covered with domes. Although not large, the building has a strong expression of a finished and well-articulated form. The plan for this library was originally conceived for a restaurant, which has raised heated discussion about the honesty of the design. Yet this may be accepted as a valid approach, because, as history has attested, a container form may be used for different purposes. Here Eldem puts his building on a strong base and arranges his main polygonal rooms under large eaves. All is terminated by pyramidal domes with caplike skylights. Eldem's more representative buildings, such as the Akbank Headquarters at Istanbul (1971) and the Indian Embassy (1965) and Pakistani Embassy (1966–1974), both at Ankara, prove his versatility and ability to play with the same idiom in different kinds of buildings, yet end up with an elegant but cold classicism.

Turgut Cansever's Turkish Historical Association Building at Ankara[17] may be considered the best example of a modern approach that has a genuine feeling for traditional forms without necessarily repeating them.[18] He uses a plan that immediately alludes to the traditional semiclosed courtyard, adding to the charm of the interior. The use of local stone, the good workmanship, and the care taken in details contribute positively to the final effect. Much more than Eldem, Cansever avoids any modern cliché. This characteristic attitude is also seen in his Şişli Terakki School in Istanbul (1970–1980).

Apart from these two architects, the search for a synthesis of the traditional and the modern has not been seriously considered by the younger generations of architects until recently.

In the 1960s and early '70s Turkish architecture at its best had two basic qualities: functionalism and modesty. This was the result first of university education in which the early puritanism of the International Style found echo; and second of the impact of the politico-cultural atmosphere of the period, in which social and economic considerations were strongly emphasized. The bulk of official buildings designed by noted architects express this trend.

In the '60s competitions for large university campuses became another field of experimentation for architects. The

Tatko office building, Istanbul (left). An example of an experiment with bold, three-dimensional effects, yet firmly rooted in the International Style. Above: Headquarters of the Turkish Language Institute, Ankara, by Cengiz Bektaş (1979).[19] The accommodation is planned around a spectacular atrium. Right: Atatürk Library, Taksim, Istanbul, by Sedat Hakki Eldem. Originally designed for a restaurant, the cluster of hexagonal pavilions is able to serve adequately the functions of a library.

Middle East Technical University (METU) at Ankara, the University at Erzurum, and those of Trabzon and Diyarbakir were large projects won in the competition and commissioned. Among them the most outstanding is the campus of the Middle East Technical University, by Behruz Çinici. Çinici, who has become one of the best-known architects of the country, is a man of experiment and phantasy.[20] Criticized by orthodox professional opinion for his exuberance, he is an imaginative architect who sometimes approaches the superfluous in his detail. He might be accepted as the first postmodernist in Turkey when architectural public opinion opposed to phantasy and strict economy subsides.

Government-sponsored buildings such as museums and cultural centers have provided another opportunity for freer design. Çinici's recently completed Public Relations Building of the Parliament at Ankara underlines on a larger scale the new postmodernist trends in Turkey and shows Çinici's mature style at its best.

After the late 1960s modern design and its Turkish modalities were assimilated. Design experiments were begun with bolder, three-dimensional effects. The relative development of building technology helped architects to change their attitude toward the use of newer techniques and materials, and they adopted ready-made panels, metallic window frames, new synthetic materials, and modern fixtures. The architecture as image and symbol of big business also became fashionable in Turkey. Large office buildings of important banks and business firms are now the preeminent examples of modern architecture.

Buildings for transportation have gained importance relative to the growth of highways and bus transport. Lacking still in momentum and quality, they started nevertheless to attract the attention of the best architects. Only a single airport terminal can be mentioned here, that at Istanbul, opened in 1983 but designed earlier by Hayati Tabanlioğlu.[21] It expresses the still prevailing influence of Central European taste, with its subdued dimensions, good but not arrogant in form.

The development of industrial architecture has paralleled fast industrialization. Foremost among the architectural offices involved in industrial design are Tekeli and Sisa, whose Lassa tire factory at İzmit,[22] short-listed for the 1983 Aga Khan Award for Architecture, is the most appreciated work. Aydin Boysan is another architect who built a sizable number of industrial buildings, among which are the Arçelik factory at Istanbul and a ceramic factory at Bozüyük.[23]

The poorest efforts went into the development of modern religious architecture. This may be the outcome of a very strong and long tradition of mosque architecture in Turkey. However, in the 1950s the competition for the Ankara Great Mosque, for which many participants submitted modern interpretations, was won by Vedat Dalokay, the same architect who won the international competition for the National Mosque at Islamabad.[24] But politics and religious reaction impeded the Ankara Mosque's realization.[25]

Problems of Preservation and Reuse.   Monumental restoration has a long history in Turkey. But preservation of historic areas and historic houses and reuse are fields in which only very recently have some efforts been made. Several caravansaries have been remodeled as hotels, such as Oküzmehmet Pasha at Kuşadasi, by Orhan Tunçer (1964);[26] Rustem Pasha at Edirne, by Ertan Çakirlar (1966–1972),[27] a 1980 Aga Khan Award winner; and the Haseki Complex at Istanbul (unfinished). Large old mansions found readier opportunities for reuse, and several were reconstructed by the government as museums or private houses. The best known of these is the Ertegün house at Bodrum, by Turgut Cansever, also a 1980 Aga Khan Award winner.

The theory of the preservation of historic city cores has been on the agenda of the architectural debate for a long time. Master plans have been prepared for the preservation of some cities, such as the ancient site of Side, about 60 kilometers east of Antalya, by Ersen Gürsel, Mehmet Çubuk, and Nihat

Güner; Gaziantep, which I planned with a team from the Institute of Restoration of the Istanbul Technical University; Safranbolu, by Ismet Okyay and me; and Antalya's old town, by Gönül Tankut and a team from METU. These plans have not been realized, however, and only a project for a tourist facility, Antalya Harbor, by the Bank of Tourism, has been partly implemented.

Residential Architecture.   Housing in Turkey, both in its functional and aesthetic aspects, exposes all the discrepancies of a society in transition: changes in technology, dwelling concepts, and taste; adoption of foreign images without digestion of their content; economic exploitation and land speculation; and all the ills connected with inadequate regulations, bad planning, or lack of planning. On the other hand it is a field in which architects can have more freedom to exhibit their preferences and talents. Elaborate design and good quality are to be found in expensive mansions, apartments for the wealthy classes, and the architecture of tourist villages in resort areas. But the overall picture is very deceptive, because Turkish housing is notorious for its illegal and nonprofessional building activity, and decent professional designs constitute only a very small portion. Yet its formal bases and functional goals were established during the 1930s by architectural schools and by noted architects eager to follow the precepts of the International Style of economy and pure expression. By the '50s there were sufficient clichés in the plan types and simplified facade designs with horizontal windows, which constituted the basis of residential architecture produced by simple contractors.

Due to fast urbanization, the limited funds of public authorities and the inadequate rationalization of building techniques, housing was left to the private sector, which was totally unprepared for a task of this magnitude. With the sole aim being speculation, the avidity to maximize the use of space, the poor quality of construction, and the repetition of clichés created the face of modern Turkish cities.

The weaknesses in urban planning and building regulations helped the fast development of a simple, ugly jargon of apartment typology all over the country. New apartments replaced historic quarters and crowded suburban areas. They in turn were surrounded by *gecekondu*, or squatter housing, which constitutes in some large cities as much as half the total number of individual dwellings.

In the housing field the *gecekondu* is an urban problem per se. According to figures issued by the National Institute of Statistics, in the last twenty-five years, out of every hundred families coming to the cities from rural areas forty-five have moved into squatter housing. Although from 1950 to 1980 authorized housing in the whole of Turkey increased from 1.3 to 2.8 million, the city population increased from 7.1 to 20 million.[28] These figures are sufficiently revealing to demonstrate the enormous dimensions of the illegal-housing problem.

At the end of 1983, when housing production became part of the government priority program, it was observed that there were eight varieties of housing production in Turkey:[29] 1) the unorganized single house; 2) housing co-operatives; 3) the so-called build-and-sell type in the hands of both small and large contracting firms; 4) mass building companies; 5) production through the cooperation of local administrations and the unions of building cooperatives, mostly operating in the recently developed zones; 6) self-built squatter housing; 7) squatter housing partly organized by speculators; 8) governmental housing production, which is not usually classified because it is so negligible.

Individual house production, which was almost the only pattern in the 1930s, is of limited numerical importance in Turkey today. Before the Second World War, when urban land had not yet gained speculative value and urbanization was still very slow, the building of single houses on individual lots was common practice. Only Istanbul had an older tradition of apartment houses. Nevertheless in the '30s apartment buildings up to five stories started to be introduced. After the war, however, as a result of increasing urbanization and the rapid escalation in the value of urban land, individual houses became inaccessible to all but high-income groups.

In the design of the modern Turkish house or of residential architecture in general the great traditions of Turkish domestic architecture have become one of the poles of attraction. Sedat Hakki Eldem, who had been the prime instigator, as we have seen, of the prewar seminar on the Turkish house, has been searching all his life for a modern Turkish style based on the analysis of old Turkish domestic architecture. Over the years he has elaborated his style and produced several mansions on the shores of the Bosporus.

Eldem's style in its final phase, which may be called structural classicism, is refined in its proportions and its careful handling of details and materials. It has ended up with a physiognomy of '30s functionalism (a style similar to that of Giuseppe Terragni, an Italian architect of the modern movement, for example) but incorporating stylized elements of traditional house design. In planning he shows a decided preference for symmetry. Among the following generation, from the Academy of Fine Arts, another seeker for a synthesis of the traditional and contemporary is Turgut Cansever. Plenty of architects of the same generation, however, were by no means absorbed in tradition. Structuralism, for example, remained a favorite attitude.

The next generation of architects, which graduated in the 1950s, does not look at tradition as a source, yet some of the architects belonging to that generation, such as Behruz Çinici, still flirt with it. His faculty housing at METU incorporates overhanging eaves with visible rafters, and he uses wood, stucco, and brick as a reminder of the traditional vernacular. Günay Çilingiroğlu is among the group of architects who do not show any preference for tradition. He is a structural mannerist and has a taste for superabundance of form in all his buildings. At the opposite pole to Çilingiroğlu, there is a pure modernist, Mehmet Konuralp, who has a taste for geometry, which associates his buidings with the earlier functionalism. Cengiz Bektaş, another prolific representative of this generation, builds with a clear geometry that is combined with finesse in the handling of facades and the respect for regional tradition.

Ahmet Gülgonen, who works mostly in France, has a complicated and intellectual approach that brings him closer to postmodernist tendencies. Abstract and recherché, these tendencies are well illustrated in his own house at Vaniköy, where the reminders of the past are somehow tortured by spatial phantasies.[30] Recent trends in housing design show the considerable influence of theoretical writings and discussions on the traditional Turkish house and the campaigns for its preservation. In this field architects who graduated in the 1960s respond positively to the challenge of traditional forms. Another factor underlining this trend has been the proliferation of resort housing. Large vacation villages, mostly on the Aegean and Mediterranean shores, with their beautiful topography, are a new field of building that attracts architects. The traditional/regional fits well with the picturesque and commerical spirit of tourism, but it also provides a free hand for experiment.

Special mention must be made of Nail Çakirhan, not a professional architect, but a writer and contractor. He built in the province of Muğla, in southwestern Turkey, fifteen houses, reinterpreting local house plans and using local craftsmen. One of his houses received an Aga Khan Award in 1983 (page 154), which created a great debate among the professionals on the role of the professional as well as on the use of tradition in modern design.

One might predict that the experiments in tourist architecture will eventually influence the architectural style of the coming decade. Actually both the use of the old for its picturesqueness and the reuse of traditional buildings have already had a strong influence on architectural design, an influence that has been strengthened by the international tendencies of postmodernism. In this context Cansever's conversion of the Ertegün house at Bodrum and many single traditional houses restored for cultural and tourist purposes or simply for private use open vistas.

In the field of housing, city apartments have been the most common and widespread source of criticism. Toward the end of the 1950s the build-and-sell type of production by contractors became the most favored and seemingly profitable means of investment, because of the exorbitant increase in land prices that spread to all the cities. Geared to profit making, it ended up as the major source of aesthetic decay of the cityscape. The build-and-sell contractor, who was only a small businessman and not a developer in a proper sense, usually took over a lot in exchange for apartments and built blocks one after another in a given district in accordance with a few clichés of poor design, supposed to be favored by the population. A smaller group of these investors built apartments with expensive finishes and decoration in the smart quarters of the city, which brought higher profits. Despite the marble facings, aluminum frames, expensive tiles, and floor areas reaching 200 to 300 square meters, perhaps with some kitsch treatment of the facades, these apartments rarely had any architectural merit. This kind of business activity has been readily pursued by many architect-contractors and even by large industrial and commercial firms for a reliable investment.

Such multistory apartment blocks were produced with common technology and at a rather slow rate. The commercialized shapes of the build-and-sell apartments have not risen above the monotony of vertical or horizontal repetition and a certain coarseness of mass, the latter the effect of building regulations and the use of the maximum permitted volume.[31]

Nevertheless since those involved in this type of activity constitute the bulk of the profession and since the income

groups who prefer this type of housing have been on the increase, apartment blocks of a higher quality of design, built in fashionable quarters by eminent architects, have also increased in number. They have a distinguished appearance because of their materials and finishes and because of the relative elegance of their architecture, yet their architectural idiom remains mostly within the limits of the *déjà vu*; recently, however, the new interest in using traditional elements and in working outside the international routine seems to be changing their physiognomy. It is too early, however, to make an objective evaluation of the results.

Significant examples of city apartments are mostly built by the landowners themselves. As in individual house design all shades of styles can be found in their architecture. Haluk Baysal and Melih Birsel, sensitive designers, built two attractive examples, in a refined International Style, at Bebek, Istanbul. Although this style has been followed by many architects, these two buildings retain their superiority of design. The apartment house designed by Cansever at Çiftehavuzlar, Istanbul, shows his effort to stylize the traditional elements of the Turkish house, as well as the consistent use of flat pyramidal eaves, which were introduced by him in his Open Air Museum (1954–1961) at Karatepe, Adana, and which became fashionable all over the country. One must acknowledge Cansever at this point as one of the most talented and serious of modern Turkish architects. In all his buildings he has consistently searched for a synthetic style, and on each occasion he has been able to produce an original composition.

A trend in large-scale housing projects has been the involvement of social insurance agencies, banks, and private firms as developers. They establish their own building companies and erect housing that is usually intended for high-income groups. Although they sometimes use advanced systems of construction, their present level of production hinders the reduction of building costs.

In Istanbul, the Fourth Levent housing, planned by Kemal Ahmet Aru and Associates (1960) and the large suburban development of Atakoy (started in 1957 and still ongoing, the first group by Tugrul Akçura, Eyüp Kömürcüoğlu, Muhteşem Giray and Associates) are well-known examples of large-scale private housing. At Ankara, housing built by the Central Anatolia Construction Joint Stock Company (OR-AN) and de-

Arçelik factory, Çayirova, Istanbul, by Aydin Boysan (1975–1976). This paper plant makes efficient use of advanced building technology and is one of the few distinguished examples of industrial architecture to be found in Turkey.

signed by Tuğrul Akçura, Turgut Cansever, İlhan Tekeli, and Şevki Vanli (started in 1969 and still ongoing) and the Meram blocks at Konya, again by Şevki Vanli (1967), are successful efforts in bringing architectural quality to a commercial venture.[32] Although not in the same genre, it is necessary to mention Vanli also for the dormitories for military students at Ankara, one of his best designs, which he carried out in collaboration with Ersen Gömleksizoğlu.

In the present decade private organizations and large building firms have started building larger residential developments, mostly on the outskirts of cities. They usually own the land and prefer using industrialized building systems or at least prefabricated components. They differ radically from ordinary contractors in their choice of designs. Thus to increase the selling value of individual apartments, they combine various housing types and try to raise the quality of design, for both efficiency and appearance. The multistory mass housing of Mesken Sanaxii (ME-SA) at Ankara (1970–1980) is an example worth mentioning.[33]

The general design approach tends to vary, each city having some characteristic of its own. İzmir has airy design, due to the climate, and relatively good craftsmanship. Ankara owes some of its qualities to its privileged status as the capital, which attracts many talented architects.

In the mid-'70s social-democratic mayors led the way in the construction of mass housing by getting local administrations to work with the unions of the building cooperatives. Although these projects, which were directed toward low-income groups, attempted to produce cheaper dwellings, they failed to promote good design standards as an essential goal of economic housing. Among the projects is the mass housing started by the municipalities of İzmit (1974) and Ankara (1975).[34] The İzmit New Settlement Project of 30,000 dwellings started with the expropriation of the land. A new experience for Turkey was the efficient program of interviews that was organized with the prospective users of the houses. A plant for the construction of ready-made elements was de-

OR-AN housing, Ankara, by Şevki Vanli (above). A successful effort in bringing architectural quality to a commercial venture. Right: Gecekondu, Etiler, Istanbul. Squatter settlements have ruralized the city. Their contribution to the housing program has been recognized, and they are often upgraded.

signed, but unfortunately the scheme was never realized.[35]

The Batı-Kent (Western City) project, which was started by the municipality of Ankara, had more luck perhaps because of a more limited user participation, and because it was less laden with political implications. Its final aim was 60,000 dwelling units and the basic structural system adopted was the common reinforced-concrete skeleton, which greatly increased its applicability. Thus a first group of dwellings was recently completed (1983) but without any pretence at good design.[36]

The Problem of Gecekondu and Mass Housing.   Since the 1950s, in an ever-widening trend, belts of *gecekondu* (squatter housing, literally "done in one night") have been surrounding the cities. The official figures show that the number of squatter houses went up from approximately 430,000 in 1966 to 1.2 million in 1982 and that more than 50 per cent of the populations of Ankara, Istanbul, and İzmir live in this kind of housing.[37] The original *gecekondu* was the individual house built by the peasant recently moved to the city, mostly on state-owned land and in a very short time (maybe one night where there was no control), consisting of a single room to be extended later. This type of dwelling proliferated all over the country. Subsequently the construction of squatter housing became more organized, being built by local masons on shared lots owned by members of one family.

The extension pattern of *gecekondu* areas shows a great similiarity to the traditional patterns in rural and semirural areas. They are usually single-story houses that the owner enlarges horizontally as he collects the required building material. But at a later stage buildings in the old squatter areas are extended vertically and finally small apartments are built. Compared to apartments in inner-city areas they have the advantage of being near open country, of having room for a little garden and a few trees around them, and allowing their occupants to indulge in a rural kind of neighborhood relationship. Governments have tried to settle the squatter population in mass housing or at least to provide the necessary infrastructure of roads and services. Such official efforts, however, have failed to keep up with the vast dimensions of the problem.

The *gecekondu* man is a villager who keeps part of his family and possibly some land in the village or township from which he comes. His new house is neither a village house nor a town house. It is a traditional house in transition that transfers the village to the city. It still shows a preference for horizontal living organically connected with the surroundings. This architecture without architects has been officially accepted and even integrated into the metropolitan areas. It may be short on design content or lacking in urban character, but it offers the sort of environmental qualities that architects and planners often seek.

In the last decade, as the number of squatters have multiplied, market mechanism began to operate and migrants from rural areas fell into the hands of organized speculators. Squatter-house production was started by gangs who would sell a shared real-estate deed to the new settlers. The area would be divided into tiny lots, roads leveled, and the topography ironed out. The development itself could be equally brutal. This mechanism slowly replaced the old self-build methods, and it has resulted in unhealthful suburbs and in the loss of the *gecekondu*'s rural character. Today, the inhabitants are affected by the same sort of alienation, which has caused the speculative apartment block of the inner city to be one of the most unpopular building types ever conceived.

Government housing projects to replace or to clean up these areas are extremely few in number, have no particular architectural quality, and have proved to be totally ineffective. This calls to mind the housing built by the Turkish government in areas frequently hit by earthquakes, which has certainly been more effective but equally lacking in architectural quality.

Today the construction of both authorized and unauthorized buildings is in decline because of the recent inflation of the economy. Housing experts are insisting once again on the necessity of undertaking the rapid construction of mass housing, in which a law, enacted in the summer of 1981, has given the government an active role.[38] According to this law, the government will give 5 per cent of its yearly national budget to a mass-housing fund, will help in securing land and financial sources, and may take over some of the construction. However, because of the precarious state of the building economy, the law has not yet been properly put into effect.

Two basic conclusions may be drawn. First, a sufficient development in the field of housing parallel to the rapid growth of the cities has not been realized. While the housing shortage has become an epidemic, the architectural quality of the average residential development has dropped. The spread of squatters, in addition to the general loss of design and construction quality, has created cities without individuality. Urban politics intermingled with speculation has largely destroyed the historical character of the cities. The loss of the old image and the lack of urban consciousness in the citizen of rural origin have played havoc with the quality of the towns.

Second, in this general chaotic development, the contributions of a few architects remain insignificant except as personal expressions. Architectural quality remains the privilege of high-income groups and therefore elitist in nature. To find a proper style for the new urban house may be a burning question, but the urban physiognomy is decided at economic and functional levels, while the dominant aesthetic, if any, remains the most unsophisticated secondhand image of the modern International Style.

RECIPIENTS OF THE SECOND AGA KHAN AWARD FOR ARCHITECTURE 1983

STATEMENT
OF THE
MASTER
JURY

Members: Habib Fida Ali, Turgut Cansever, Rifat Chadirji, Mü-beccel Kiray, Charles Moore, Ismail Serageldin, Roland Simounet, James Stirling, Parid Wardi bin Sudin.

As members of the master jury we have carefully considered the 216 nominations for the second Aga Khan Award for Architecture in two separate meetings in Geneva, January 24–28 and June 20–24, 1983. At the first meeting, thirty-six projects were selected for detailed technical review *in situ.* In the second meeting we selected the eleven winners. Our deliberations in both meetings were considerably facilitated by the thoroughness and technical competence of those who prepared the project dossiers and undertook the detailed technical reviews, as well as by the outstanding support given to us by the Award office, the Award staff, and the secretary general.

In our task, we were guided by the terms of reference for the Awards, which stress recognition of those projects that "demonstrate architectural excellence at all levels"; that respond to their "social, economic, technical, physical and environmental challenges"; that nurture "a heightened awareness of the roots and essence of Muslim culture"; and that "have the potential to stimulate related developments elsewhere in the Muslim world." We have also tried to respond to the felt need for reducing the numbers of winners to enhance the importance bestowed by the Award on the projects selected. It proved difficult largely because of the diversity of viewpoints among the jury members, and for some because of the breadth and variety of the projects considered, which reflect the scope and diversity of the Muslim world with its myriad challenges as well as the many different responses that imaginative individuals and groups have made to these challenges.

The eleven schemes premiated were retained by the jury, which was satisfied that they, in addition to their individual merit, collectively represented a sampling of the geographical range of Islam, from Mali to Malaysia, the problems of rural and urban populations, and of widely varying incomes in very different environments. The jury was in agreement that the projects, eleven from nine countries, fairly (though of course not completely) represent the richness and variety of the cul-

Detail of qibla wall and minaret (left), Great Mosque of Niono, Niono, Mali. Pages 76–77: Detail of roof woodwork, Tanjong Jara Beach Hotel, Trengganu, Malaysia. Both designs incorporate traditional indigenous elements.

---

tures of Islam. Here the agreement ended: no one on the jury saw the projects as equal in accomplishment, merit, or importance. The most widely held sympathies, probably, were for the three restoration projects. The Hajj Terminal, almost everyone felt, is in a class by itself, its structure a magnificent achievement of twentieth-century technology.

At the other end of the spectrum between the familiar and the surprising, even more controversially, lies the mud mosque in Niono, Mali, the work of a master mason building in the rich tradition of his country. Some jury members felt strongly that in spite of its elegance and beauty, it was not in a class with the architecture of more sophisticated societies, that it represents the last efforts of a traditional culture that cannot survive for long; other jurors saw it in its continuity and poetry as representing a major source of continuing inspiration.

In between these two comes the "white flower," as one juror put it, Sherefudin's White Mosque, probably the most widely (though certainly not universally) admired of all eleven, full of originality and innovation (though with an undeniable debt to Corbusier's chapel at Ronchamp) laden with the architect's thought and spirit, shared richly with the community, connecting with the future and the past.

The same spirit has gone more humbly into the Ramses Wissa Wassef Arts Center, a traditional mud-brick building with a casual though learned plan, in which the great glory is the light, falling on a collection of sculptures.

The other four entries are housing; they represent on the one hand the central importance housing has to our world and on the other the compromises and miscarriages that diminish the clarity of housing design and increase directly with the inhabitants' number, and inversely with their wealth.

The easiest housing problem then and the most elegant solution can be expected to be for a private house. The jury premiated an airy and handsome house on the Turkish coast, finely crafted in the local tradition. Another problem that promises achievable elegance is the tourist hotel: the jury picked two, in Malaysia and Tunisia. More difficult to confront is urban housing for middle- and lower-income inhabitants. The Hafsia quarter of Tunis is an important effort to deal with the problem, though flawed in execution and detail.

The jurors believe the projects should not be seen as equivalent in social importance or sophistication or elegance or technological innovation or depth of poetic feeling, but rather, as the 1980 master jury put it, as reflecting "the present stage of transition, experimentation, and continued search in Muslim societies. In most instances they represented not the ultimate in architectural excellence, but steps in a process of discovery, still an incomplete voyage toward many promising frontiers." As they did, we in 1983 also have selected some of the projects for their excellence in architecture but recognize that most of them "stand as accomplishments in this continuing search for relevant forms and designs that has already started and that must be supported."

Finally, we would like to salute the generous and continuing support His Highness the Aga Khan is giving to this most important search.

Left: Detail of the upper-level madrasa, *Fountain of Abd al-Rahman Kathuda, Darb Quirmiz quarter, Cairo, Egypt (see pages 92–97).*

HAFSIA
QUARTER

Tunis, Tunisia, completed 1977. Clients: Association de Sauvegarde de la Médina de Tunis (A.S.M.), acting for the municipality of Tunis; homebuyers of quarter. Architects: Arno Heinz with Wassim Ben Mahmoud; Saleh Younsi, Serge Santelli, Michel Steinback. Planner: Jelal Abdelkafi, A.S.M.

Master Jury's Citation: For a noteworthy attempt to deal with the problem of urban public housing in a sensitive and humane fashion. The Hafsia quarter represents a considerable effort in achieving the scale of the old medina, sensitively inserting new "infill" housing into the urban tissue of the medina. The use of the covered suq as a device for linking the two parts of the medina separated by the demolished quarter, while simultaneously screening off the large-scale buildings from the new development, is also excellent.

On the other hand, the project is surely flawed: physically in its detailing and execution, socioeconomically in its inability to cater to the needs of the lower-income residents of the medina. Yet such shortcomings are not unexpected in a first attempt by the Tunisian authorities in dealing differently with the problems of urban housing in the medina. Subsequent phases of the program will build upon the experience gained in this first step of a continuing search for culturally sensitive and economically viable design solutions.

Objectives. The reconstruction of the Hafsia quarter is the first large-scale renovation project of its kind in an Islamic country. The aim of the project was to reconstruct a residential and commercial sector of the medina of Tunis that would maintain the character of the old city and at the same time provide suitable housing for the poor from neighboring areas.

Historical Background. Located east of the central area of the medina, the Hafsia is the former Jewish quarter of Tunis. During the colonial period its original inhabitants began to desert this sector for newer European areas. In 1928 the French authorities declared the Hafsia quarter a health hazard and between 1933 and 1939 many of its buildings were demolished. Further destruction occurred with the bombing of the site during the Second World War. While some construction did take

Pages 84–87: Reconstruction of the Hafsia quarter in the medina of Tunis, with contiguous courtyard houses separated by winding alleys, is a milestone on the road to a more appropriate urban architecture. At the same time, white walls with small shuttered openings continue the local tradition.

place in the years following the war, renewed demolition occurred during the 1960s and a population of poor immigrants settled into the remaining derelict houses, causing overcrowding and further decline.

Site.   The site of the Hafsia quarter is almost flat, with a very gentle slope of 1 in 100. It is somewhat protected from the northern and western rain-laden winds by the topography of the medina. The soil is a mixture of clay and limestone, with the water table lying 1 to 1.5 meters below the ground.

Local Architectural Character.   The architecture of the area surrounding the Hafsia is traditionally characterized by courtyard houses and narrow winding alleys. Its aesthetic and historical value, however, is not as high as that in other parts of the city, and it is also less well maintained.

The modern buildings bordering the site include three 4-story apartment buildings, a market, two schools, a children's club, and a recently completed social club.

1: The plan shows the snaking form of the Suq el-Hout with the eleven house types, mixed to avoid monotony. 2, 3, 4, 5: As the section and views indicate, the suq is of the traditional vaulted form. The aerial view (3) shows the low, spreading nature of the development in contrast with the other, adjacent modern buildings.

Access.   The former Suq el-Hout, a pedestrian route running north-south, has been severed by a straight east-west vehicular avenue linking the modern quarters of Tunis to Achour Street through Bab Carthagena. This avenue had already attracted development west of the *suq* (market) in the form of tall, modern apartment blocks.

Brief.   The brief focused on the reconstruction of the Suq el-Hout with about a hundred shops. Its structural frame was designed to allow for flexibility in the allocation and size of shops. A further twenty-two shops were to be constructed adjacent to the dwellings and facing a pedestrian street, with private offices for professionals provided above them. Ninety-five housing units were also planned, some with central courtyards and others with only a garden or terrace.

The brief as well as the design concepts were elaborated by the Association de Sauvegarde de la Médina (A.S.M.). The functional requirements of the quarter were defined by the A.S.M.'s multidisciplinary team after a survey of the neighboring population's needs. The survey included detailed studies of the income levels and social backgrounds of the future inhabitants, their requirements regarding the internal organization of dwellings, and a commercial report on the shops needed outside the *suq*.

Existing pedestrian routes were to be continued, with the

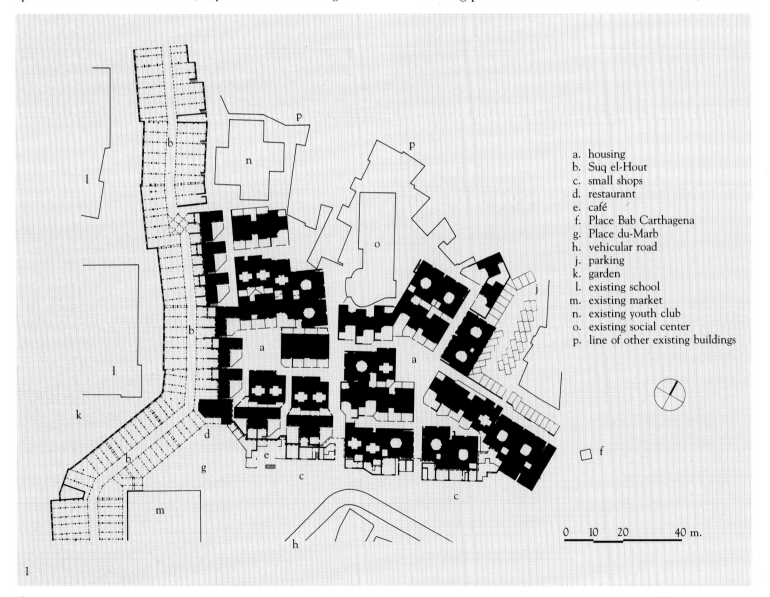

a. housing
b. Suq el-Hout
c. small shops
d. restaurant
e. café
f. Place Bab Carthagena
g. Place du-Marb
h. vehicular road
j. parking
k. garden
l. existing school
m. existing market
n. existing youth club
o. existing social center
p. line of other existing buildings

0   10   20   40 m.

1

new Suq el-Hout serving as a covered walkway, connecting the existing *suqs* of El Grana and Sidi Mahrez. The straight vehicular avenue running east and west and cutting across the Suq el-Hout was to be rebuilt along a zigzag route, and a pedestrian street established along its former length. Two parking lots for the inhabitants and customers were to be located at either end of the vehicular avenue, near the Bab Carthagena and beside the market.

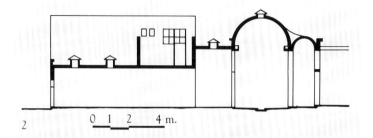

2

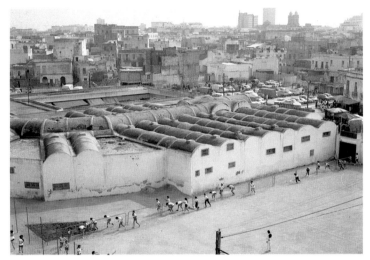

4

An examination of 900 applications clarified the requirements of potential inhabitants even further. These included a preference for a quiet housing area, separated from the noisy commercial district and throughways; independent housing units with private entrances; and courtyard houses with the internal circulation protected from winter weather, with the reception area and living room near the entrance, and with the kitchen and more private area toward the back. Since some of the requests were contradictory, they could be satisfied only through the provision of several different types of houses. Each type was defined by its floor area and by the inhabitants' income level as well as their needs and aspirations.

The nature of the shops outside the *suq* was also decided by a survey. The shops were to include a restaurant, a café, a laundry, a barbershop, a shoe-repair shop, and a photographer's studio. Offices for lawyers, dentists, and other professionals would be placed on the floor above.

Design. The politicians as well as some local and foreign architects and planners would have preferred a high-rise solution following the then-prevailing Western models. Despite their opposition and despite the abandonment of rehabilitation plans for neighboring areas, the design was developed according to the guidelines set by the A.S.M.

The politicians insisted, however, on attaching greater prestige to the operation by eliminating the poorest applicants. This meant that the housing standards had to be raised during the course of the project. Eleven house types were defined, ranging in area from 60 to 163 square meters, and assembled in different configurations. The four main types were courtyard houses on one level, courtyard houses on two levels, row houses with individual enclosed gardens, and row houses built adjacent

5

to the *suq*. None of the courtyards overlooks the interior of the house.

The units were standardized to facilitate the design and implementation of the project, but the types were mixed so as to avoid repetition and monotony. A few special house types such as bridge houses spanning the pedestrian street were also included. Certain traditional architectural concepts were retained, such as white walls contrasting with colored openings and a small window set just above the exterior doorway to light the interior.

Structure.   The housing units and shops were built with a post-and-beam structure (because of the water table) while the *suq* was designed with a concrete frame supporting concrete vaults. In general *in situ* concrete was used for structural members and brick for the exterior walls and internal partitions. The floors were constructed of brick filler blocks covered with concrete and paved with terrazzo tiles. Exterior walls were rendered and painted.

Assessment.   The buildings integrate well with the old city, and the quarter is not easily identifiable in a rooftop view of the medina. The scale, shapes, and colors are also discreet when viewed from the preexisting traditional streets to the north. Unfortunately a substantial amount of abandoned land, especially to the south, still surrounds the new housing.

Anticipating the possibility of such changes by homeowners as the external addition of rooms or roof terraces, the architects provided a certain flexibility in their plans and overdesigned to accommodate such additional loads. The transition to these houses is gradual, starting from the fully public external areas, through the internal semipublic streets and squares and semiprivate gardens, to the fully private house areas. The irregular layout and the bridge houses provide a variety of views and even more a degree of formal complexity. The orientation of the gardens of the L-shaped houses protects them against rain-

laden winds from the north and west, while the courtyards of the other houses are naturally sheltered.

As for utilities, the project was due to be connected to city gas mains at the end of 1983. Although electrical and telephone cables were initially buried below the street, anarchic connections have proliferated along the walls and across the streets.

There is a variety of shops along the length of the Suk el-Hout differing in size, length, width, height, orientation, and lighting. The *suq* also serves as a barrier separating the new residential area from the existing tall apartment blocks and the large-scale facilities to the west. The specialization intended for the other shops did not materialize, and many of them sell cheap clothing. Unfortunately the provision of offices was a failure, and most have been converted to dwellings or storage areas. The commercial life of the quarter nevertheless is quite vigorous.

Conclusion.   Before its reconstruction the Hafsia was socially a relatively undesirable living area, and most of its current inhabitants would have preferred to live in a villa in one of the city's suburbs. Yet the comparatively low cost of the quarter and its location near the city center were attractive incentives, as were speculative motives in certain cases. Only a few of the inhabitants chose to live in the reconstructed quarter for its aesthetic qualities.

The first objective of the project, that of maintaining a harmonious relationship with the existing urban morphology, has been largely attained. The second one, of providing appropriate housing for the poor from neighboring areas, has been almost a complete failure because the houses were allocated according to income and solvency rather than need or previous residence in the area. Consequently only the wealthiest members of the neighboring communities could afford the quarter. A majority of the buyers came from areas outside the medina and belonged to more affluent social sectors.

By 1978, one year after completion, 80 per cent of the wealthier inhabitants had already modified the plans of their houses, eliminating or adding partitions, moving entrance, kitchen, or closet doors, and rearranging storage areas. Also

6: *A typical window with shutters.* 7: *The ground- and second-floor plan of the row houses.* 8: *The living room of one of the wealthier inhabitants. Political pressure eliminated the poorest applicants and allowed a high-income group to modify house plans.*

6

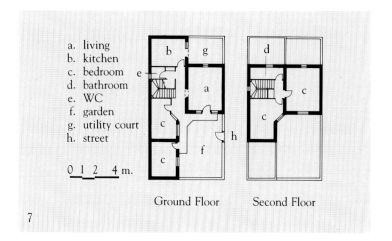

a. living
b. kitchen
c. bedroom
d. bathroom
e. WC
f. garden
g. utility court
h. street

0 1 2   4 m.

Ground Floor   Second Floor

7

16 per cent of the units had been subdivided into smaller independent units, either by the poorer inhabitants to generate additional income or by wealthier landlords for speculation. Furthermore 25 per cent of the residents had undertaken extensions involving up to three additional rooms, and 31 per cent of the units were shared by two or three households.

These modifications to the original plans generated problems. Although the architects had made allowances for some alterations, half the additions made were not anticipated and caused friction between neighbors over sunlight, ventilation, and views. In some respects, however, these extensions and modifications help to make the project a living neighborhood rather than a frozen monumental design.

The reconstruction of the Hafsia quarter, while architecturally unspectacular, demonstrates the will of the Tunisian authorities to check the gradual destruction of the medina. In 1975 the medina had 140,000 inhabitants and 15,000 dwellings covering an area of 270 hectares. The scale of the problems of the medina are immense and have led to the consideration of several renovation projects following Hafsia. One, known as Hafsia 2, has been officially adopted by the Tunisian authorities with financial support from the World Bank. There is every evidence that lessons have been learned from the first phase, especially at the socioeconomic level, and that the same

mistakes will not be repeated in the Hafsia 2 project. This evidence can be found principally in the new renovation concepts and principles that the project embraces:

1) "Integrated" projects. All architectural, urban, demographic, socioeconomic, and employment data should be simultaneously taken into consideration.

2) User participation. Financial and institutional incentives should be given to private owners to undertake rehabilitation.

3) "Urban continuity." Renovation areas should not adjoin derelict areas but should be entirely surrounded by rehabilitation zones.

4) "Social solidarity." In order to displace as few as possible of the urban poor already living in the neighborhood, the incoming, more affluent inhabitants should pay a higher share of the costs.

5) Replicability. To ensure the spread of the rehabilitation projects to the rest of the medina, appropriate funding and agencies should be set up and cost recovery of expenses should be as high as possible.

The Hafsia 2 project combines the sale of properties to private developers with the cross subsidization of rehabilitation loans for the deteriorated residential structures. It meets the needs of the urban poor and at the same time shows a respectable economic rate of return on invested funds.

DARB QIRMIZ QUARTER

DARB QIRMIZ QUARTER

Cairo, Egypt, Phase 1 completed 1980. Client: Egyptian Antiquities Organization, Islamic Section. Restoration: Egyptian Antiquities Organization (Abd al-Tawab) and German Archaelogical Institute, Cairo (Michael Meinecke, 1973–1979; Philipp Speiser, 1979–; Muhammad Fahmi Awad). Master craftsmen: S. M. al-Habbal, S. H. Muhammad, I. Abd al-Mun'im.

Master Jury's Citation: For the ambitious restoration program executed as part of the rehabilitation of a whole area of the Old City of Cairo. The effort made to restore seven important monuments, which had fallen into considerable disrepair, is exemplary. The high quality and purity of the restoration work is evident throughout as is its positive value for the surrounding community. The project has provided the opportunity to sustain and develop rapidly disappearing artisan skills. On the way to implementing successfully its ambitious program with limited resources, the Darb Qirmiz already stands as an important example of conservation in the Islamic world.

Darb Qirmiz is a residential quarter in the center of what is now Old Cairo. In the 1970s restoration work began on the monuments of this ancient quarter with the aim of encouraging a more general rehabilitation and revitalization of the area.

The conservation program is to be carried out in four phases and entails the restoration of seven monuments as a first step in the eventual rehabilitation of the quarter. Two monuments that were restored during the first phase and that have already contributed to community life are the Madrasa (Koranic School) of Sabiq al-Din Mitqal al-Anuki, a Mamluk building dating from 1368 and restored between 1973 and 1976, and the Tomb of Sheik Sinan, dating from 1585, also restored between 1973 and 1976. The second phase, now in progress, includes the restoration of the five remaining monuments of the quarter. These are the Fountain of Abd al-Rahman Kathuda, dating from 1744–1745, and under restoration since 1979; the Madrasa of Tatar al-Higaziya, built between 1347 and 1360; the Palace of Bastak al-Nasiri, built in 1339 and under restoration since 1983; the seventeenth-century Wakalat

Left: The Fountain of Abd al-Rahman Kathuda, with its upper-level madrasa, is one of the smallest of the restored buildings, but its strategic position at a fork in the road makes it one of the most important visually. Pages 92–93: The fountain's ornate timber ceilings have been carefully restored and its wall tiles faithfully copied.

Bazaar; and the Madrasa of Gamal al-Din Yusuf al-Ustadar, dating from 1407.

The third and fourth phases, still in the planning stage, will concentrate on upgrading the infrastructure and residential buildings of the quarter, and will include the construction of new housing on empty plots.

Location.   To the north of the quarter and adjoining it lies the area where the original Fatimid Palace once stood. To the west the quarter is flanked by the main thoroughfare of Old Cairo, since the Middle Ages called Darb Qirmiz, from which the quarter gets its name.

Background.   The fact that the earlier monuments are still standing can be attributed to two factors: their solid construction of thick stone walls and a regular program of repair and maintenance. During the last thirty years, however, this maintenance has been neglected, and all the monuments were found to be in an advanced state of disrepair, bordering on collapse, when the German Archaelogical Institute in Cairo chose this quarter as an experimental project for the conservation of the Old City.

Lacking the historical significance of the monuments, the residential buildings of the quarter have suffered even more from insufficient maintenance. Despite having been reconstructed in most cases between the eighteenth and early-twentieth centuries, they are nevertheless in a fairly advanced state of disrepair.

The life of the quarter has become less vibrant over the years. The wealthier inhabitants have moved to other areas, and residential buildings have consequently deteriorated. At the same time traditional crafts and trades, once the predominant means of livelihood for the inhabitants of Darb Qirmiz, have been replaced by modern ones, notably aluminum works and the recycling of waste paper.

Local Architectural Character.   On average, both the monuments and residential buildings are 15 meters in height, with the former constructed throughout most of their height of stone-faced walls with a core of rubble. Occasionally their upper levels are constructed of brick. The roofs are made of shaped wooden beams carrying a wooden platform with a layer of earth and clay serving as the roofing material. Floors are often of patterned marble or plain stone slabs. Poorer-quality materials have been used in the construction of the residential buildings. Here the walls are timber with an infill of brick and rubble. They are often plastered on the outside and colored in dark ocher or cream.

The Work of Conservation.   So far the procedure followed for the restoration of the monuments has been fundamentally the same for all. Stone in the lower levels of the walls that corroded as a result of rising damp has been replaced as have similarly damaged paving stones. All plaster that came loose or was damaged, once again because of rising damp, has been replaced with new plaster both made and laid in the traditional way. Damaged decorative work has been replaced, keeping as closely as possible to the original technique and appearance; damaged

wood in doors and screens has either been repaired or replaced; original painted surfaces have been carefully cleaned and where possible repaired, especially those containing inscriptions. Missing features that were clearly identified have been replaced and new glass lamps have been hung in all seven monuments. Finally, all roof surfaces have been repaired and reconstructed with original materials.

Details. Madrasa of Sabiq al-Din Mitqal al-Anuki. The central floor of the *madrasa* courtyard was re-created in its original form with the help of patterns found at the Egyptian Antiquities Organization. The *mihrab* was dismantled and everything below its arch rebuilt. For this purpose old marble, which matches the particular type of marble originally used here, had to be found and special ceramics made. The *minbar*, which had fallen apart, was reassembled with the addition of new wood where necessary. One of the two badly burned wooden screens on the upper level, which looked onto the courtyard below, was partly reassembled from old pieces, while the other was remade with completely new material.

Tomb of Sheik Sinan. The most important repair work on the mausoleum was done on the damaged dome, which was carefully replastered inside and out. Internally the building was cleaned and repainted and the cresting was repaired.

Fountain of Abd al-Rahman Kathuda. Some of the most severe damage to the fountain was on the timber eaves and pendants at the top of the building. This was all repaired and the roofs resurfaced to make them waterproof. The paving of the *madrasa* on the upper level was relaid and the surfaces cleaned.

1: The madrasa *on the upper level of the Fountain of Abd al-Rahman Kathuda is a light, lofty structure of stone columns and arches surrounded by a timber balcony screen. 2: Tiny yet monumental in the street scene is the Tomb of Sheik Sinan. 3: The plan of the whole quarter identifies the seven monuments.*

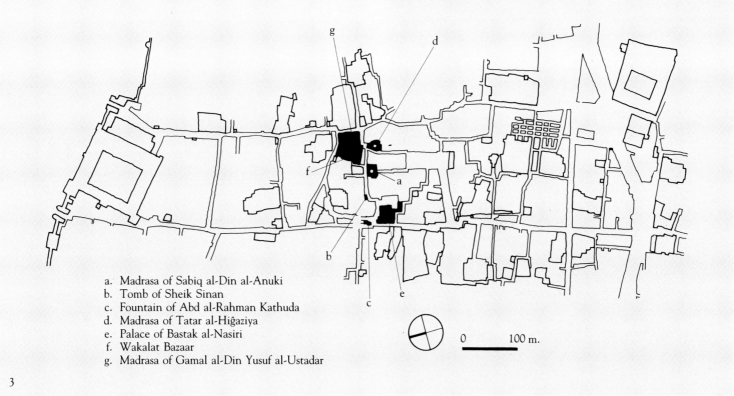

a. Madrasa of Sabiq al-Din al-Anuki
b. Tomb of Sheik Sinan
c. Fountain of Abd al-Rahman Kathuda
d. Madrasa of Tatar al-Higaziya
e. Palace of Bastak al-Nasiri
f. Wakalat Bazaar
g. Madrasa of Gamal al-Din Yusuf al-Ustadar

0   100 m.

3

The restoration of this building has been held up because of difficulties in getting tiles made to match the originals. The experimental tiles produced were not considered to be of adequate quality, and further experiments are being undertaken.

Madrasa of Tatar al-Hiğaziya. This building was in worse condition than the preceding three: only fragments of the original decoration remained and most of the plaster had fallen off. Re-creating the original appearance of the *madrasa* was therefore more difficult. All the gypsum screens had to be re-made, as well as large portions of the original, highly decorated calligraphic frieze around the courtyard and the *mihrab.*

One of the splendors of this *madrasa* is the Tomb of Tatar al-Hiğaziya and particular care was taken in cleaning the gilt

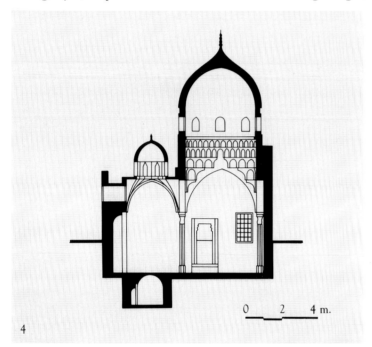

4

and polychrome woodwork of its interior. The magnificent quality of the windows, both in terms of design and craftsmanship, became obvious once they had been carefully cleaned. Rising damp on the northeastern corner of the building was a particular problem, but this was solved by leaving vent holes in the walls to allow evaporation.

The top of the minaret, removed and stored at the Antiquities Organization when it seemed that it might collapse, has still to be replaced. The correct identification of its stones seems to be in some doubt.

Palace of Bastak al-Nasiri. Work on the conservation of the palace—the most ambitious project undertaken so far—was begun in 1983. When complete the main reception hall, which overlooks the Darb Qirmiz thoroughfare through a number of large screened openings, will probably be the finest example of interior domestic architecture surviving from the Mamluk period in Egypt.

Conclusion. Shortage of funds made major restoration work in certain areas impossible. Consequently it was decided quite

4, 5: The major domed space of the Tomb of Sheik Sinan. The section shows the relationship of the major and minor spaces; the interior was merely cleaned and the painted surfaces repainted. 6: The fourteenth-century Madrasa of Tatar al-Hiğaziya has a ribbed dome that sits on an octagonal base. 7, 8, 9: An interior view shows the mihrab and minbar, and the elaborate tiling and calligraphy adorning the walls, details of which are also shown. So sensitive has been the restoration that nowhere is the newness usually associated with such projects apparent.

6

early in the conservation process not to undertake the extremely expensive task of trying to control rising damp. Instead it was determined that continual maintenance and repair work on the buildings would be necessary in the future until this problem could somehow be brought under control.

In some respects the shortage of funds was an advantage. For example, very little work has been carried out on those parts of the old fabric still in reasonable condition, with the result that the image of age that the buildings conveyed before conservation work began has been largely retained.

The original restoration program has been somewhat modified because the quarter is becoming increasingly commercial. Two new commercial complexes have been built on sites that

had been earmarked for residential development. Fortunately, the buildings are relatively inoffensive and the German Archaelogical Institute has been able to ensure that their height does not exceed the average height of the older buildings in the area. The increasing commercial prosperity of the quarter is a welcome step in the direction of rehabilitating and revitalizing the old city.

The quality of the restoration work is generally of a high standard and the sense of retained authenticity is very strong. The impact of the project on the surrounding community has been considerable. Two local mosques have again become available for use. These have been beneficial to the local community not only by providing centers for prayer, but since

mosques are commonly used as *madrasas*, for religious instruction as well. The restored Tomb of Sheik Sinan is a fine addition to the street scene. It is hoped that the Palace of Bastak al-Nasiri will become a center for the organization and public display of projects relating to the development of the old city.

A problem in the quarter has been the main cross lane, Darb Qirmiz, which was blocked by the erection of a house across it at the beginning of this century. One of the aims of the conservation program is to open a way through this house to allow traffic once again to pass from one half of the quarter to the other, thus assisting in the process of revitalization.

Finally, apart from the importance of preserving the historical heritage of a nation, such restoration projects also help revive the traditional crafts of an area. The project has led to the employment of some of the finest masons, plasterers, and carpenters in Cairo, and their continued employment is helping to keep their crafts alive.

10: The courtyard of the Madrasa of Sabiq al-Din Mitqal al-Anuki with its re-created marble patterned floor and mihrab *in the sanctuary. 11, 12: Below is a detail of the entrance porch to the* madrasa *with its castellated parapet, and at right the sanctuary with the* mihrab *and* minbar. *All the glass lamps are new.*

SHEREFUDIN'S WHITE MOSQUE

Visoko, Yugoslavia, completed 1980. Client: Muslim community of Visoko. Architect: Professor Zlatko Ugljen. Engineer: D. Malkin. Contractor: Zvijezda, Visoko. Craftsman: Ismet Imamovic.

Master Jury's Citation: For its boldness, creativity, and brilliance. Located in the center of Visoko, Yugoslavia, it replaces a previously destroyed mosque and includes a new public library. While acknowledging the tradition and necessities of a Bosnian mosque, the design extends the architectural vocabulary of the mosque into the twentieth century and therefore contributes to the changing architectural heritage.

This building is a unique achievement in a period when the great problem confronting all architects is integrating and absorbing the "modern movement" into the developing architectural scene. The combining of modern and traditional architectural elements is done with great skill. Similarly, the combining of technological and vernacular building is extremely convincing. The lighting and ambience of the interior, though modern, exactly maintain the traditional atmosphere of the mosque, and the choice and conjunction of materials, old and new, is refined and elegant.

An examination of plan and section reveals the extent to which the architect has been able to fuse traditional custom with a modern spatial ensemble. The community who have commissioned this mosque are to be praised for their boldness and support of this avant-garde building.

Objective. One of the major problems confronting architects in Islam today is how to reconcile the use of valid design principles established by the modern movement in architecture with the continued use of traditional Islamic forms. The problem is particularly evident in the design of mosques, in which function and meaning have hardly changed, and is therefore examined further in two separate essays (pages 30–63). Sherefudin's White Mosque is situated in the center of Visoko, a Yugoslavian town located at the southeastern end of a valley in the formerly Turkish province of Bosnia (now Bosnia and Herzegovina). The design represents a bold attempt at reinterpreting the traditional forms of the mosque in a contem-

Pages 102–103: Sherefudin's White Mosque with its minaret dominates the red-tiled roofscape of Visoko. The strongly sculptured exterior contrasts with the sense of containment and protection of the outdoor prayer area, (at left), with its ablutions fountain.

porary language; while acknowledging the needs of a Bosnian mosque, the design extends the architectural vocabulary into the twentieth century.

Background. Built to replace the old mosque of the same name, which had been recently demolished, Sherefudin's White Mosque has become a prominent architectural landmark in Visoko. The town's history dates back to the late-medieval period when, owing to its location on a caravan route, it began to serve the surrounding cities as a trade-exchange center. Visoko often served as the capital residence of Bosnian kings during the periods when Bosnia was an independent state. While agricultural activity is important, Visoko is better known today as a leather-manufacturing center. The town developed its Muslim character under Ottoman rule (1463–1878), and today a majority of its 30,000 inhabitants are Muslim. Some seven mosques have been built to accommodate the religious activities of the community.

Local Architectural Character. In 1911, a fire destroyed most of Visoko's traditional architecture, which consisted mainly of the wood houses common to all formerly Ottoman towns in the Balkans. The new buildings constructed in their place took the form of two-story masonry structures with pitched red-tiled roofs, reflecting the influence of a more urban and modern architectural tendency.

While the appearance of the buildings changed, the ratio of built-up areas to open spaces—such as streets and backyard gardens—remained the same. In this respect the relation of the residential fabric of the town to the mosque has been maintained on the same scale.

Brief. Social, political, cultural, as well as religious considerations were taken into account by the architect in designing the new mosque. It was decided that the new construction would not only continue to be the largest mosque in Visoko but would also be larger in size than the destroyed one. A larger praying area was considered essential to accommodate the town's growing Muslim community. At the same time the current tendency in Yugoslavia of giving religion a new emphasis, especially in the Muslim communities of Bosnia and

Herzegovina, resulted in the design's providing increased space for both cultural and intellectual activities. A new small-scale complex (*kulliya*) was thus created in Visoko.

Two additional factors that had also to be considered in the mosque's design were the existing graveyard and local climatic conditions. While the old graveyard had to be preserved and integrated as part of the mosque complex, the climate dictated the need for larger protected spaces, both internal and external. The architect therefore decided to situate the main worshiping activities at a lower level than that of the market area and access road, which would make possible an interior providing a greater sense of protection and privacy.

Plan. The mosque comprises five functional areas: the access space and first courtyard, the mosque proper, the annex building, the graveyard, and the minarets.

Access is by means of a curved, sloping path leading down to the partially open outer courtyard with its ablutions fountain. The courtyard functions as an outdoor prayer area.

Situated on the lower floor, the large central space of the mosque is designed to obtain the largest possible space for praying and at the same time to allow other religious activities such as lectures and discussions to take place under suitable conditions. The arrangement of steps and corresponding platform groupings makes visual contact and participation more efficient. The large glass division between the indoor and outdoor praying areas was conceived to achieve the best visual integration of these spaces, thus allowing for the highest possible participation at prayer time.

Adjoining this indoor prayer area is the annex building, whose simple rectangular geometry contrasts with the free volumetric organization of the mosque. The annex consists of a small auditorium and an office or work space separate from

1: In the section, the complex form of the roof over the indoor prayer area is apparent, as are the two levels—the sunken level, with its courtyard and prayer areas, and the street level with its annex building. The upper, street-level floor plan shows both the curved path down to the courtyard and the separate entrance from the street to the annex building. 2: The powerful forms of the mosque are best seen from the graveyard.

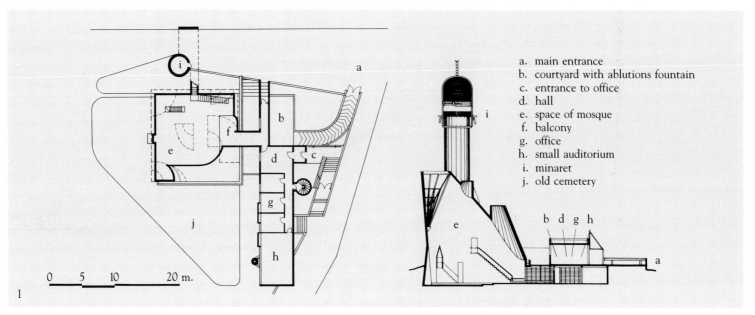

a. main entrance
b. courtyard with ablutions fountain
c. entrance to office
d. hall
e. space of mosque
f. balcony
g. office
h. small auditorium
i. minaret
j. old cemetery

0   5   10   20 m.

1

the prayer areas. A separate entrance from the street to the annex, as well as its location on a different level, ensures its total functional independence from the rest of the mosque. The two minarets, one of which is served with a loudspeaker system for the call to prayer, were built largely for their symbolic effect.

In traditional Bosnian mosques graveyards act as a buffer between the mosque and the buildings of the surrounding community. These graveyards usually encircle the main block of the mosque and are left simply as outer courtyards, without any preconceived formal arrangements. In Sherefudin's White Mosque, however, the graveyard is isolated from the rest of the mosque, because it constitutes the backyard of the complex and the mosque itself does not have windows opening onto the graveyard.

The layout of the mosque is based on the plans of traditional Bosnian mosques: a courtyard leading to a simple square praying area, over which rises a cupola. In its unusual and perhaps dramatic arrangement of this concept, however, Sherefudin's White Mosque differs from its Bosnian counterparts. The ground level, for example, though typical of a traditional Bosnian mosque with its clear, simple courtyard area, is even better integrated into the rest of the building than is usual because of the large glass panels. Moreover, the use of a warped quarter cupola pierced by five roof windows, which cast dramatic shafts of light on key areas of the interior, creates a sharp contrast between the simple plan and the dynamic form of the roof. The five roof windows are a symbolic reference to the five principles of Islam. Symbolism is also apparent in the shape of the cupola at the southeastern facade, which

points forward toward the Ka'ba, the small building in Mecca containing the sacred Black Stone that is the point Muslims face during prayer.

Both the interior of the mosque, with its undulating roof, and the exterior have been painted white, creating a simple and unified effect with slight differences of illumination. From the exterior this same mosque has the appearance of an amorphous rock typical of an architectural style found in some Mediterranean and Aegean churches.

The fountains, *mihrab*, (symbol indicating the direction toward Mecca), *minbar*, (pulpit), and decorative elements are modest in scale and successfully designed as simple objects. The calligraphy decorating the interior is simple and readable, and it contrasts with the highly stylized tubes applied to the taller minaret that are reminiscent of Kufic script.

Only three colors have been used: beige for the floor; white for the walls, roof, and minarets; and green for a few linear metallic elements consisting of frames and tubes.

Structure and Materials.   The structural system for the whole building is reinforced concrete: generally an orthogonal system of columns and beams supporting the floors. For the mosque block, two reinforced-concrete walls provide support for the cupola, with one part of the latter starting at the ground level. The building materials used for construction of the mosque were very limited: plastered concrete for the walls and cupola; white mortar for the inner walls; a combination of pine wood and white mortar surfaces for many interior elements such as the *mihrab* and *minbar*; local travertine tiles for exterior paths and courtyard paving; and iron tubes for the tall minaret. The interior floors are covered with green carpeting.

Conclusion.   The design concept of the mosque has been guided by three aesthetic principles: unity, hierarchy, and contrast. The principle of unity is reflected in the choice of one basic color—white—and in the simplicity of the elementary forms, which consist of squares, rectangles, and cylinders. The pyramidal massing of the mosque, beginning with the large minaret and cupola and continuing down to the annex and features of the open spaces, illustrate the hierarchical principle. Finally, contrast is apparent in many aspects of the mosque's design: pure geometry versus warped forms; rectangular and curvilinear shapes; the easy continuity of horizontal surfaces in contrast to asymmetrical and vertical dynamism; the austere starkness of the inner space and the formal richness of the mass; the change from illuminated to dark spaces. Contrast on an urban scale is also apparent between the highly sculptured pyramidal mass of the white mosque and the pitched red-tiled roofs of the surrounding houses. This emphasizes the landmark effect of the mosque compared to the anonymous uniformity of the nearby pitched roofs.

The mosque is currently in use, with ten to fifteen people attending each prayer session during weekends. On Fridays, however, attendance mushrooms to nearer 300 and swells to about 400 for certain religious lectures, confirming that the mosque is the Friday Mosque, or main mosque, of Visoko.

3, 4: *Indoor and outdoor prayer areas are separated by a large single sheet of glass. The rectangular geometry of the courtyard contrasts with the warped roof form of the interior.* 5: *Shafts of light penetrate roof windows and illuminate great circles of calligraphy.* 6: *The mihrab and* minbar, *which make use of pine, stand out against the plain white walls of the indoor prayer area.*

All the technology and materials used, as well as the labor employed, were indigenous to the region, and as much as 94 per cent of the cost was covered by voluntary donations from the members of the community.

The simplicity of the mosque's interior space, its decorative features and recognizable objects (*mihrab, minbar, minaret, fountain*), its introverted atmosphere, the presence of the gravestones, and finally the organizational pattern of a religious-cultural complex within a market area make a significant contribution to a modern community that remains not only profoundly religious but also linked culturally and historically with Ottoman tradition.

ANDALOUS
RESIDENCE

ANDALOUS RESIDENCE

Sousse, Tunisia, completed 1980. Client: Consortium Tuniso-Kowëitien de Développement. Architect: Serge Santelli.

Master Jury's Citation: For the search toward a contemporary expression of the structural principles underlying the traditional architecture. The simplicity and functional elegance of the design, the successful use of local architectural elements such as courtyards, interior gardens, pools, stream water, and of traditional materials such as tiles make this apartment hotel one of the best examples of the search for a new synthesis of the traditional and modern architectural vocabularies.

Particularly praiseworthy is the restraint with which materials and forms have been used and the subdued nature of the color scheme, which enable this group of buildings to achieve its imagery while avoiding pastiche.

Objectives. The design of the Andalous Residence, an apartment hotel in the Diar el-Andalous resort complex near Sousse, is simple and regular, and it avoids the falsely exotic character of neo-Moorish architecture now widespread in Tunisia. This was intended deliberately by the architect, whose objective was to achieve a contemporary expression of the structural principles that govern traditional Arab-Islamic architecture. He therefore avoided adding Moorish decorative features such as arches, sculptured capitals, and green tiles to the facades, believing that such additions correspond to standards that are essentially international and Western in origin.

Location. Located 140 kilometers south of Tunis in the newly created resort of Port el-Kantaoui, 7 kilometers north of Sousse, the Diar el-Andalous complex consists of a 282-room luxury hotel, two apartment hotels, and various recreational and entertainment facilities situated on 19 hectares. The 3.3-hectare site of the Andalous Residence is a gentle slope 300 meters from the sea.

Historical Background. Built on a Phoenician foundation, the city of Sousse revived at the end of the seventh century after

Pages 110–113: The Andalous Residence turns its back on a flat, featureless site by the sea to create its own architectural landscape of inner and outer interconnected courts, laid out with pools, channels, fountains, pergolas, and trees. The view at left, showing a sequence of courts, crosses the main axis of the central oblong court.

its destruction in Byzantine times. It developed under the Aghlabites and by the second half of the ninth century contained many fine public buildings and monuments, reflecting a prosperity derived from trade. This was interrupted during its subsequent history by Spain, France, and Venice. The modern city was damaged in the Second World War during the Tunisian campaign in 1942 and '43.

Local Architectural Character.   Traditional Tunisian houses are designed around courtyards giving access to the rooms, none of which are connected with one another. Where an upper level exists, the rooms are connected by a gallery running around the four sides of the courtyard. All houses have usable terraces and roofs that are accessible. In traditional Tunisian Muslim homes, where privacy is all-important, the central courtyard cannot be reached by a straight path from the street door. Instead the hall imposes a zigzag route on visitors to prevent the interior of the house from being seen from the street. In larger houses the hall may also give access to service rooms or to secondary inside corridors.

Design and Construction.   The relatively flat site limited the design options available to the architect. To take advantage

of the Mediterranean by giving the hotel rooms a sea view would have meant designing a tall building totally out of keeping with the horizontal lines of the site and its surroundings. An informal plan, ignoring the sea but reaching out into the landscape and making the most of the immediate environment, might have been a solution if the site had contained interesting physical features and not been an arid expanse dotted with a few olive trees.

The only approach was to make the project itself an architectural landscape that was at the same time in keeping

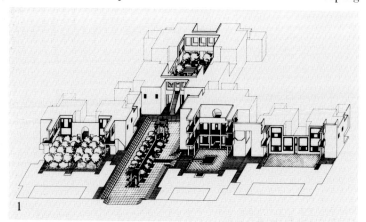

1

with its geographical and cultural setting. The architect achieved this by creating a new environment interesting and attractive enough to distract the user from the otherwise monotonous surroundings. The built area, about one-third of the plot, has sixteen studio apartments, thirty 2-room and seven 3-room apartments, a four-room restaurant, a bar, a terrace café, a reception area, and two other public rooms for guests. Offices and service facilities open onto a separate courtyard.

Plan. The three-story hotel is arranged around a series of inner and outer courtyards. The apartments are entered directly through the inner courtyards, which in turn link up with the outer ones. All the courtyards are connected along a main longitudinal axis, attached to which is a secondary network creating passages and sequences of spaces that recall courtyards and gardens in traditional Arab-Islamic palaces.

Paved and bordered by two or four porticoes similar to those in Tunisian *fundouks* (workshops), the outer courtyards are regular and simple in form—either square or rectangular. The size and form of the interior courtyards vary, but they are smaller than the outer ones, creating a more intimate atmo-

1, 2, 3: Flanked by trees and pergolas at each end, a long pool dominates the central court. At the center of each long side, porticoes, as in Tunisian fundouks, *lead to smaller courts. Outside staircases lead to second-floor galleries, which in turn lead to the apartments. Small windows maintain privacy in the apartments, and recesses in the walls of the court provide built-in seating. The pool and steps are lined with traditional ceramic tiles and the smoothly rendered walls are painted white in the Mediterranean manner.*

sphere. Some of the courtyards are paved and others planted with orange trees and jasmine. All the courtyards are treated as interior gardens, with such features as small streams, pools lined with traditional ceramic tiles, fountains, and pergolas. A small water channel links a square basin in one courtyard with a long basin of water in another. Most of the courtyards have built-in niches for seating, which offer satisfactory protection from the glare of the sun.

The Apartments. With the exception of the seven 3-room apartments, all the others have either one or two rooms. While one-room apartments are designed for up to three persons, the two-room ones can accommodate four or five persons and the three-room ones up to six. The rooms have French windows that open onto a private garden at ground-floor level or, in the case of the upper level, onto a private terrace protected by a high wall. Smaller windows with wooden *mashrabiyas* (latticework screens) open onto the inner courtyards. The private garden or terrace attached to each apartment is an important feature from the point of view of comfort. It allows the occupants to sunbathe and have a meal or a cool drink in the open air without being observed.

The design of the Andalous Residence creates subtle variations in the natural lighting from one place to another in the building. Luminosity decreases as one moves from the big courtyards located on the axis of the building to the smaller lateral courts and still farther into the apartments. There the light penetrates only through openings, all of which have *mashrabiyas* and curtains, allowing the occupant to obtain whatever intensity of light he desires.

Each apartment is equipped with a kitchenette, which includes a stove, a refrigerator, and all the necessary utensils, dishes, glassware, and cutlery. Household linen is provided, and the apartments are cleaned daily with a more thorough cleaning twice a week. The one-room apartments contain a shower, the two-room apartments a bathroom, and the three-room apartments both. Central heating is provided in winter and, although originally only the public rooms had air-conditioning in summer, all the apartments are now being equipped with it. Restaurant and bar facilities are provided for residence guests, who can also enjoy the services provided by the Diar el-Andalous complex, which include swimming pools, tennis courts, and discothèques.

Services. The residence provides full services independently from the rest of the Diar el-Andalous complex. It has its own service quarters consisting of a courtyard onto which the various service rooms open. These are not visible from the areas or traffic routes used by residence guests. There are two such rooms per floor for each courtyard, which makes service both efficient and discrete.

Security is the responsibility of a team of eight watchmen equipped with radios. The outside doors of the patios, made of wrought iron, are locked at night, leaving only the main entrance by the front office open.

Material, Structure, and Technology. The building is a bearing structure with outer walls of poured-in-place concrete 18 centimeters thick. While the mode of construction proposed by the architect was traditional stone and concrete blocks, the construction firm that won the contract preferred cast-concrete technology in order to save both money and time. Unfortunately these advantages were not realized. The work force, which had no experience with this new technology, had a difficult time adjusting the metal forms properly, with the result that the openings for doors and windows ended up being crooked. A considerable amount of time had to be spent in

straightening these openings and smoothing the walls, canceling out any time gained by the use of metal forms.

An inner skin of hollow brick is separated from the outer walls by a 4-centimeter air space; the complete wall measures 35 centimeters in thickness. The interior partitions are also of hollow brick, coated on both sides with cement mortar to a finished thickness of 10 centimeters.

The floors of the apartments are covered with blue and white tiles, and those of the salons and public rooms with gray marble or Agglo-marble—a locally quarried stone. The floor finishes for the galleries and passageways are pink cement tiles, stone, or marble.

The ceilings of the reception rooms and bars imitate the painted wooden ceilings of Tunisian houses, whereas living-room and bedroom ceilings in the apartments are plastered. The outside walls are covered with a rustic-style sprayed surface in ocher, and the interior wall surfaces, though originally rendered smooth and white, are being changed so that they will have a sprayed texture similar to that of the outside walls.

The windows of the inside courtyards are surrounded by bands of traditional tiles from Nabeul, accented by black borders like the decoration in the courtyards of traditional Arab houses. Some courtyards have niches covered with faience of the traditional *maadenoussi* type, whose brilliant texture and strong color contrast with the flat white surface of the surrounding masonry. The courtyard where guests are received is completely covered with faience in framed panels highlighting the outlines of the openings.

The windows, all of which are small in size and flush with the outside wall, are made up of two frames with attached inside shutters. When open, they are contained within the

4: Smaller courts have galleries with wooden balustrades. Windows are contained within a decorative framework of tiles from Nabeul edged with black borders. 5: One-room apartments have deep sleeping niches with built-in beds. 6: The wall around the entry to the reception area is completely covered with tiles.

thickness of the wall. On the outside, *mashrabiya*-type screens protect the windows and allow light to filter in. All the doors are of wood painted light-green with dark-green frames. The wooden shutters of the French windows are also painted green.

While some outside galleries are protected by white-painted concrete rails, others have wooden balustrades painted green. At the ends of some galleries *mashrabiya*-type wooden panels help protect the courtyards from wind and sun, and add to the decorations. These are also painted green.

Conclusion. The typical Tunisian hotel tends to be a monolithic block turned toward the sea. The Andalous Residence has avoided this stereotype successfully and has attained the objective of the architect to build an apartment hotel agreeable to stay in, pleasing to the eye, and at the same time related to Tunisian architectural traditions.

The figures provided by the residence manager reveal a reasonably satisfactory level of occupancy: 45 per cent in 1981, rising to 54.44 per cent in 1982 for the nine months the hotel is open. Most of the hotel guests are European, with Tunisians making up about 2 per cent.

The project has been of considerable benefit locally. Only local materials were used in its construction, which was carried out entirely by Tunisians. The hotel is run by a Tunisian-Kuwaiti company employing a Tunisian staff, with extra employees, also local, hired for the summer.

6

HAJJ
TERMINAL

HAJJ TERMINAL

King Abdul Aziz International Airport, Jidda, Saudi Arabia, completed 1981–1982. Client: Ministry of Defence and Aviation, Jidda, Saudi Arabia. Architect: Skidmore, Owings and Merrill, New York and Chicago.

Master Jury's Citation: For the brilliant and imaginative design of the roofing system, which met the awesome challenge of covering this vast space with incomparable elegance and beauty. The Hajj Terminal structure has pushed known building technology beyond its established limits while demonstrating that such a massive structure can still be light and airy, a twentieth-century echo of the traditional tent structures that have worked so well in desert climates.

The size of the structure and the uniqueness of the hajj phenomenon itself that prompted its erection place it beyond the pale of direct replicability, but the design will undoubtedly serve as a source of inspiration to designers throughout the Muslim world for generations to come.

Hajj, the yearly pilgrimage to the holy city of Mecca, Saudi Arabia, is required of all Muslims who have the means and ability to undertake the journey. With the number of Muslims growing, economic development in the Islamic world, and the increasing reliance on air transportation, the *hajj* has indeed become a unique phenomenon of religious practice, facilitated by modern means of transportation. Estimated at about 500,000 in 1979, the number of pilgrims is expected to double by the early 1990s.

The *hajj* season takes place within a period of about six weeks, resulting in unusually heavy air traffic during this rather short time span. To cope with this the Saudi government began planning for a *hajj* terminal in the early 1960s. Construction was started in 1974 with the American firm of Skidmore, Owings, and Merrill as architects and engineers. Given the large number of pilgrims that had to be accommodated, as well as the diverse requirements of the *hajj,* the terminal was designed and built not merely as another air terminal but in many respects as a large village.

Pages 118–123: The light, airy structure of the Hajj Terminal echoes in gigantic form the traditional tent encampments of nomadic tribes. The elegant open structure allows the air to circulate, while the translucent fiberglass roof fabric maintains a tolerable temperature inside the terminal for the tens of thousands of pilgrims that may find themselves there at any one time.

Location. The Hajj Terminal is one of three terminals in the recently constructed King Abdul Aziz International Airport (KAIA), Jidda. The others include the New Jidda International Airport and the Saudia Terminal. KAIA was built when the old airport, located to the northeast of the old city of Jidda, became obsolete as a result both of urban growth and a phenomenal increase in air travel since 1975. Located approximately 70 kilometers west of Mecca and 64 kilometers northwest of Jidda, KAIA occupies an enormous site of about 105 square kilometers of desert plain, with the Hajj Terminal covering 40.5 hectares. To give some indication of its vastness by means of comparison, the Hajj Terminal covers an area larger than the combined areas of the international airports of New York, Chicago, and Paris. A network of roads connect KAIA to Mecca, Medina, and Jidda.

Plan. The plan of this terminal is extremely regular geometrically, consisting of two separate but identical tent-roof pavilions 320 by 686 meters, separated by a landscaped mall. (An elaborate landscape has been planned for this mall to resist the yearly El-Kamassen sand storm that engulfs the region). Each pavilion is divided into five equal modules. Each module in turn consists of twenty-one identical lightweight tent units, arranged seven units long by three wide and covering 4 hectares.

The *hajj* aircraft land at one of twenty gate processing areas—ten on each side of the terminal. Each gate has equal areas within the terminal for passenger processing. The enormous problem of the numbers of people to be catered for, as well as the time lag while pilgrims wait for road transport to take them to Mecca, decided the designers to form two zones

under each module. The first zone consists of a number of air-conditioned buildings and the second of the vast waiting and support areas, which are not air-conditioned.

Passengers disembark onto a second-level air-conditioned building to go through immigration and health formalities. Baggage collection and customs are on the ground-floor level, after which the pilgrim enters the terminal support area, which is not air-conditioned but covered with a fabric roof, providing shelter from the intense desert heat. Designed to shelter the pilgrims before they depart for Mecca, this area consists of restaurants, shops, toilets, and mosques, with facilities for food preparation, washing, resting, and sleeping.

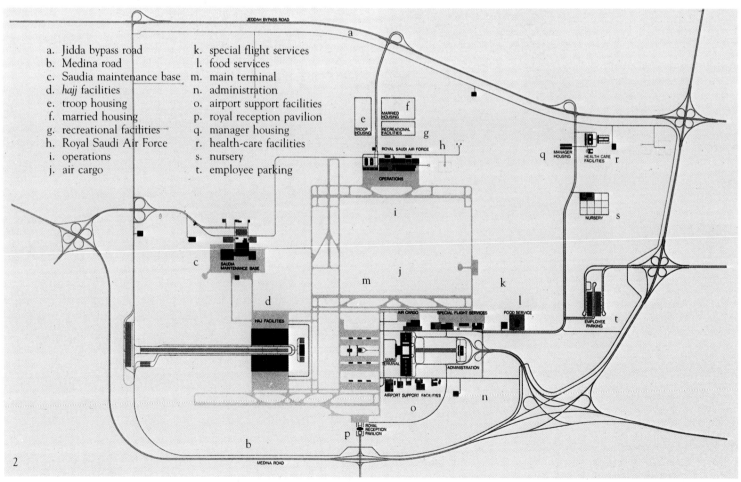

a. Jidda bypass road
b. Medina road
c. Saudia maintenance base
d. *hajj* facilities
e. troop housing
f. married housing
g. recreational facilities
h. Royal Saudi Air Force
i. operations
j. air cargo
k. special flight services
l. food services
m. main terminal
n. administration
o. airport support facilities
p. royal reception pavilion
q. manager housing
r. health-care facilities
s. nursery
t. employee parking

2

One of the essential factors in the concept of the support area is that it does not impose the conventional "airport discipline," which would be both alien and uncomfortable to most pilgrims. Most have saved all their lives to make the journey, and this is probably the first and last time they will be traveling by air. The informal and flexible design of the support area, therefore, conforms with the spirit of *hajj*. The thousands of pilgrims arriving at the terminal during this period often have to wait, sometimes for up to thirty hours, for certain formalities to be completed. Large rest areas have therefore been provided with benches that allow pilgrims ample room to lie down comfortably. At the same time the enormous floor space allows them to roll out rugs and offer prayers without obstructing anyone.

1: The Hajj Terminal has the capacity to handle the 950,000 pilgrims expected in 1985. 2: The master plan shows the terminal in the context of the new King Abdul Aziz International Airport, 64 kilometers northwest of Jidda. 3, 4: The terminal is in two halves, each consisting of five equal modules, one of which is shown in the computer drawing; each module comprises twenty-one tent units suspended from tapering steel pylons.

From the support area the pilgrims have direct road access to the Mecca and Medina freeways.

In 1979 approximately 500,000 pilgrims flew to Saudi Arabia for the *hajj* season. By 1982 this figure was expected to increase to 600,000, which would average out to roughly 30,000 passengers a day. The capacity of the terminal at any one time is estimated at 50,000 pilgrims for a period of up to 18 hours during arrival, and 80,000 pilgrims for periods of up to 36 hours during departure. The time lag is due to waiting for the arrival of buses. In its present form the terminal has the potential of catering for the needs of the 950,000 pilgrims expected by the year 1985.

Structure. The roof of the Hajj Terminal, consisting of a number of tent units, is the world's largest fabric structure enclosing the world's largest covered space. The idea of the tent structure was the third solution proposed by the architects. First a concrete structure was proposed. This plan gave way to a lightweight steel structure. Finally, a tent structure was accepted as the most appealing and practical solution.

Each tent unit is 45 by 45 meters at its base, rising conically to a 5-meter-diameter center support ring at the top. The con-

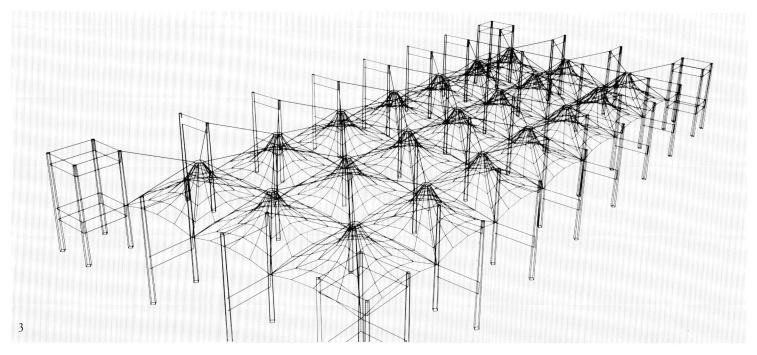

3

4

struction of the tent unit is unusual. Unlike most tents its lowest edge does not touch the ground but is some six stories, or 20 meters, above it, with the fabric rising to 33 meters. The fabric surface is supported by thirty-two steel radial cables, which span from the upper tension ring to a lower tie-down or catenary. The twenty-one tent units of each module were raised simultaneously into place by means of electronically synchronized equipment.

The overall stability and structural integrity of the system is achieved by a special arrangement of perimeter pylons. Extending around each three-by-seven-unit module, including the common row of pylons between adjacent modules, are very stiff double-pylon portal frames. In all there are 440 pylons, for which 30,000 tons of steel was used. Each pylon is 45 meters high, weighs 68 tons, and tapers from a diameter of 2 meters at the base to 1 meter at the top.

Materials.   The double-curved skin of each unit is made of heavy-weight Teflon-coated fiberglass fabric, manufactured by Owens-Corning. This specially designed fabric has a number of uses. The whiteness of the fabric reflects 75 per cent solar radiation and, together with the design of the terminal structure, which allows for air circulation, it helps keep temperatures

down. Thus when temperatures outside reach a scorching 130° F., those within the shaded area of the terminal that is not air-conditioned can be kept in the mid-80° range. At the same time the thin, translucent quality of the fabric allows it to transmit some 7 per cent of sunlight into the structure, eliminating the need for artificial day-time lighting. In addition the acoustical problems under the tents, caused by the presence of large numbers of pilgrims, are diminished by both the height of the roof and the material. The fabric is able to withstand temperatures up to 1,500° F. and will not change color as a result of the sun's ultraviolet rays. Its strength gives it a life expectancy of thirty to fifty years.

Other materials used were rolled shaped steel for the tent pylons, plastic-jacketed bridge strand cables for stretching the tents; and concrete, both cast in place and precast, prestressed for the terminal facilities.

Conclusion.   The tent structure of the Hajj Terminal is an important contribution to the development of an architecture relevant to the Islamic world. As a concept and in its execution it is a work of exceptional originality. Because of its size the terminal's support area is ideally suited for large public events. Outside the *hajj* season, therefore, it is used for such purposes as the city of Jidda's reception for King Fahd, held there after he became king.

The late Fazlur R. Khan, a Bangladeshi architect who played the major role in designing the Hajj Terminal's tent-roof structure, considered it "a very Saudi place." However, while the tent is typical of Saudi architecture, the form it takes at the Hajj Terminal makes it different. "This tent," said Khan, "does not copy tents of the past—it is a form for the future, and here it caters for today's needs—air travel."

The regular geometry of the plan, made by repeating the tent unit, does not produce a monotonous effect. On the contrary, the composition of fabric, cables, and steel columns results in a visually stimulating environment. The interplay of solid and void, dark and light, creates a continuous sense of drama, while the repetition of the tent unit provides rhythm and a strong sense of order.

5, 6: Each tent unit consists of a double-curvature tensile surface that rises conically to a tension ring. 7: The fabric surface is supported by steel radial cables (seen in the computer drawing) that span between the upper ring and lower catenary. 8: Tent units are suspended some six stories above ground with each module of twenty-one tent units separated by double pylons.

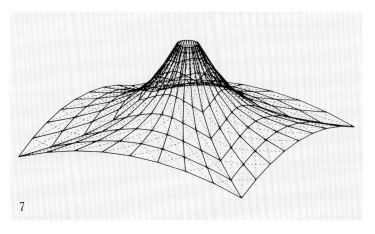

RAMSES
WISSA WASSEF
ARTS
CENTER

RAMSES WISSA WASSEF ARTS CENTER

Giza, Egypt, complete 1974. Clients: Ramses Wissa Wassef, his family, and the community of weavers. Architect: Ramses Wissa Wassef.

Master Jury's Citation: For the beauty of its execution, the high value of its objectives, and the social impact of its activities, as well as its influence as an example. For its role as a center of art and life, for its endurance, its continuity, and its promise.

The project is perfectly adapted to its environment, enhancing the role of earth as a building material, and demonstrating imagination in the organization of volumes and in the subtle use of light. The quality of the spaces, the generosity of the forms, and the ambience created by light all reflect architectural excellence.

The Ramses Wissa Wassef Arts Center has a social as well as a sculptural and spiritual dimension. It has provided a place, supportive as well as poetic, where the young tapestry weavers of the community have been free to develop a local craft that supports the village with products of great excellence and renown.

Objectives. The Ramses Wissa Wassef Art Center evolved over a period of twenty years and now comprises weaving, pottery, and batik workshops, a tapestry showroom, a sculpture museum, middle-class residences and low-cost housing, a farm, and other ancillary buildings. It reflects Wissa Wassef's rejection of modern Egyptian architecture and his search for ways of developing traditional mud-brick architecture to serve a wide range of needs. As Wissa Wassef intended, the center is also an unconventional teaching institution where the traditional crafts and building techniques of Egypt are kept alive and at the same time the innate creativity of the human being is encouraged and allowed expression.

Location. The art center, built on a flat, irregular site of approximately 50,000 square meters just outside the ancient village of Harraniya, is situated a few kilometers southwest of Cairo, with the Pyramids of Giza clearly visible on the horizon. The center's site was part of the flood plain of the Nile before the completion of the second stage of the Aswan High Dam in 1952 and lies just off the Saqqara Road, about two kilometers

Pages 128–131: The courtyard of one of the workshops and a view of the rooftops of the Ramses Wissa Wassef Arts Center exemplify Wissa Wassef's rejection of modern Egyptian architecture and his return to traditional forms that evolved with the use of mud brick.

outside the Green Belt that surrounds metropolitan Cairo. The countryside around Harraniya is agricultural and, while fruit and vegetables are grown for the market at Giza, alfalfa is the principal crop.

The soil of this area consists of clay and silt to a depth of 14 to 16 meters, below which a layer of coarse sand and gravel, running as deep as 60 meters in places, covers the subjacent limestone strata. The water table, at 1.5 to 2 meters below ground level, is stable.

Economic and Social background. Until recently Harraniya had little to distinguish it from any other peasant village in Lower Egypt. Although still predominantly rural in character, it employs only one quarter of its estimated 7,000 inhabitants in agriculture. Up to two-thirds of the young men who live here commute to Giza or Cairo to work in hotels, catering, and other service industries, while 10 per cent work as laborers. There are few craftsmen—other than those working at the center—or white-collar workers.

The social organization of the village is traditional. For example, it is still not considered normal for a woman to work outside the home. The village fountain continues to play an important role as a meeting place for the female population. Running water is rare and there is no main drainage, although a number of sewers discharge into the irrigation canals around the village. While standards of hygiene are low, the incidence of schistosomiasis has declined in recent years.

Local Architectural Character. The traditional material used for construction is mud brick. Most buildings are one or two stories, with an enclosed entrance passage leading to an internal courtyard. The room to the right of this passage normally

serves as a reception area, but in general the use of space is not highly differentiated. Roofs are flat with low parapets, and are widely used for sleeping in the summer and for the storage of camel dung, which is used for fuel.

The architectural style of the outskirts of Cairo, 2 or 3 kilometers away, has had a major influence on the architectural development of the village. Almost all the more recent buildings are concrete structures with brick infill, but interestingly traditional forms have tended to reassert themselves. External windows, for example, are reduced in area to mere slits above eye level, and concrete roofs are covered with a thick layer of earth to improve insulation.

Access and Locations. The site of the center is walled, and its main entrance is reached from the Saqqara Road by way of a bridge across a secondary irrigation canal. Separate accesses are provided to the museum and Mounir Nosshi's house, though these are not generally used. The main access for local people is a walled alleyway from the weavers' houses to Harraniya. Apart from a graveled drive from the main entrance to the various houses, the paths, courtyards, and other spaces within and between buildings are compacted earth.

The unbuilt parts of the site, apart from some modest garden plots, are used for agricultural purposes, particularly for growing fodder and dye plants such as madder, indigo, and woad. A duck pond, poultry houses, and a stable for a horse and oxen underline the rural setting of the center.

Design and Construction. There was in the strict sense no architect's brief. The center evolved over a period of years and continues to evolve in response to varying requirements. Enjoying an enviable freedom from bureaucratic or other control, the architect was able to experiment with forms and materials, and in the later stages of the experiment the participation of the users became an important element in the design process.

1, 2: The weavers' workshops are the central curved row of workshops shown on the plan. The row to the north houses the batik dyers and the straight double row to the south the potters. 3, 4: To the west lies the exhibition area with its central barrel-vaulted space and smaller domed spaces alongside. Vault and domes are pierced by small circular openings to admit shafts of sunlight. 5: The workshops are mainly single-story, but a domed second-floor storeroom and a belvedere give them appropriate prominence.

2

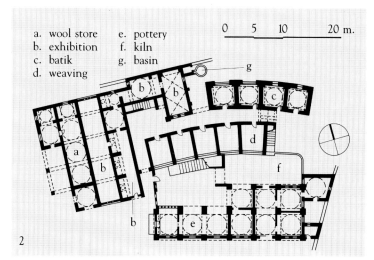

a. wool store e. pottery
b. exhibition f. kiln
c. batik g. basin
d. weaving

0   5   10   20 m.

133

Ramses Wissa Wassef was an idealist determined to put his ideas to the test, and the creation of the center at Harraniya gave him the opportunity of developing and testing theories about architecture and craftsmanship that he had already initiated elsewhere. Born into a prominent Coptic family and conventionally trained as a Beaux Arts architect, Wissa Wassef was deeply struck by the traditional architecture of Upper Egypt, which he discovered with his colleague Hassan Fathy in 1941. Vaulted brick structures were then considered revolutionary, but for Wissa Wassef they represented something essentially Egyptian, because the same forms had been adopted

in turn by Pharaonic, Coptic, and Islamic civilizations. At the same time he had been developing certain theories about the relationship between art and craftsmanship, questioning the distinction between the artist as creator and the craftsman as manual worker. He saw that "traditional craftsmanship," devoid of any creative impulse, was condemned to give way to industrial production and doubted whether the modern school system was capable of transmitting the values of craftsmanship from one generation to the next. Determined to put his ideas into practice, he chose tapestry as the medium for his experiment in applying the creativity of children from the age of eight up to a relatively simple technical task.

When he acquired the first 3,000-square-meter plot of land at Harraniya in 1952, not only did Wissa Wassef bring with him master builders from Nubia who had already worked for him in Old Cairo, but he also brought one of the three nineteen-year-old pupils who had learned weaving and whose role it would be to teach his craft to the children of the local *fellahin* (peasants).

The Nubians built the first house and workshop, and the experiment with weaving was an immediate success. The children showed themselves to be extraordinarily adept at projecting their own imaginations onto the loom, without the aid of drawings and with protection as far as possible from adult interference. Their work soon came to the notice of enlightened Egyptians and foreigners living in Cairo, and a series of exhibitions followed, starting in 1958, in different European countries. Wissa Wassef was encouraged to apply the same approach to pottery, carpet weaving, and stained glass. Since his death, batik dyeing has become one of the principal activities at the center.

Encouraged by the children's creativity and success in mastering the crafts, Wissa Wassef decided to apply a similar approach to architecture. A number of young boys aged twelve and over who had already learned to weave were taught how to prepare mud bricks using local silt and sand and how to build walls. The real experiment began when they learned how to construct vaults on the inclined, or Nubian, system and domes without centering. As intended they were eventually equipped to build for themselves without having to purchase materials.

Workshops and Farm Buildings.   The first workshop, built by the Nubians in 1954 and still used by ten adult weavers, occupied the ground floor of Ramses Wissa Wassef's own house. The interior and small courtyard remain unchanged, with their reused Coptic columns, fine dome on squinches, and fretwork shutters. Concrete extensions, necessitated by the growth of Wissa Wassef's family, were added to the south and east ends of the original building. The use of concrete was justified in order to obtain a factory permit, unlikely to be awarded to a mud-brick structure; there was also a need for a secure place to house the tapestry collection and for a strong roof to sustain the weight of the water tank.

Wissa Wassef's experiment in training his pupils to build with their own hands began modestly with poultry houses, which considering they are the work of children have stood the test of time remarkably well. The same children, aged twelve to fifteen, went on to build their own workshops and showrooms for the tapestries in the early 1960s.

The children's workshops, comprising beginners' and intermediate weaving schools and the batik dyeing and pottery areas, are designed as a separate, enclosed precinct with clearly differentiated areas for the three crafts. The main axis is east-west, and it runs between the two parallel but slightly curved rows of workshops, barely 12 meters wide. There is a deliberate reference to the traditional Egyptian town with its narrow winding lanes lined by craftsmen's workshops. To the north and south of this axis lie the areas used for potting and dyeing; in the former there is a kiln, and in the latter a large circular fountain.

With the exception of a first-floor storeroom for wool and a *maq'ad* (belvedere) used for drying unfired pottery, the buildings are all single story with the roofs used for drying the skeins of dyed wool.

The main showroom is a long barrel-vaulted room with a series of smaller domed spaces alongside it. Large lunette windows provide the workshops with both lighting and ventilation, the east-west orientation of the main axis ensuring that they catch the prevailing northerly winds. Perforated brickwork filters the light and provides a reasonable degree of privacy. With the main axis in the shade all day, there is a reservoir of rel-

atively cool air on which the south-facing workshops can draw.

The showrooms are lit by shafts of sunlight from oculi in the vaulting, and it is possible to supplement the very low level of natural light by spotlighting the tapestries lining the walls. Simple sanitary facilities are located at the southeast corner of the complex.

The farm buildings, workshops, and showrooms were built entirely of mud brick laid in mortar. The mud is flood silt excavated from the foundation trenches, mixed in porportions of two parts sand to one part mud for the bricks (three parts sand to one part mud for the mortar) and fermented for thirty days in water. The roofs are sealed with a cement, lime, and gypsum rendering, and any rainwater is thrown clear of the walls by pipes through the parapets. The interiors of the workshops are whitewashed and those of the showrooms left their natural earth color. The floors are of compacted earth, the main axis being set with rough-hewn limestone.

The workshops, situated on the northeastern tip of the site, are the most prominent feature of the center for visitors arriving at Harraniya along the Saqqara Road. Although their style is not local, they integrate well with the landscape. The domed storeroom and belvedere have a strong visual impact, while the intimate scale of the workshop areas adds to their character. Despite the fact that fifty children under the age of sixteen create a great deal of visible wear and tear, the wall surfaces and roofs have been renewed only once since completion in 1968. Scant rainfall, however, is also a factor contributing to the preservation of these structures.

Habib Gorgy Sculpture Museum.   The museum was built two years after the completion of the tapestry showrooms as a tribute to the late Habib Gorgy to house a collection of his pupils' works from the 1940s and '50s. There are three main exhibition areas of roughly equal importance: an open courtyard, reached by a doglegged passageway; a long gallery; and a dome with three *iwans* and a lesser domed space beside it. The building also contains a porter's house, consisting of two rooms off a secondary courtyard.

It is never too bright or hot in the courtyard, which although open is shaded by both the tall dome and the fronds of palm trees planted in one of its corners. Small terra-cottas are arranged in alcoves along the courtyard's east wall. The long gallery is generally dark and cool apart from some shafts of light penetrating through the oculi at its domed end. Here the sculptures are mainly ranged along the double-skinned west wall. Each piece is placed in an alcove in the inner wall, lit indirectly by light falling on it from an unseen opening in the outer wall. This is a highly ingenious form of natural spotlighting. The apertures in the outer wall do not correspond to those in the inner wall. As a result the angle of light falling on each work is individually directed. The tall dome is shouldered by eight window apertures through which shafts of light

6: *The courtyard of the potters is part of the workshops and a flight of steps leads to a flat roof. 7, 8, 9: The plan of the Habib Gorgy Sculpture Museum shows the three main exhibition areas—the open courtyard, the long gallery at one end and the elaborately domed and vaulted space with three iwans and a smaller, more enclosed domed space beside it.*

penetrate, and the north *iwan,* toward the courtyard, has an arrangement of sculptures silhouetted against a background of perforated brickwork.

The museum is constructed entirely of mud brick, with mud plaster finishes left in their natural color. The floors are of compacted earth. The museum's tall dome is a remarkably accurate example of a parabola built without centering.

Ceres Wissa Wassef and Mounir Nosshi Houses. The house for Wissa Wassef's sister, Ceres, was built less than a year before the one for his friend Mounir Nosshi. Both houses, which have the same general orientation and very similar plans, are raised about 1.2 meters off the ground. Ceres Wissa Wassef's house is on two floors, with an additional mezzanine above the garage and pump room. A vaulted entrance, kitchen, WC, dining room, and living room opening onto a large terrace make up the ground floor, while the second floor and mezzanine consist of three bedrooms, one bathroom, and two washrooms. Mounir Nosshi's house has a similar distribution but omits the mezzanine and is slightly larger, with a study on the ground floor and a fourth bedroom on the second. There is little doubt that the house built for Ceres Wissa Wassef comes closer to the architect's intention. Mounir Nosshi's house was considerably modified in the course of execution in response to newly formulated demands by the client.

The walls of both houses are up to .7 meter thick, and the design of the buildings is well suited to a hot climate. From the terraces, situated to the northwest to shelter them from the sun, one can enjoy a magnificent view of the Pyramids. In both houses much use is made of simple wooden *mashrabiyas* (latticework screens), which allow sunlight to filter through and at the same time enhance privacy. Ceres Wissa Wassef's house also utilizes some stained glass.

Both houses were built of limestone cut from nearby quarries. For Ceres Wissa Wassef's house cement mortar was used up to the second floor with mud mortar above, because it was feared that the walls of the upper story of Ceres's house might not withstand the lateral thrust of the vaults and buttresses, which are characteristic features of the house added after the initial plans had been drawn up and construction started. For Mounir Nosshi's house cement mortar was used up to the parapet level.

The vaults of both buildings are of porous red brick laid in cement mortar. In Ceres's house the dome of the main living area rises on pendentives through the second-floor level; in Mounir Nosshi's all the vaults are groined. This measure was taken partly for reasons of economy, since the amount of fill needed to level the floor above was considerably less than that required for a dome and could be reduced still further by building up the voids to floor level with little diaphragm walls. At the same time the construction of intersecting arches did require centering. The floors were laid with red brick tiles produced locally.

The finishes for Ceres's house were more expensive. Marble was used throughout the bathroom and WCs, and the antique handbasins are in carved Coptic style. Patterned brick tiles

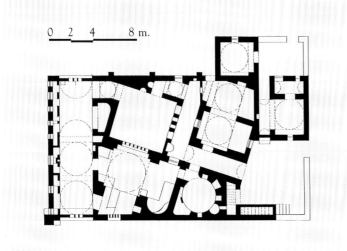

0 2 4 8 m.

7

9

with mosaic tesserae adorn the landing, and the living area is graced with an inlaid marble fountain.

There is a considerable amount of woodwork in both houses, which sent costs up considerably since all the wood had to be imported. The houses also contain tiled fireplaces, hanging glass lamps, and other decorations. The exteriors were rendered in cement, sand, and lime mortar with a final coat of a traditional earth-colored finish known as *dahara*. Interior renderings were done in cement, sand, and lime plaster with a gypsum skim and edging coated with emulsion paint.

Both houses blend well into the landscape. The design of the interior is interesting, with the link-up of spaces particularly successful in Ceres's house. A bent entrance leads into a domed entrance hall, deliberately lower than and out of alignment with the spaces beyond. The dining and living areas flow into each other, with the pivotal position occupied by the tall dome reflected in the marble fountain set into the floor beneath it. An arched aperture between the two flights of stairs draws the eye upward, and on the second-floor landing the way out onto the southwest roof terrace cunningly negotiates the shoulder of the dome.

Weavers' Houses.   Seven houses were built for seven landless weavers. The chance of owning their own homes, it was hoped, would give them a sense of independence. Ramses Wissa Wassef bought the land and divided it into seven plots. Each of the seven weavers was then given a piece of clay to model his future home. The choice was not entirely unfettered, since the group had already worked out in long hours of discussion

what their common requirements were. These included a courtyard with a living room on one side, and a kitchen and washroom with WC on the other. The courtyard would have a chicken coop and a bread oven. The weavers, however, were given complete freedom in deciding how the functions would be distributed and how the entrance, courtyards, and steps to the upper story would be laid out. A vaulted storage area and sleeping place was planned for the roof of each house.

In the end no two houses were the same. In fact there were some significant differences. The living rooms, however, are all vaulted with *iwans* containing *mastabas* (masonry benches), and all seven houses have direct access to the village of Harraniya by means of a walled alleyway created especially for the purpose. The walls are made of limestone with mud mortar and the ground-floor vaults of porous red brick with cement mortar. The upper stories have groined vaults built with centering and made of mud brick laid in mud mortar.

As an example of user participation the project is of undoubted interest. Yet of the seven houses, only three are now lived in permanently by their beneficiaries. This has come about because the young weavers came under considerable pressure from their families to leave. In this sense the experiment was perhaps premature, anticipating changes of attitude that, ten years later, are only now taking place. At the same time the style of architecture still tends to have negative con-

10: Ceres Wissa Wassef's house is on two floors, with an additional mezzanine over part of it. The plan is a free arrangement of square domed or vaulted compartments; when a rectangular compartment is required the space is extended in one direction with an arched alcove. 11, 12: The living area on the ground floor has an inlaid marble fountain and is roofed with a dome that rises on pendentives through the second-floor level.

a. hall
b. living
c. dining
d. kitchen
e. bathroom
f. WC
g. bedroom
h. terrace
j. garage/carport

Mezzanine

Second Floor

Ground Floor

0 2 4   8 m.

10

notations in that mud is associated with poverty and domes with religious buildings. With Wissa Wassef's death in 1974, before the houses were finished, his paternalistic concern for the welfare of the weavers, which might have prevailed upon them to stay, was also lost.

Conclusion. In general the buildings of the center are well adapted to their uses. Their response to climatic conditions is good, and maintenance, drainage, and sanitation are adequate. Wissa Wassef's application of the empirical approach to architecture has proved successful, as reflected by the buildings themselves. Training provided on the job has produced a versatile and talented team of builders. The response of the users is generally positive. In the case of the experiment with the weavers' houses the relative lack of success has to be viewed in the context of subsequent social change.

The existence of the center has had a profound impact not only on Harraniya but on many of the surrounding settlements. Since Wissa Wassef tapestries became well known, other tapestry workshops have sprung up in neighboring towns and villages. In at least one of them, Kirdâsa, the main industry is now the making of inferior copies of Wissa Wassef tapestries. Real Wissa Wassef tapestries are individual works of art and command higher prices in Egypt and abroad, with the weavers of Harraniya earning, with bonuses, up to three times the local average. Consequently this has earned respect for weaving and other crafts and given the weavers a great deal of independence and a feeling of self-sufficiency. Female weavers in particular have won the right to continue working after marriage and even to live in their own houses and not necessarily with their husbands' families. Economic viability has therefore led to social gains. There has also been some impact on the physical environment. The children working at the center have been set higher standards of hygiene and are generally better fed and clothed than other village children.

The center demonstrates that traditional architecture using local materials and relatively unskilled labor is better adapted to the climate, cheaper, and more spacious than conventional modern buildings, using imported materials and technology. There appears to be a future, therefore, for nonindustrial modes of production in Egypt. The influence of the small group of architects led by Wissa Wassef and Hassan Fathy is felt by many younger Egyptian architects, working both in Egypt and elsewhere. The art center offers a rare opportunity of studying in one place the development of Wissa Wassef's ideas over the twenty-year period preceding his death.

12

TANJONG JARA BEACH HOTEL AND RANTAU ABANG VISITORS' CENTER

TANJONG JARA BEACH HOTEL AND RANTAU ABANG VISITORS' CENTER

Trengganu, Malaysia, completed 1980. Client: Tourist Development Corporation of Malaysia, Kuala Lumpur. Architects: Wimberly, Whisenand, Allison, Tong, and Goo, Honolulu, with Arkitek Bersikutu Malaysia, Kuala Lumpur. Interior designer: Juru Haisan Consult, Kuala Lumpur. Master craftsmen: Abdul Latif, Nik Rahman. Landscape architects: Bert, Collins and Associates, Honolulu.

Master Jury's Citation: For the courage to search out and successfully adapt and develop an otherwise rapidly disappearing traditional architecture and craft, and at the same time meet the demands of contemporary architecture. The program, while attempting to provide a resort facility in an otherwise underdeveloped area, is part of a broader strategy for the development of local architecture and the economy. In this the project has succeeded. It has provided employment at the resort and at the industries that service the resort. Through the use of traditional architectural forms and materials, the project has revived a number of building-material industries, crafts, and traditional constructional skills.

Though architecturally the adaptation of traditional forms to new uses raises several technical and ideological problems, the consistency and seriousness with which this approach has been pursued at all levels of design and execution has generated an architecture that is in keeping with traditional values and aesthetics, and of an excellence that matches the best surviving traditional examples.

Objectives. The northeastern coastal state of Trengganu on the Malay Peninsula has, like other states on the east coast, lagged behind in Malaysia's drive for modernization. Since the 1970s, however, the government has taken an active interest in developing Trengganu by utilizing its cultural heritage and picturesque settings with the aim of establishing a tourist industry. The first project undertaken as part of this scheme was the Tanjong Jara Beach Hotel (T.J.B.H.) and the Rantau Abang Visitors' Center (R.A.V.C.) which the government's Tourism Development Corporation (T.D.C.) decided to establish in 1976.

In designing both these sites a number of objectives were borne in mind, the primary one being to create a project in

Pages 138–141: The Tanjong Jara Beach Hotel has revived building-material industries, crafts, and constructional skills through the use of traditional architectural forms and materials. Its buildings were inspired by the two-story palaces of earlier sultans.

harmony with the surrounding environment. To this end local craftsmen and materials were employed and the essence of the region's architectural traditions honored. It was also intended that the projects provide the local community with an impetus for economic growth by creating jobs and making use of local crafts. In addition the T.D.C. sought to encourage efforts at conserving the natural sea life of the area, create a training center for hotel staff, and finally to set the pace for future developments in the region.

Although the project comprises two physically separate entities situated 10 kilometers apart from each other, they share the same owners and management and are regarded as a complementary whole.

Location.   Sites for the project, located south of the state's capital of Kuala Trengganu, were well chosen. The buildings are surrounded by an area with remarkable physical features: the Kuala Abang River; steep hills contrasted with golden beaches along the South China Sea; lush foliage; palm trees, a natural stream, and a lagoon.

Access.   It takes about eight hours to reach the site by car from the country's capital of Kuala Lumpur. Alternatively the journey can also be done by car with an hour's flight from Kuala Lumpur to Kuala Trengganu, from which the hotel can be reached within an hour by car.

Local Architectural Character.   The varied forms apparent in Malaysia's architecture are a reflection of the foreign influences to which the country has been exposed. Interspersed with architecture of a distinct Chinese style are mosques with domes and minarets and buildings with a formal style prevalent during the British colonial period.

The traditional architectural idiom of the east coast takes the form of buildings raised on stilts for flood protection, constructed from wood with inexpensive red Trengganu tiles used for the roofing. Today, however, this architectural form is giving way increasingly to the influence of the modern International Style. Tiling for roofs is more often than not being replaced by tin or asbestos sheets, and new housing schemes are usually not raised on stilts.

The prime source of inspiration for the design of the project was the *istanas,* the two-story hardwood palaces of the earlier sultans of the region. Perfected over centuries, their style blends in with the local environment and is ideally suited to local weather conditions. Only a few examples of the building form remain today. The *istana's* raised position on stilts, some .9 to 2.44 meters above the ground, protects it from flooding and encourages air circulation. Ventilation is also provided by open-sided rooms, lattice soffits, steep pitched roofs with grilled gables and bisque roof tiles. The latter are left exposed on the inside, thereby allowing the interior to breathe and warm air to escape through the roof. The hot tropical rains saturate the

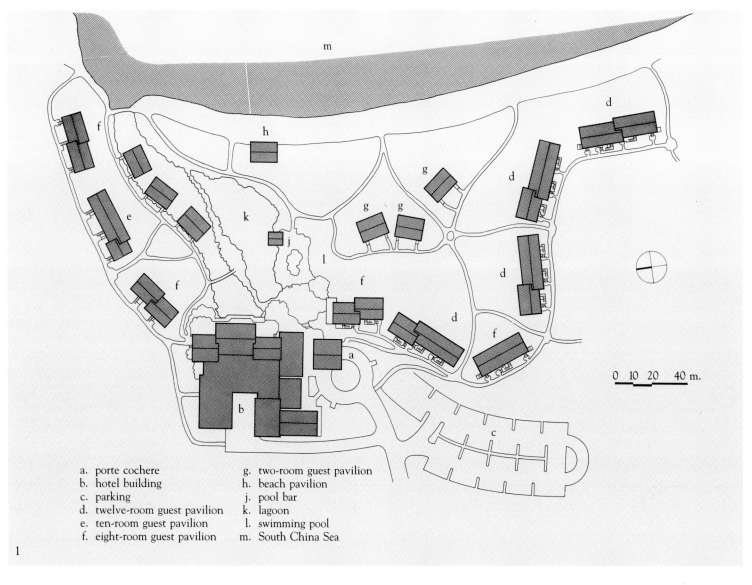

a. porte cochere
b. hotel building
c. parking
d. twelve-room guest pavilion
e. ten-room guest pavilion
f. eight-room guest pavilion
g. two-room guest pavilion
h. beach pavilion
j. pool bar
k. lagoon
l. swimming pool
m. South China Sea

1

porous tiles; then once the sun comes out and the water evaporates, cooling the spaces below. Interior temperatures in the *istanas* are therefore always comfortable, almost eliminating the need for air-conditioning. All these traditional design features have been incorporated in the design of the Tanjong Jara Beach Hotel.

Tanjong Jara Beach Hotel.   Situated 65 kilometers south of Kuala Trengganu the hotel is spread over 31.44 hectares around a crescent-shaped beach of golden-yellow sand. The northern end of the site begins at a steep hill and stretches to the south over a sand berm running parallel to the ocean. A wier, placed at one end of a natural stream running across the property, has allowed a lagoon to form. The hotel's two-story cottages, reflecting traditional *istana* designs, are situated within it. Behind them and at a higher elevation near the base of the hill are a series of two-story buildings, each containing eight to twelve guest rooms. A similar arrangement and relationship is repeated for the guest units to the south of the site.

All the hotel structures are oriented toward the ocean view. Placed in clusters, they derive maximum advantage from the ocean breeze because of their high ceilings and their verandas and balconies, which face the ocean. A large public house bridging the lagoon contains dining, conference, social, and recreational facilities.

A number of large shady trees and palms, already growing on the site when construction was started, were preserved to form the basis of a lush planting scheme.

Rantau Abang Visitors' Center.   Spread over 6.07 hectares sandwiched between the coastal road and the ocean, the Rantau Abang site lies 10 kilometers north of the beach hotel, or about 55 kilometers south of Kuala Trengganu. Running parallel between the road and the ocean is the Kuala Abang River, separated from the ocean by a high sand-dune berm. The museum, restaurants, and shops are built over this river.

Originally only an information center was planned for this site, which is noted as one of the world's few breeding grounds for leather-backed turtles and is a major tourist attraction. The center was to provide visitors with regional information especially about the giant green turtles and their annual egg-laying migration. The idea was eventually expanded to encompass other facilities: a museum concentrating on regional sea life as well as the traditional arts and crafts of the east coast of Malaysia; a snack and refreshments bar; a series of shops and bazaars featuring local crafts; a botanical garden; and eleven low-priced traditional Malaysian-style kampong bungalows situated on the banks of the river nearer the highway and particularly suited for local families on holiday.

Adapting the project to the site's topography meant taking into consideration a number of factors: the rising and falling levels of the fresh-water lagoon throughout the year; the proximity of the major east-coast highway; and of particular importance, the effects of development on the life cycle of the

turtles using the beach as their nesting ground. The species is very sensitive to light and movement. The Malaysian representative of the World Wildlife Fund has done much to protect and support them, and was adamant that nothing should be done to disrupt their breeding cycle.

The museum is raised on piers above the river and sand dunes to avoid disrupting the site's natural features. This elevated position has the added advantages of raising the museum to the level of the prevailing breeze and of allowing a panoramic view of the turtle hatching grounds on the adjacent beach. A wooden bridge connects the museum and restaurant, (which serves exclusively Malaysian cuisine) with the information center and crafts bazaar located on the highway side of the river.

Local hardwoods have been used in the construction of all buildings, with Trengganu tiles for the roofing completing the traditional appearance from the exterior. Local arts and crafts, employed in the interior decor from lamp shades and wicker chairs to soap dishes consisting of half of a coconut shell, add an informal touch and complete the indigenous character of the buildings.

The layout of the visitors' center is based on the casual rambling form of the Trengganu fishing village. Spaces between buildings convey a feeling of leisure and relaxation in contrast to the congestion and artificiality experienced in urban settings. As with the hotel none of the buildings is over two stories. Coconut palms extensively in evidence are therefore always higher than the built-up areas. Local plants and shrubs enhance the tropical setting and also act as windbreakers; in certain cases they provide privacy.

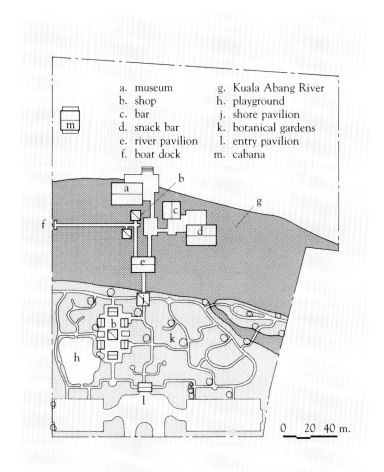

a.	museum	g.	Kuala Abang River
b.	shop	h.	playground
c.	bar	j.	shore pavilion
d.	snack bar	k.	botanical gardens
e.	river pavilion	l.	entry pavilion
f.	boat dock	m.	cabana

0   20   40 m.

1: The site plan of the Tanjong Jara Beach Hotel shows the free arrangement of hotel building and guest pavilions around the lagoon.
2: The Rantau Abang Visitors' Center is built more compactly, mainly on stilts over the Kuala Abang River, as the site plan shows.

2

Structural System.   The structure consists of a post-and-beam construction in the traditional ethnic style. The roofs are carried by timber trusses covered with local traditional clay tiles on hardwood battens and rafters. Sarking is generally left out in order to enhance the visual expression and experience of the ethnic style from the inside as well.

Materials Used.   Four kinds of wood, both hard and soft and abundantly available in the area, were utilized as the basic materials. *Nyatoh*, a kind of plywood, was used for interior paneling and *kapor* for the flooring except in the reception

3: A roof detail of the beach hotel shows the elaborately carved fascia boards, the traditional local clay tiles, and the characteristic roof structure, which is made up of compression members rather than of Western triangulated trusses. 4, 5: The group of buildings belonging to the visitors' center, which includes the museum and river pavilion, are raised high above the water level to contain the rising river and to protect the leather-backed turtles whose breeding ground it is.

area, where Thai marble was preferred; *balan*, a softwood, was used for carving, and *chengol*, the strongest and hardest, for the main structural elements. A carpentry shop and sawmill were set up on site for the duration of the project. Timber columns, beams, and trusses were manufactured on the premises, while carved panels and moldings were centrally fabricated. The design of the buildings provided a welcome opportunity for the wood craftsmen of the area to exercise their craft. Tiles used for the roofing were kiln-fired in the nearby villages and supplied through local contractors.

Conclusion.   It is common practice for architects to incorporate as many new construction techniques and innovative design features as available or affordable into major projects like hotels. With the hotel and visitors' center, however, a deliberate attempt was made to seek inspiration from the region's Muslim heritage and to incorporate the best of both worlds into the design.

The buildings function well together both as an integrated whole and as individual units. They are well lit and comfortable, the design of each building providing guests with the option of either natural ventilation or air-conditioning. Maintenance according to the hotel's manager is a "year-long affair." This is understandable, given the never-ending scraping, polishing of wood, and spraying against insects and termites that are necessary.

A Western-style hotel of similar size, though more com-

pactly planned, would have required considerably less man-power. The town's Development Corporation, however, takes the view that for a labor-intensive economy the more jobs created the better. The project has already started to yield a profit, and the impact in terms of improved life-styles for the local villagers is very apparent. The project also is expected to provide long-term benefits in terms of training individuals both regionally and nationally. A school has been established by the T.D.C. to train personnel for the specific jobs required by the hotel.

At the same time the project has revived a sense of pride in the Malay heritage and arrested the decay of local skills in the arts and crafts. The use of the traditional *istana* style, the

informal Malay village layout, handcrafted wooden construction techniques, and numerous indigenous decorative crafts constitute a successful contemporary use of traditional Malay building idioms.

More significantly and on an intellectual level, the project has helped change the image of backwardness attached to whatever was local and appropriate for the environment. It has shown that Malay architectural forms from the past can still be meaningful for Malaysia's contemporary needs.

The success of this project, the first resort hotel of international standards in the Trengganu area, has assisted the T.D.C.'s efforts to transform the east coast of the Malaysian peninsula into a major resort region.

GREAT
MOSQUE OF
NIONO

GREAT MOSQUE OF NIONO

Niono, Mali, completed 1973. Client: Muslim community of Niono. Designer/master mason: Lassiné Minta.

Master Jury's Citation: Islamic culture has only recently begun to emerge from a past whose aesthetic values were based on craft toward a future whose aesthetic values will surely be based on machine production. The continuing existence of traditional forms—both sophisticated and primitive—is one of our strongest allies in retaining architectural character and cultural identity as large-scale modern industry and worldwide building models assert their presence. Hence the will and the conscious intention to continue the traditional should be commended and encouraged.

The Great Mosque of Niono is an example of such efforts. Lassiné Minta, the master mason of the mosque, in conceiving and constructing the mosque, has reflected the deep and powerful tradition of vernacular architecture. Only when he introduced new fenestration has the work faltered stylistically if not functionally. Yet this ongoing process of change, reflecting life itself, deserves careful attention if we are ever to secure sufficient continuity—free of stylistic flaws—for the benefit of present and future cultural development. Hence the conscious volition of the master mason and community of Niono to continue their tradition in a contemporary building, thereby retaining indigenous cultural identity, deserves recognition.

Objectives. In 1955 the mosque at Niono, which had become too small for the needs of the local Muslim community—although originally built between 1945 and 1948—was enlarged. Fourteen years later, in 1969, it was decided to enlarge it still further and replace its oldest parts, whose scale and overall concept were no longer compatible with the more recent reconstruction.

Location. The village of Niono lies near the southwest tip of the Upper Niger Delta, between two irrigation canals in an alluvial plain. The already flat, monotonous landscape is being rendered more so by drainage works that are under construction for the irrigation of crops. To the west of the village lie ad-

Pages 146–149: The Great Mosque of Niono, completed in 1973 after eighteen years, follows the traditional form of Malian mosques like those of Djenné and Mopti. The long qibla wall (east), with its three minarets, and the external walls generally include an unusual feature—frequent windows louvered for ventilation.

ministrative buildings, while its eastern side contains living quarters established during the French colonial period for African workers.

The mosque occupies a central position in the residential area of the village, which has several long streets running parallel to the canals, intersected by streets crossing at right angles. The main entrance to the mosque is on one of the busiest avenues not far from the market.

Historical Background. Niono as it is constituted today is mainly a creation of the Niger Office from around 1937. This institution, at that time run jointly by the colonial authorities and the French Government, was established in 1932 to reclaim the land of the Upper Niger Delta with the object of using its agrarian and industrial potential in creating a huge agroindustrial complex to produce mainly rice and cotton. This ambitious project, aimed at reclaiming 900,000 hectares to be divided more or less equally between the cultivation of rice and cotton, swiftly ran into serious difficulties. First, there was a shortage of funds, and second, the type of soil in certain areas was not conducive to the growing of cotton, which had to be abandoned in favor of rice. The Niger Office, now an arm of the government of Mali, controls only about 60,000 hectares of reclaimed land. The inhabitants of the village, originally from a variety of regions, give the community a unique stamp.

The Niono mosque was originally constructed on a site of 119 square meters. In its original form it comprised eight bays placed crosswise and three lengthwise, with the *mihrab*, which indicates the direction of Mecca, situated on the axis of the fourth bay from the north. In 1955 the mosque committee decided to extend the mosque by adding six transverse bays on the south side. When in 1969 it became necessary to enlarge the mosque still further, the results were an extension of the main building to 726 square meters, the entire reconstruction of the original central part, the building of a separate prayer

1: The western side of the mosque, with its single tower minaret and principal entrance, faces the court and the long narrow women's prayer hall. 2: The section and plan show the hypostyle hall of pillars and its relation to the qibla wall. The plan also shows how the mosque is now too large for its walled site. 3: The structure was designed and built by Lassiné Minta and the local community.

hall for women, and the construction of a long, narrow building of 140 square meters and several annexes, all of which were contained within the boundary wall. By 1973, the main work was complete. Since then, the building orginally used as the caretaker's quarters has been turned into a sepulcher in which the first imam of the mosque, who died in 1983, is buried.

Local Architecture. The architecture of the local houses is very basic, even when compared to houses in other towns of the same region, notably Djenné, Mopti, and Bandiagara. The structural features, whose gentle lines help to minimize the effects of erosion, are made entirely by hand and serve purely functional needs. Since decorative features are extremely rare, their use in the decoration of mosques is particularly striking. With the exception of the colonial-type buildings found in the government quarter, all the other houses, most of which

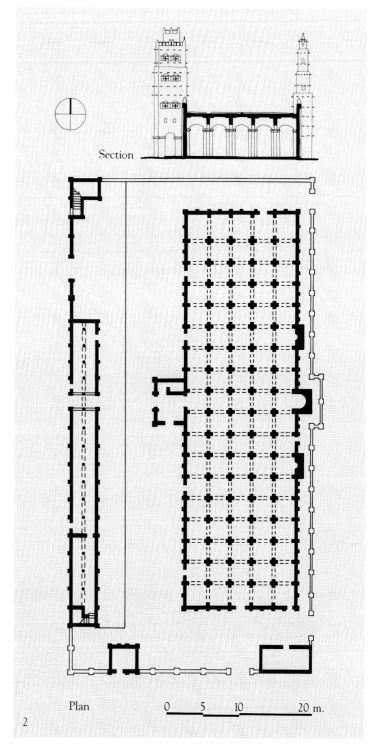

Section

Plan   0   5   10   20 m.

2

do not have an upper story, are constructed of local materials: sun-dried clay; mortar rendering made from clay and hardened rice bran; and timber, especially palmyra. The layered system used for the roofs is both ingenious and decorative, consisting of a layer of clay resting on a ceiling of wooden beams, the latter usually twisted and short in length.

Modern materials, usually imported, are gradually gaining ground. Cement, for example, is sometimes used for foundations, for roof coping and for rendering. While corrugated iron is used both in joinery and for cladding doors and windows, steel sections are used for frames and also in joinery.

Although buildings constructed entirely from these "hard" materials are still rare in Niono, this situation will probably not continue for long. Unfortunately these buildings have a very commonplace character and their spread will not only lower aesthetic standards but, from an economic angle, drain local financial resources, since most of the materials will have to be imported. Already architecture in the style of the mosque is disappearing.

Access. Situated in the center of the village a few dozen meters from the market, the mosque is easily accessible to all inhabitants. There are several points of entry opening onto the three roads surrounding the mosque, with the one on the southeast facade used only by women.

Functional Requirements. The most important consideration in planning the Niono mosque was that it should serve the religious needs of the Muslim community. It had, therefore, to provide suitable shelter for Friday and daily prayers, as well as for feast days and other religious occasions. Consequently the space requirements were fairly simple—enough room to allow the people standing in rows to offer their prayers and make the necessary movements that accompany the prayers. In addition space had to be provided for those not participating in the prayers to circulate freely. A prayer room exclusively for women was also planned, which although separate from the rest of the building would not be isolated from it.

To stress the significance of prayer as a central function of the mosque, it was considered important to create an atmosphere inside both prayer rooms that would be conducive to prayer and meditation. Maintaining a comfortable temperature indoors was also an important factor in the mosque's design, since temperatures in Niono can be unpleasantly hot. At least one courtyard was needed to contain the overflow of people on days when the mosque had an exceptionally large attendance. The addition of accommodations for a caretaker was considered necessary because of the size of the mosque, and a storeroom was designed where objects to do with both ritual and the maintenance of the building could be housed.

Evolution of Design Concept. The Niono mosque as it is today is the result of an evolutionary process that lasted almost 25 years—from 1948 to 1972. During the course of these years it was enlarged and transformed from its original size of about 119 square meters to 725 square meters. This evolution, a

result of changing needs, ambitions, and increased funds, has created problems of space. The site of the mosque for example is small by comparison with the buildings sited on it, particularly in view of their large proportions. The present size of the mosque makes it one of the largest of its type, other examples of which are the mosques at Djenné and Mopti, which in fact served as models.

Since temperatures in Niono can be uncomfortably hot during part of the year, a system of electric fans, widely used for regulating indoor temperatures in the area, is installed in the mosque. For several months each year, however, both the humidity and temperature in the village are too high even for the fans to have much comforting effect. The only solution therefore is effective ventilation. In this respect the Niono mosque, unlike most of the other, older mosques in the area, is fortunate in having a large number of windows.

Response to User Requirements.   The plan of the mosque, like the plan of any hypostyle mosque, is based on the bay as a unit. The size of the bay is determined by the structural limitations of the materials available and by the dimensions of a standard prayer mat, which accommodates one kneeling person. All this results in a very sober and functional area, with slight differences in dimensions gently stressing the east-west orientation of the mosque. This emphasis is absent in the women's prayer hall, where the pillars are rounded and generally less well-proportioned.

The use of space is both simple and functional and follows patterns commonly found in the region. The entrances and corridors of the mosque do not offer enough room for movement and can become quite congested on festive occasions when there is a large gathering. The layout of the mosque adheres to the traditional pattern, with the main building (for the exclusive use of men) occupying the eastern part of the plot. To the west of this building is a courtyard, with the women's prayer hall situated along its far side.

The main entrance of the mosque is on the south side, giving onto one of the main streets of the village. The western side has an entrance opposite the large minaret as well as an area reserved for private use such as funeral rites. The caretaker's quarters, now the first imam's tomb, consist of two small buildings situated at the southern limit of the site on either side of the main entrance. They make up two distinct outside areas—the courtyard of the main entrance and the large western courtyard—separated by the volume of the minaret on the west facade, with the ablutions area discreetly hidden in the southwest corner.

Decorative Aspects.   The massing of the buildings and their relation to one another are extremely simple. The external effect of the deep hypostyle plan, chosen in part for its traditional significance and in part to fit the site, is somewhat diminished by the disposition of the subsidiary buildings and the minaret on the western side, as well as by the vertical treatment of the facades. This treatment, characteristic of mosques of the area, is at the same time very personal and has to do with the architect's idiosyncratic variations on a basic theme. One of these variations is the duplication of the internal arches on the facade. The pilasters are not linked by

arches and do not extend the whole height of the facade in the usual manner. Nevertheless they are topped by sugarloaf pinnacles that pick up the rhythm, and even at the main doors this rhythm is continued rather eccentrically with pinnacles that do not correspond to the pilasters. The use of elements varies from mosque to mosque. Sometimes the pilasters and pinnacles match exactly and sometimes the number of pinnacles is a multiple of the number of the pilasters. At Niono this vertical rhythm is accentuated by the towers, those on the east facade being treated more conventionally than the minaret on the west facade. The dominant appearance of the latter seems unusual and suggests outside influences.

Another unusual feature of the Niono mosque is the large number of windows surrounded by reinforced concrete on the facades of the main building. This kind of treatment is, however, becoming increasingly common in more recently built mosques.

The windows of the large minaret on the west side and the women's prayer room are more elaborate. These are double windows, each flanked by cylindrical portions of pillars. Above each window is an opening in the form of a segment of a circle. The only decorative elements used inside the mosque are the capitals of the pillars and traditional decorative motifs, probably pre-Islamic in origin, which are placed in a niche above the main entrance on the south side. The two distinct types of motif are curiously reminiscent of the white-ants' nests found in the area.

Structure, Materials, and Technology.   The mosque's structure consists of load-bearing walls and pillars of sun-dried clay bricks, from which arches spring along the longitudinal and

transverse line of the bays. Over the arches, closely packed round wooden joists are laid diagonally across the corners, thus ingeniously reducing the span to suit the materials available.

The materials used include sun-dried clay bricks and clay mortar, with or without decayed rice bran; local wood for the roofing; imported wood and corrugated iron for the joinery; precast concrete for the window frames; steel sections for the enclosing doors; quicklime for the whitewashing; and tubular steel posts for the veranda. Traditional building techniques were used, with labor provided largely gratis by members of the congregation. Local artisans made the joinery in wood and metal in their workshops. Both the choice of materials and building techniques were appropriate to local conditions. While imported materials were kept to a minimum, which helped reduce costs and the flow of funds out of the region, the use of local wood for construction purposes has exacerbated the problem of deforestation in an area whose vegetation is already sparse.

The problem with sun-dried clay-brick construction is the need for annual repairs to the external rendering, as well as the regular maintenance of inside surfaces. The life expectancy of such a building is otherwise reasonable, and a sun-dried clay-brick house, if properly looked after, probably has the capacity to outlast buildings employing many more costly types of construction. Another advantage is the possibility of reusing the sun-dried clay bricks when the building falls into disuse. In fact the reuse of building materials, already a growing industry in some developed countries, is likely to find increasing favor in a world that is becoming more ecologically conscious day by day.

Conclusion.   The appearance of the mosque is undoubtedly striking, particularly its eastern side. While the other facades maintain the exuberance of the design as a whole, they are not of quite the same quality. The upper part of the large minaret on the west facade, for example, is a comparatively weak and unconvincing design. Although the size of the mosque is large for the size of its site, the external spaces have been skillfully disposed. The interior spaces, while also somewhat restricted, especially in the main building, are of harmonious proportions.

Together with the market area, the Niono mosque is located in the center of the village and is its focal point. Financed and maintained by the local community, the mosque represents the people's needs. In practically every way the Niono mosque can be considered homegrown. Its architecture and the use of materials and building techniques all originate in the region. It suggests that there are places where it is still possible to talk of a continuing tradition and where a traditional approach to architecture can still be dynamic, integrating new features, but mainly playing variations on age-old vernacular themes.

4: A star and crescent forms one of the finials seen in the view on pages 146–147. 5: The hypostyle prayer hall is based on an approximately square bay as a unit, the dimensions determined by the structural limitations of the wooden joists spanning the bay and the size of a standard prayer mat. Pillars and arches are built, like the external walls of the mosque, of sun-dried clay bricks whitewashed with quicklime.

NAIL
ÇAKIRHAN
HOUSE

NAIL
ÇAKIRHAN
HOUSE

Akyaka, Turkey, completed 1971. Clients: Nail and Halet Çakirhan. Architect/contractor: Nail Çakirhan. Carpenters: Ali Duru, Cafer Karaca.

Master Jury's Citation: For the purity and elegance in design and decoration resulting from the direct continuation and reflection of traditional values. The design of the house goes well beyond the simple reproduction of past models; its ornaments are judicious, sober, and genuine. Its extraordinary harmony with nature, as well as its multipurpose use and the ambience of its inner space, gives it great distinction.

This airy and attractive house deserves special attention for its sensitive revival of craftsmanship and cultural sensitivity as a whole.

It was as a retirement home for himself and his wife, Halet, that Nail Çakirhan designed and supervised the building of this traditional Islamic Ottoman house in his home province of Muğla. What is particularly interesting about this project is that Çakirhan, a poet and journalist by profession, was never formally schooled as an architect but became interested in construction in his forties while accompanying his wife, an archaeologist, on her field trips, and he was over sixty when he began work as an architect.

Since completing his house he has designed and supervised the building of thirty other houses (eighteen in Akyaka itself), renovated several older ones, and completed a hotel. While the first of these projects were weekend houses for nonresidents, some of the later ones were designed for the villagers themselves. Çakirhan's work is further assessed and put in context in the essay on contemporary Turkish architecture (pages 64–75).

Location. The village of Akyaka lies to the southwest of the Anatolian peninsula and is surrounded by a pine-forested, mountainous region that is becoming increasingly popular as a resort center. The site of the house, occupying .2 hectares, is on a cliff overlooking the sea some 150 meters to the south. A road to the north of the house connects it with the cluster of small houses that make up the village, 500 meters away.

Pages 154–157: Nail Çakirhan's finely crafted timber house, built for himself and his wife, takes its inspiration from traditional Islamic Ottoman houses and includes a central hall, an outdoor haney *(loggia) and two living/sleeping rooms.*

Although Akyaka has a long tradition of highly crafted timber houses, concrete structures are becoming increasingly common. The climate consists of hot summer days tempered by a cool sea breeze, and mild winters with cold nights.

Brief.   Corresponding to the rather simple needs of Nail and Halet Çakirhan, the house was to be quite straightforward. It was to include two separate areas, one for the Çakirhans and the other for their guests. Although referred to as living/sleeping rooms, these areas are multipurpose as in traditional Turkish homes. Between them was to be a *divanhane* (central hall) in which the Çakirhans and their guests could gather.

A sheltered outdoor *haney* (loggia) was to provide additional living space during the warm season, with separate shower rooms for the couple and their guests, and a kitchenette and a lavatory completing the program. A caretaker's lodge, situated next to the entrance, was considered necessary since the Çakirhan's were away quite frequently. A garage and storeroom were added later.

Plan.   Following the tradition of master builders the plan was more or less directly laid out on the ground, with only a few sketches considered sufficient. Çakirhan's house does not belong to Akyaka's simple architectural tradition but in fact gets its inspiration from his native town of Ula, about 30 kilometers away, where a variety of traditional houses can still be found on lots usually no smaller than 1,000 square meters. These fall into three broad categories: the 150- to 200-year-old houses, which contain a single multipurpose room and a *hayat* (courtyard); 100- to 150-year-old houses, comprising two rooms flanking a *mabeyn* (porch) used for storage, as well as a *haney*

and a *hayat*; and two-story houses, 50 to 100 years old, with a lower floor devoted to storage and an upper floor similar to the previous type. In some cases the *haney* was turned into a polygonal *divanhane*, which can either be open and supported on columns or closed with an abundance of windows. In either form the *haney* faces south or southwest.

Nail Çakirhan's single-story house includes both *divanhane* and *haney* in the same plan, with the *mabeyn* reduced to a rather open area between them. Unlike traditional Turkish homes the kitchenettes and lavoratories are not located outside the main building but retain a marginal place in the plan.

The design of this house goes beyond the simple reproduction of past models and was built in three phases. The foundation, framework walls, and roof were completed in forty-five days, the woodwork and finishes in twenty-four and the built-in furnishings in fifteen days.

The southern facade of the house is shielded by an open loggia supported on columns. From here one has access to two lateral living/sleeping rooms flanking a porch which draws one into a large polygonal *divanhane*, corresponding to the tradition of the central *eyvan* (hall) in Ottoman houses. The two identical living/sleeping rooms flanking the porch also flank the *divanhane*. They are adjoined by shower rooms (where clothes are also kept), a kitchenette on one side and a lavatory on the other, which can also be entered from each end of the loggia. The caretaker's lodge, two multipurpose lateral rooms separated by a lavatory and shower room, also has a loggia toward the south, which can be entered from the sides.

The house is thermally insulated by the large air space left beneath the tiled gables of the roof, with hot air vented through the wooden ceilings. In summer the house remains cool and comfortably ventilated, yet without drafts and with the deep loggia and generous eaves providing a band of deep shadow over the windows and around the house. In winter the fireplaces are lit and their burning coals placed in the bra-

1: The house, which is one of eighteen at Akyaka designed by Çakirhan, has a caretaker's lodge at the bottom of the garden. 2, 3: The plan shows the symmetrical distribution of the three main rooms. The sheltered loggia, which provides additional living space during the warm season, has access to the central hall, the living/-sleeping rooms, kitchenette, and lavatory.

a. Nail Çakirhan house
b. caretaker's house
c. gate
d. water pump
e. pond

0   10   20   40 m.

1

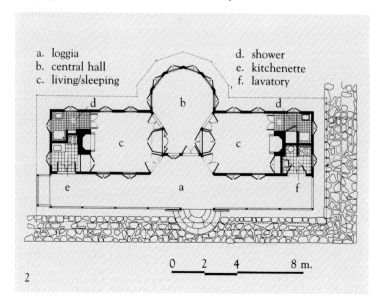

a. loggia
b. central hall
c. living/sleeping
d. shower
e. kitchenette
f. lavatory

0   2   4   8 m.

2

zier of the central hall which, when the doors of the adjoining rooms are left open, heats the entire house. Heavy blankets provide adequate warmth at night.

The details of the house have been judiciously designed. For instance, doors are set diagonally across the corners of the rooms in the old *farisi* way. This arrangement allows the doors to fold back into the spaces reserved for them against the cupboards when they are open. When all the doors are open, the various rooms, including the loggia, merge into a single space.

With the exception of tray stands, book stands, traditional braziers and low couches with cushions placed below the windows of the central hall and side rooms, no movable furniture has been used in the house. There is a fireplace in each living/sleeping room flanked by two cupboards, where bedding is stored during the day. A traditional *serpenc* (shelf), on which books can be kept as in the living/sleeping rooms, or decorations displayed as in the *divanhane,* passes continuously over the doors and windows of every room. Both the cupboards and shelves display a high level of craftsmanship, as do the traditional windows and richly ornamented wooden ceilings.

The loggia is supported on wooden columns with decorated capitals and contains the traditional *ayazeh* (raised seat) at its west end, where the breeze is strongest. A traditional semicircular flight of steps in local pink stone leads from the loggia to the garden.

Structure. A traditional timber frame, which provides the house with the elasticity necessary to resist earthquakes, has been set on a rubble stone base. The roof, covered with the round red *alaturka* tiles of the region, has no truss but simply posts and beams with wooden planks forming its gables. The walls are made of brick and rendered with lime plaster and whitewash. With the exception of the shower rooms, kitchenettes, and lavatories all the floors are covered with wood over a 5-centimeter air space. The ceilings and built-in furniture are also made of wood. All major elements were manufactured on site, and the woodwork was crafted by hand.

Conclusion. For Nail Çakirhan the concrete structures one sees increasingly all over Turkey are like a "frightening cancerous growth." He strongly favors a new spirit in architecture, which is in harmony with the climate, environment, and cultural background of Turkey, and he is a critic of the slavish imitation of Western architecture unadapted to the needs of his country.

His houses have attracted the attention of the authorities responsible for planning and development both regionally and nationally. The governor of Muğla, who is also opposed to the construction of inappropriate concrete structures, wants future building projects in his province to be designed in the spirit of Çakirhan's Akyaka houses.

Timber-frame houses are less likely to be damaged by earthquakes than other types of construction because of the movement the wood allows. Nail Çakirhan's houses are therefore particularly suited to the province of Muğla, which lies within Turkey's earthquake belt. During the last major earthquake in the province, the old timber houses, including those in a whole village where most of the houses were constructed in timber, were hardly damaged. Even the windowpanes remained intact. However, buildings made of other materials, particularly concrete, were completely destroyed. While concrete houses have become a status symbol for the rural population, it is hoped that the practicality, visual appeal, and comfort of Çakirhan's traditional timber houses will in the future encourage the construction of buildings more in harmony with the environment.

Building in timber is also much cheaper than concrete, contrary to certain prevailing misconceptions. Although more timber is required for a timber house than for the timber forms to make a corresponding concrete house, the timber used for the concrete forms is later discarded. Concrete structures also require the addition of reinforcing steel, which is becoming very expensive in Turkey. The better quality of wood required for timber construction still works out cheaper especially when several houses are being built. With a large amount of timber of second- or even third-rate quality, a sufficient quantity of good-quality timber can be found in the core of the wood and set aside for the finer parts of the building, while the lesser quality is used for supporting posts and lintels and for constructing the roof.

Timber houses also require fewer man-hours to build than concrete structures of the same size, which means saving both on money and time. Nail Çakirhan's house was completed within seventy days. The foundations, walls, roof, and chimneys of a timber house can be completed in the same amount of time needed for laying the foundation of a concrete building.

The demand for traditional timber houses has also revived many crafts, especially woodworking, with many young apprentices beginning training in this field. Carpenters, whose work had been limited to making the frame and formwork for concrete buildings, have begun to work with traditional joinery once again.

The simplicity and elegance of Çakirhan's architecture results not from imitation but from the direct continuation and reflection of traditional values. He has succeeded in reviving a vernacular architecture not merely at the superficial level of appearances, but by convincingly reintroducing the compact multivalent spatial organization of old Turkish houses. At the same time he has demonstrated successfully that the form and construction of his houses continue to make economic sense.

4: A high-level shelf for decorative objects or books forms a strong architectural feature of the rooms. The shelves, built-in cupboards, windows, and ceilings are all made of wood and display a high level of craftsmanship. Doors are set diagonally across the corners of the rooms and fold back into recesses reserved for them so that all the rooms merge into a single space. 5: The sense of space is greatly enhanced by the absence of conventional movable furniture.

AZEM
PALACE

AZEM PALACE

Damascus Syria, *haremlık* completed 1954, remainder under restoration. Client: General Directorate of Antiquities and Museums, Damascus. Architects: Michel Ecochard (before 1946), Shafiq al-Imam (since 1951). Director of workshop: Zaki al-Emir (before 1946).

Master Jury's Citation: For the thirty-four years' efforts to preserve, restore, and reconstruct a badly damaged eighteenth-century palace, one of the masterpieces of Islamic architecture. The high quality of the restoration is complemented by imagination in dealing with the destroyed parts of the building. Such rebuilding as took place demonstrated respect for the existing structure and more generally for the heritage of the period. Furthermore this palace now performs an additional cultural service as a well-attended museum that has helped to make people conscious of the beauties and values of the Islamic architectural heritage.

This long project has been an important one in reestablishing cultural identity and cultural continuity and in developing expertise and artisan skills. The reconstitution of the Azem Palace has been an important event in the Islamic world, its significance being more than that of a case of restoration.

The purpose in restoring this badly damaged eighteenth-century Ottoman palace was twofold. First, there was the need simply to preserve, restore, and reconstruct one of the masterpieces of Islamic architecture badly damaged by French shelling during the Syrian uprising of 1925. Second, the client wanted the palace to be more than just a fine example of restoration by adapting part of it to serve as a folk museum.

Location and Access. The Azem Palace is situated in the old city of Damascus not far from the *qibla* wall (which orients the worshiper toward Mecca) of the Ommiad Mosque. Most of the old houses surrounding it have been built around courtyards that contain pools and fountains and, together with the old shops of the area, are generally constructed in stone and wood with lime-and-gypsum plaster. The walls of poorer buildings are usually made of mud brick, also used for the roofs

Pages 162–165: The courtyard of the haremlık, *with its pools, fountains, orange trees, and elaborately patterned floor of different-colored marbles, is by far the largest of the four courts of this lavishly decorated eighteenth-century palace. One of the buildings facing this courtyard has a wide, arcaded loggia.*

of all buildings, which are supported on timber poles carrying wooden plank ceilings.

The palace is accessible from the *suq*, which is close to the Ommiad Mosque.

Historical Background.   It was as a residence for one of the last great Ottoman governors of the province of Damascus, Assad al-Azem Pasha, that the Azem Palace was originally built in the mid-eighteenth century.

The palace is constructed around three courts, of which the *haremlık*, or private family court, is the largest and central one. To the southeast of the *haremlık* and about half its size lies the men's *selamlık*, or public court where visitors were received and which was normally reserved for formal use and business. To the north of the palace lies the smallest of the three courts, surrounded by kitchens and storerooms. Originally the *selamlık* acted as the entrance court, from which access to the *haremlık* was obtained. There was in fact no other

access to the *haremlık* from the exterior except through the two smaller courts.

In 1922 the French government, whose mandate over Syria after the fall of the Ottoman Empire lasted from 1920 to 1946, bought the *haremlık* for 4,000 gold liras. The craftsmen engaged in the decorative work of this courtyard when it was purchased were retained by the French to encourage the revival of traditional crafts. It was during this period that a direct entrance was opened into the *haremlık* from the original entrance portico of the palace.

In 1925 the entire palace was extensively damaged when the French shelled the old quarter of Damascus to quell the Syrian uprising against their rule. The *qa'a* (main reception room) and the baths of the *selamlık* were set on fire, its roof burned and the upper parts of its walls destroyed. When hostilities ceased, the French set about reconstructing the *haremlık*. Subject to certain limitations, these were restored exactly as they had been. The limitations included a lack of evidence concerning the original form of the building and a scarcity of both the right materials and workmen with the relevant skills. It was therefore necessary to accept a modified and less ornate reconstruction.

In 1930 the French government gave its buildings in the palace to the newly set up French Institute. A new house for the institute's director was commissioned within the grounds

1: As seen from the plan, the large palace fits into the irregular pattern of the old city of Damascus, turning its back on its neighbors, and facing inward onto a number of courts, the most important of which is the haremlık. *2: The view from the loggia is into the* haremlık *court, where the water and the trees help to cool the air in the heat of the summer.*

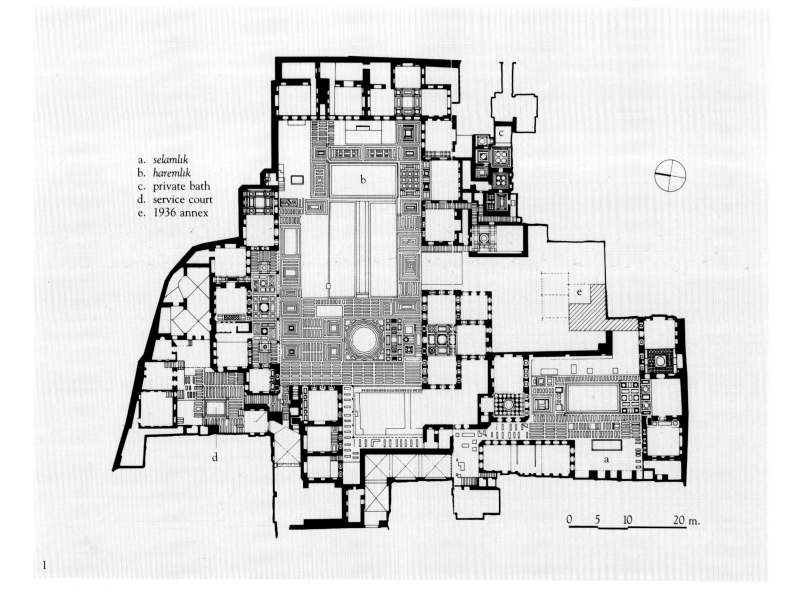

a. *selamlık*
b. *haremlık*
c. private bath
d. service court
e. 1936 annex

0   5   10   20 m.

1

and was built in a relatively empty area lying between the *selamlık* and the *haremlık* and set back in a position where it was hardly visible from the latter. The design was uncompromisingly modern and the house was constructed of concrete. By utilizing the original materials and plasters for the infilling of the concrete work, however, the building blended perfectly into its eighteenth-century setting. The institute was evacuated from the premises after Syrian independence.

In 1946 the *haremlık* was handed over by the French to the Syrian government and remained closed for the next four years. Upon leaving the country the French agreed to pay further reparations for the damage done to Syrian buildings, including the rest of the palace, during the bombardment of Damascus and other towns. No repair work, however, was undertaken at this time on the extensively damaged *selamlık*, which continued to be occupied by members of the Azem family. In 1951 the Syrian government bought the remainder of the palace from the family for a sum of $30,000 (U.S.) with the intention of creating a national folk museum there.

The work of conserving the palace still continues. In recent years the authorities have been concentrating on the restoration of the kitchens and cellars of the palace with particular attention to the latter in an attempt to reduce rising damp. New drains have been introduced and the cellars cleaned and replastered with the hope of utilizing some of them as rooms for lessons in history and crafts.

The Process of Restoration.   Since 1951 the director of all conservation work has been the curator of the museum, Shafiq al-Imam, whose approach has been to invent nothing. With the help of master craftsmen he undertook a detailed study of the palace, ascertained the original condition of the building as well as the original techniques employed in its construction, and gradually restored it as far as possible to its eighteenth-century condition.

The work was done very economically. Stone and decorations were acquired for practically nothing from other buildings of the same period that were either being demolished or altered. Fortunately old materials often came on the market during the 1950s and early '60s because of demolition work being carried out in the old city to make room for the building of new roads.

One of the first steps taken in the restoration process was an attempt to hold the effects of humidity in check. Consequently the ground level around the palace was lowered and a drain laid around the outside in order to reduce the damp in the walls. At the same time a new water supply was introduced. The paving, which had become uneven, was lifted, and the same stones relaid after the ground was leveled.

Restoration work on the *selamlık* was begun in the early 1960s. For evidence of its original structure and design, plans made by the French in the early 1920s as well as descriptions by members of the Azem family were relied upon.

The destroyed upper stories were rebuilt with new materials and plastered. Here the roofs, like those in many of the buildings, were constructed in the original way except for a reinforced concrete slab instead of a layer of earth. Care was taken, however, to ensure that this was not visible from below or

above. The parapet was covered with traditional plaster and the roof surface given a finish of earth over the reinforced concrete.

In 1964 a large-scale program was undertaken for the rebuilding of decayed and leaning walls. Once again the paving was taken up after careful drawings were made. The system of canals originally laid for the drainage and irrigation of the site underneath the paving was uncovered, cleaned out, and repaired to make it waterproof once again. This done, the paving was put back in its original position.

Two separate underground cables were installed to provide electricity, ensuring that, in the event of a power failure in one part of the city, it would be possible to switch to an alternate electrical supply.

Conclusion.   The restoration of the upper levels of the palace by both the French and Syrian authorities does not follow the original design exactly, but this does not seriously detract from the general effect of these rooms or of the palace as a whole. The introduction of the reinforced concrete slab above the ceilings does not seem to have been harmful to either the structures or their appearance, though the fact that some of the ceilings are losing their paint may be the result of condensation caused by the concrete slab. Concrete is an inferior insulator to earth, so that extremes of temperature also may be causing this deterioration. The earth surfaces have not been maintained annually as they would have been when the build-

ings were first erected, and the concrete slabs are not waterproof. The result has been that in the last few years bituminous felt waterproofing has been laid over the concrete slabs. Unfortunately this method of waterproofing has failed because the bitumen soaks out of the felt during the heat of the summer.

It is also distressing to see that the same engineers have undertaken to repoint small areas of the stonework in the *haremlık* courtyard using modern cement. This serves to highlight the persistent care with which the building was restored during the previous sixty years: only traditional mortars were used.

The restoration of the palace has been beneficial in more ways than one, not the least of which is the revenue it has earned. Environmentally it has helped preserve the traditional buildings surrounding it. Although these are supposedly listed, Shafiq al-Imam believes they would probably have fallen victim to commercial exploitation had it not been for the presence of the palace.

What has been particularly gratifying, however, has been the remarkable response of the Syrian public to one of their restored historical sites, evident from the large numbers that visit the palace regularly. When the *haremlık* was opened to the public as a museum in 1954, the crowds so exceeded expectations that a new staircase had to be designed for the *qa'a* to enable them to enter at one place and exit at another.

Ever since its opening to the public the palace has been crowded with visitors. According to Al-Imam's records for 1961, during the relatively quiet season from January to May

there was a record number of 161,000 visitors, which averages out to about 3,800 daily. The revenue collected from entrance fees for the period amounted to $4,000 (U.S.), which is commendable since many of the Syrian visitors to the palace are not required to pay the fee. In that same year there was an average of 5,000 to 6,000 visitors daily during the peak period of September. Today the annual income from the palace is somewhere near $27,000 (U.S.) Over the last thirty years, therefore, the Syrian government has got back in revenue four to five times the amount it has spent on restoring the palace.

The presence of the folk museum is a mixed blessing. While it certainly attracts some of the interest of the Syrian public, its displays are inconsistent with the character and original use of the buildings. The curator hopes that a proposal for the acquisition of neighboring properties will be implemented, thereby allowing him to move some of the more alien exhibits out of the palace so that it can be furnished in the proper traditional manner. In this way he hopes ultimately that the Azem Palace will be seen as a great house museum, preserving once and for all the atmosphere and detailed character of a lost Damascene way of life.

3: This detail from the two-story building that separates the haremlık *from the courtyard with the 1936 annex is an example of the elaborate care taken in the restoration. 4: The* haremlık *is now used for a folk museum. 5: Over the rooftops of the* haremlık *courtyard a minaret of the neighboring Ommiad Mosque can be glimpsed.*

TOMB OF
SHAH
RUKN-I-'ALAM

Multan Pakistan, completed 1977. Client: Government of Punjab, Lahore. Architect: Muhammad Wali Ullah Khan, director, Awqaf Department, Lahore. Restoration: Awqaf Department, Lahore. Master craftsmen: Talib Hussain, Bushir Ahmed, Haji Rahim Bukhsh, Abdul Wahid, K. Allah Divaya, Kashigai Nazar Hussain, Imtiaz Ahmed.

Master Jury's Citation: For the restoration of an important fourteenth-century mausoleum of the Tughluq period in Multan and for its contribution to reviving some of the great crafts of 600 years ago and promoting similar building activity throughout the country.

This remarkable program was the brainchild of Muhammad Wali Ullah Kahn when he was architect to the Antiquities Department. It was further developed when he became director of the conservation section of the Awqaf Department of the government of Punjab in 1970. His main concern has not only been the restoration of the monument but the establishment of a training program for Pakistani craftsmen in the traditional crafts of glazed Multan tilework, wood carving, and terra-cotta.

This commendable effort of Muhammad Wali Ullah Khan has not only resulted in the rescue of a great monument from decay and thoughtless disfigurement, but has led to an awareness of the need for the conservation of other great monuments in the country.

The fourteenth-century Tomb of Shah Rukn-i-'Alam in Multan is one of the outstanding architectural treasures of Pakistan and is considered to be the culmination of the Multan-style tombs, which derived their inspiration from Central Asian models. The earliest example in Pakistan of this style is the twelfth-century Gardezi Tomb at Adam Wahan.

The way of conserving this fourteenth-century monument was to restore all the damaged parts of the building as nearly as possible to their original appearance. Those parts of the tomb only slightly damaged, however, were left untouched in order to convey a sense of age.

Historical Background. Shah Rukn-i-'Alam, for whom the tomb was built between 1320 and 1324, was an accomplished mystic by the age of twenty-five and established a *khanqah*

Pages 170–173: The restoration of the fourteenth-century Tomb of Shah-Rukn-i-'Alam was seen not only as an end in itself but also as an opportunity to establish a training program in glazed Multan tilework, wood carving, and terra-cotta for Pakistani craftsmen.

(shrine) and *madrasa* (Koranic school) in Multan during his lifetime. He also held the title of Sheik ul-Islam (Grand Mufti) bestowed on him by the Sultan of Delhi.

Situated at the eastern end of the fortified hill on which the Tomb of Shah Rukn-i-'Alam stands is the large domed tomb of his grandfather, Hazrat Shah Baha ul-Haq Zaqariya, also the holder of the title of Sheik ul-Islam during his lifetime. One version of the construction of the tomb has it that the monument was originally intended by the Delhi sultan, Ghiyas al-Din Tughluq, for himself. But after his death his successor, Sultan Muhammad Tughluq, rededicated it to Shah Rukn-i-'Alam, who in the meanwhile had already been buried in the tomb of his grandfather. The body of the holy man was transported to his present tomb by a sultan who came later, Firuz Shah Tughluq.

There are, however, no authentic records for this version of events and the more likely story is that the immense reverence in which the aged saint was held at the time of his death resulted in the construction of a magnificent monument solely in his honor.

Location. Because of its raised position on a fortified hill, the tomb dominates the view of the surrounding countryside in many directions. The top of the hill has been leveled at the western end to provide a platform for the structure, with high retaining walls on three sides.

Access is by means of a narrow road leading from the town square below and winding up the hill to the front gates of the tomb. Large numbers of vendors, hawkers, doctors, masseurs, and musicians set up shop daily on either side of this road, assured of a clientele of pilgrims that visit the tomb from all over the country.

The architectural character of the surrounding buildings is typical of Multan: kiln-dried bricks are used for walls, floors, roofs, and for paving streets. The walls and roofs of buildings are usually plastered and painted in light colors. Most buildings have flat roofs, with domes and vaults usually being reserved for tombs and mosques.

The Process of Restoration. The need to restore Rukn-i-'Alam's tomb and check its severe deterioration was initiated many years ago by Muhammad Wali Ullah Khan, then an architect at the Antiquities Department of Pakistan. On becoming director of the conservation section of the Awqaf (religious endowments) Department of the Punjab, and with the help of the governor of the province, Muhammad Wali Ullah Khan's campaign was successful in raising funds to implement the project. With a budget of $200,000 (U.S.) work commenced in late 1971 and was completed in 1977.

Before starting, the authorities had to find traditional craftsmen with some knowledge of the fourteen different masonry and wood crafts employed in building the tomb and its

1, 2, 3: Standing on a level platform at the top of a hill, the tomb commands a dominating position. It consists of a domed chamber that is octagonal in plan, its thick walls stepped back on the outside to form two platforms, of which the top platform supports the dome. The octagonal form is emphasized by eight rounded buttresses that rise above the parapets into domed pinnacles.

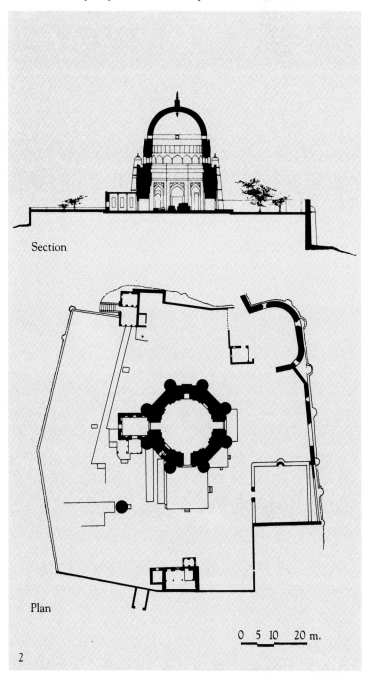

Section

Plan

0 5 10   20 m.

2

surrounding areas. Although passed down through the generations, these crafts had either been discontinued or had been significantly modified through time. The task, therefore, was a difficult one. An outstanding mason, a tilemaker, and a wood carver were eventually found. Together they trained a total of thirty-three craftsmen and so revived techniques that had been perfected by trial and error over a long period. In order to maintain a regular check on the quality of the new tiles to ensure that they conformed to the originals, a small laboratory was set up on site for the tilemakers.

Work started with the clearing of the platform area around the tomb. This entailed taking the controversial action of removing all but two of the tombs that had been built over the years both inside the porch and on the platform. The fate of the two surviving tombs has yet to be decided in court. At the same time the original drainage system was cleared of all loose debris.

Next attention focused on the foundations. A complete reconstruction was not considered justified since the foundations had not moved to any great extent. The dome, for example, which has a direct bearing on the state of the foundations, had suffered only from a crack a few millimeters wide. It was discovered, however, that the dome had tilted by 5 to 6 centimeters. Since it would have been too dangerous to correct this, the tilt was left but subtly disguised externally with additional plaster to create thickness.

Since reconstructing the foundation was not necessary, the architects concentrated on rebuilding the lowest sections of the brick walls on the side nearest the city (the western-facing section), wherever the walls were cracked both below and above the platform level.

Once these measures had been taken, the whole of the platform area was surfaced with a 7.5-centimeter bed of very strong concrete, on which new tiles, similar to the original in size and color, were laid. New precast-concrete grilles, matched with the large tiles in size and pierced with holes to allow water to drain into the underground drainage system, were also laid among the tiles. Floodlighting was installed on the platform, and flowering trees and shrubs, with openwork brick structures built around them for protection, were planted to enliven it. An outer vestibule—a later addition to the original entrance—was removed. The entrance to the platform, a portico that lacked authenticity, was demolished and a new one built in the Multan style.

The original enclosure wall was strengthened in two ways. First, wherever necessary, the original foundation was widened and a stepped, buttressed toe wall was provided underground. Second, two new retaining walls were built at intervals in the sloping ground below the enclosure wall. To consolidate the site further the slopes were planted with grass and shrubs, and the area around the top of the hill adjoining the platform enclosure was landscaped with grass and trees.

Materials. One of the most outstanding features of the tomb is its tilework. When the tomb was built in the fourteenth century, local clay was used to make the tiles. Today, however,

the same clay has a very high saline content, owing to a drop in the level of the water table over 600 years. In remaking the tiles, therefore, clay had to be brought in from much farther away and washed thoroughly with fresh water in order to remove any impurities.

The wood reinforcing the masonry walls and the carved woodwork of the doors, niches, and *mihrab* were all repaired

4: The domed pinnacles of the buttresses have extravagantly shaped finials. 5, 6, 7, 8: Perhaps the most spectacular of the craft revivals has been that of the tilemaker, whose work is everywhere apparent. 9: A view into the dome shows the transition from octagon to circle and the pattern of window openings that light the space. Since the restoration of the monument, the number of pilgrims coming from all parts of the country has greatly increased.

with wood carefully selected from the Forestry Department's timber supply some 80 kilometers from Multan. In each case the wood was selected with meticulous care to match the color of the old wood.

In relaying the brickwork of the enclosure wall and some parts of the tomb, cement mortar (one part cement to three parts sand) was used to within 2.5 centimeters or so of the surface. The remaining section was filled, like all the cracks in the existing mortar joints of the brickwork, with *surkhy* mortar, a lime mortar with a catalyst of burned earth. Portland cement was used to repair and waterproof the substructure of the platform area surrounding the tomb, where it would not be visible.

Conclusion. Visually, the technical quality of the repair of the monument is remarkable. Only the keenest eye can tell the difference between the restored parts and the original. The brick and tile restoration falls little short of perfection. The colors of the tiles have been matched perfectly and, like the

original, have scarcely any glazing cracks or textures. The wood carving is equally superb, if not quite matching the artistic sense of the original, since it was executed more mechanically. This, however, is a fault only visible at close quarters. The match in color and overall appearance is otherwise perfect.

The immense pains taken over every detail in the restoration of this monument may suggest that the building has been overrestored. This might have been the case if the slightly damaged tiles, bricks, and terra-cotta work had not been retained. However, by designing a new main door to the tomb and a new outer portico to its enclosure, the architect can perhaps be said to have given these parts of the structure an excessively new appearance.

Apart from its contribution to the preservation of the architectural heritage of Multan, this restoration project has also had another beneficial effect on the people of the area. As a result of it some fourteen ancient building crafts that had fallen into disuse over the centuries have been revived. These crafts are now receiving patronage in other conservation efforts as well as in new buildings. Master craftsmen trained at Rukn-i-'Alam either continue to be employed by the Awqaf Department or have set up independent businesses. The master tilemaker who received an award for his tilework, subsequently left the employment of the Awqaf and is now successfully engaged in his own business, the manufacture of tiles of a traditional kind.

9

TECHNICAL REVIEW

By SAMIR ABDULAC

INTRODUCTION

The Award's aim "to recognize completed projects which meet today's needs, while being in close harmony with their own culture and climate," is a challenging task. This is why on-site investigations have proved necessary during the final selection process. First the master jury screens all nominated projects, based on materials gathered by the Award office, and prepares a short list. Since it is not feasible to send the master jury to each of these sites, a technical reviewer for each is entrusted with collecting information for the jury. This includes:

1) Visiting the project, surveying its context, and interviewing the main contributors and the users.

2) Verifying the documentation (statements by participants, descriptions, and visual materials) already in the Award's file.

3) Gathering missing information and answering specific questions from the master jury.

4) Formulating a detailed, objective analysis of the project, covering all the Award's areas of concern.

The technical reviewer's report includes:

1) Objectives of the project.

2) Description of the site—topography, climate, historical background, local architectural character, access, etc.

3) Design and construction information—architect's brief, evolution of design concepts (physical constraints, user requirements, formal aspects), description of structure, materials, technology, and their sources.

4) Construction schedule and costs—history of the project, main sources of finance, cost analysis, general and comparative economic data for the country.

Pages 178–179: Ramses Wissa Wassef Arts Center. Batik dyers rinse excess dye from fabric in the courtyard fountain of the batik workshop.

5) Technical assessment—use, climatic performance, choice of materials and technology, aging and maintenance.

6) Aesthetic assessment.

7) Project significance—achievement of objectives, client/user response, relation to cultural context, environmental impact, originality, and replicability.

8) Proposed apportionment of credit.

Technical reviewers meet in the Award office immediately after the preliminary screening. They are briefed for two or three days, in general meetings and individual conversations, by a member of the steering committee, the secretary general, his assistant, and other staff. Projects and countries are allocated among the reviewers, who begin to prepare by reading the project dossiers, planning their travel schedules, and coordinating with the photographers. The photographer's visit should coincide with the reviewer's, so that the latter can point out specific needs on the spot. Photography sessions depend on good weather and may require special authorization, because of security, revolutionary activity, or even war. Getting visas is a problem for holders of certain passports, although a few countries restrict entry to all foreign nationalities. In some cases a local contact is found to arrange interviews and to act as an interpreter.

Site visits are only part of the work of a technical review. Afterward the reviewer must identify each of the documents in the dossier and prepare a detailed report synthesizing old and newly gathered data and providing the analyses described above. Finally the reviewer makes a slide presentation to the master jury, which may then ask questions on any points that still seem obscure. It is extremely difficult for the reviewer to remain fully neutral and not to be tempted to advocate or criticize a project. But experience has shown that such intervention tends to backfire.

The technical review is one of the most original features of the Award, although it developed logically in response to the Award's goals. In 1983, eleven technical reviewers were selected, representing as many nationalities. The following day-to-day journal will give the reader an idea of how a site visit is conducted. Each visit, however, is very different from the others, and it is rare that several short-listed projects are located in the same city. The general quality of the projects should be evident from the description, although this one, the Cité al-Ahmadi, did not ultimately receive an Award.

JOURNAL OF A TECHNICAL REVIEWER: REVIEW OF A PROJECT IN TUNISIA— THE CITÉ AL-AHMADI AT LA MARSA

Wednesday, March 2. I landed about half an hour ago at the Tunis airport, and by now it is already dark. I find a taxi immediately. On the way to the city center the driver says that the weather has just cleared this evening after several days of rain.

On arriving at the Hotel International, I learn that our photographer, Kamran Adle, is also staying here, while my fellow technical reviewer, Dorothée Vauzelles, is at the Africa. Both have been here for several days. Kamran is still out, and while unpacking I recall our previous reviews together in Iran three years ago: the splendors of Isfahan, with the Ali Qapu and the Hasht Behesht, the heat of the Gulf at Bandar Abbas, and also Ahvaz, Khorramshahr, and the unfortunate people of Khuzestan. We had an ideal working relationship.

Half an hour later I call again, and salute Kamran in Farsi. At first he is startled; then he recognizes me and greets me warmly. The three of us meet at half-past eight. Dorothée, who is responsible for two other short-listed Tunisian projects, is a little ill but has nonetheless steadfastly pursued her work. Kamran is quite concerned about the weather because of the number of photographs he must take in a short time. He also hasn't yet received his visa for his next reviews and will probably have to return to Paris a day early. I am dismayed by this news, which means that I will need to revise my own schedule.

After dinner at the Château in the old medina, I return to the International to spend several hours carefully rereading the background materials on the two projects that I am to review: the renovation of the Hafsia quarter in the medina of Tunis and the new Cité al-Ahmadi, a residential neighborhood of La Marsa, a resort area near Tunis. The Award's portfolios must be completed with the missing information and documents.

Thursday, March 3. Telephoning in Tunis requires great patience. One has to get an early-morning start to obtain a line. After a long and exhausting struggle, I finally reach Abdul Mejid Sahnoun, one of the directors of the Ministry of Housing. Immediately he sends a car to take me to his office.

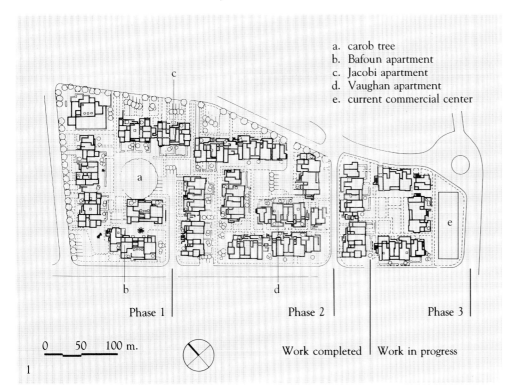

a. carob tree
b. Bafoun apartment
c. Jacobi apartment
d. Vaughan apartment
e. current commercial center

Phase 1   Phase 2   Phase 3

0   50   100 m.

Work completed | Work in progress

1

1: Overall plan. 2: Typical staircase and entrances to the apartments. 3: Outside staircase. 4: Internal square. The gannaria to the left belongs to Jaouida and Paul Vaughan's apartment.

Arrangements are made, such as authorizations for photography. A few introductions are provided, and several appointments are made from the office. By chance Sahnoun's assistant, Henri Jacobi, from the World Bank, happens to live in the Cité al-Ahmadi. He agrees to show me his apartment on Saturday afternoon and to try to arrange visits to other apartments occupied by friends. He will also try to gather some figures for me on average construction costs in Tunisia, their breakdown, and their escalation in recent years.

By now it is late morning, and I have to return to the hotel to meet Dorothée and Kamran for lunch. Although he has not yet heard about his visa, Kamran is relieved that the rain has stopped so that he can finish the photography of a rehabilitated palace that Dorothée has reviewed. Now he is free to start working with me.

To avoid getting stranded in remote spots, Dorothée has rented a car, so she drops us off in the Hafsia quarter for our first photography session. A few hours later we have to call on her again for help, having spent over an hour after dark looking desperately for a taxi to take us back with all our equipment.

Tonight we have dinner in a small, simple restaurant near the hotel. Afterward I work until almost four again, to prepare for tomorrow's interviews.

Friday, March 4. My morning is spent interviewing Abdel Aziz Daouletli and Jamila Binous from the Association de Sauvegarde de la Médina in their beautiful Dar Lasram Palace, while Kamram continues photographing nearby in the Hafsia quarter.

Though my appointment with Wassim Ben Mahmoud has been postponed from eleven to twelve, I am nonetheless a little late. On the way I mentally review my next interviewee's background. Wassim is a young architect educated both in France and the United States, which is rare among Tunisians. I first met him three months ago while preparing a seminar that took place in Tunis. He was instrumental in both the projects I am reviewing, a happy coincidence that will save me some time. The statements he has already filled out are quite complete, so I need only limited information from him now.

In his office I find him as efficient and busy as usual. He has already made lunch reservations in La Marsa and is ready to go. First, I insist on giving him a list of plans that I will need to take back with me, to be gathered by his staff. For the Cité al-Ahmadi, I particularly request a better site plan, the latest layout, copies of plans, sections, and facades as well as some characteristic construction details. Not unexpectedly the drawings are not instantly available, but Wassim promises to have them ready by Monday. He will also arrange a meeting for me with the developer before my departure on Tuesday.

My interview continues en route to La Marsa. I need to verify carefully who all the significant participants in the project were. It is essential information since the Award is to be shared not only among the designers but also among those who contributed most as clients or as executors of the project. One of the Award's aims is to encourage all types of involvement.

The situation seems fairly clear in this case since Wassim was completely in charge as the only private architect. His assistant in this project was a young French architect now in the Philippines, certainly much too far away to be interviewed. The one exception is the cantilevered *mashrabiyas*, locally called *gannarias*. Those were designed by a decorating firm based on a survey of existing traditional models in Sidi Bou Said and Tunis.

Our restaurant in La Marsa is by the sea, but we are seated in a closed room since the weather is still cool. The house specialty is of course fish. The conversation continues, casually mixing Hafsia and Al-Ahmadi. Although I prepared a comprehensive list of questions beforehand, I prefer to let them come as naturally as possible.

Some important changes occurred during the project implementation: a second supermarket was added at the north, the number of dwellings was modified, the internal layout of flats was simplified, and the variety of *gannarias* was reduced. Major conflicts with the contractors occurred, causing a change of general contractor for Phases 2 and 3.

I also learn that climatic constraints are not severe enough to generate particular and sophisticated solutions, as occur in the architectural traditions of other Arab countries. Wassim explains, however, that it is best to orient a project so that it is closed toward the northwest and open toward the southeast.

After lunch, Wassim takes me briefly to his project. It looks exciting, but we have to hurry back to Tunis. Wassim is not able to arrange visits to flats for me, but he gives me the name of a resident whom he knows personally. He also explains that all modifications and additions such as pergolas are to be designed exclusively by him.

On our way back to Tunis, we discover that we studied architecture at the École des Beaux-Arts in Paris at the same time. The school has so many students that we never met. Wassim makes a detour to drop me off beside the medina. My afternoon program consists of interviews and photography in the Hafsia quarter.

In the evening, we assess our general plans: Kamran should definitely go to Paris on Sunday to get his visa. Dorothée's flight to the south of

5: External staircase between two blocks. 6: Jaouida and Paul Vaughan's living room. 7: The Vaughans' entrance hall. 8: Connection between the staircase and the living room in Alia Bafoun's apartment. 9: One of the blocks on the eastern side, in which Henri Jacobi's apartment is located. 10: Dorothée Vauzelles. 11: Pointing out a view I want a shot of to Kamran Adle. 12: Individual villas around the Cité al-Ahmadi.

Tunisia was canceled because of strong winds. Therefore her assignment is finished, and she will be leaving us tomorrow. She will leave her car at the airport, so I must book another one before closing. I also request a driver at the nearby, less expensive rental office. This driver will prove indispensable.

Saturday, March 5. A private arrangement is made with the driver to carry Kamran's heavy and cumbersome equipment. After a few last shots of the Hafsia from the tops of neighboring buildings, we hurry across the streets of the old medina to take some views of the project's surroundings. Following a delay in the twelve-o'clock traffic jam, we pay a quick visit to Sidi Qacem, a newly restored monument outside the old city walls. The photographs are intended only to enrich the Award's general documentation since this project has not been short-listed.

Our lunch with Dorothée is a little sad because of her impending departure. We agree to meet again in Paris.

Henri Jacobi's apartment in the Cité al-Ahmadi is not easy to find, but we are guided by helpful neighbors. His door is reached by an external staircase. He and his wife await us, and he shows us around—on the lower floor, a living room, dining room, and kitchen; upstairs, three bedrooms and bathrooms. As usual Kamran and I decide which views should be taken before I start my interview.

Since Jacobi is also an architect, his praise for the organization of the apartment is especially meaningful. His wife likes the built-in cupboards, but explains that there are not enough in the kitchen. The apartment receives satisfactory natural light, but this is not the case for the ground-floor dwellings. Noise is a problem where kitchens share a light well. The district is not yet connected to the city gas mains, so the inhabitants depend on individual gas cylinders. Leaks sometimes occur in the ceilings just below the roof, and the wooden window frames are not waterproof.

Kamram has now finished his work indoors and is eager to continue with photographs of the outside access to the apartment.

The Jacobis' rent is 165 Tunisian dinars ($264 U.S.) per month, but they say that it would normally be about 200 dinars. Many foreign advisers (*coopérants*) live in the complex. The Jacobis estimate that they constitute roughly 50 per cent of the population, but this will require checking. Occupants who are owners seem to be in the minority. Even so, subrentals are rare, despite the fact that the proportion of Tunisians increases during summer vacations when the Cité becomes more like a seaside resort.

Kamran reappears looking quite worried: he has dropped one of his 35-millimeter cameras, and its meter is not working. He tries to fix it.

The gardens outside are well-kept but require regular care by gardeners. The monthly maintenance charges amount to approximately ten Tunisian dinars ($16 U.S.) per dwelling, but many Tunisian residents find this unreasonably high and therefore refuse to pay.

Kamran has finished his repairs but is still anxious about the quality of his remaining photographs.

Next we go to meet Jaouida Vaughan, a Tunisian model married to an Irish publisher. She is a very active person and used to run a beauty parlor in the neighborhood's commercial center. Our meeting is scheduled for half-past four in front of Touta, the local supermarket. Since she has not yet arrived half an hour later, we decide to visit Alia Bafoun's apartment with Henri Jacobi before it gets too dark for photographs.

Alia Bafoun is a university professor and, as a sociologist, should be able to provide us with some valuable insights. Unfortunately she is out, but her son is at home. We are surprised that he already knows about the Award, and immediately he produces a booklet about the 1980 Award winners. Kamran is proud to show everyone his photographs of Isfahan.

This dwelling belongs to the first phase of the project and is more sophisticated than the Jacobis' apartment. The change in level between the entry and living room is going to be photogenic. We quickly agree on the views to be taken, and Kamran starts work. Meanwhile I try to put some apparent order into a place where a photographer has clearly not been expected. Kamran gets increasingly nervous. He has been subjected to too much pressure today.

Next we hurry to the Vaughans' apartment, still accompanied by Henri Jacobi. Fortunately Jaouida is back by now. She apologizes because there was no way to warn us about her delay. Her husband, Paul, is also home from work, and their two daughters are playing in the background. Henri Jacobi leaves. This time Kamran listens quietly to the interview over a drink since it is too dark for photography.

The Vaughans have lived here since September 1981, when their block was completed. Introduced to the neighborhood by the Jacobis, they were attracted by its proximity to the French *lycée* (for their children) and to commercial facilities. There is easy transportation to Tunis by the main road or the railway, which are both close by. Many conveniences are immediately available, including a bank and doctors. "There is practically no need to leave the neighborhood," says Jaouida.

The size and homogeneity of this housing estate are quite exceptional for the Tunisian private sector. It is also a good property investment. Ninety per cent of the owners rent their flats, and some own as many as three or four units. The Vaughans can't think of any foreigners they know among the owners, but there are many Tunisian tenants, including high-ranking civil servants. Like the Jacobis, they estimate that 50 per cent of the residents are foreigners. As I insist on this particular point, they explain that their impressions are based on what they know about their immediate neighbors, as well as on their experience as active members of a residents' committee.

The estate seems ideal for the upper middle class. Children make friends easily within the neighborhood, but used to fight local children who previously played on the site. Social relationships with the surrounding inhabitants don't seem to have developed.

The Vaughans describe Tawfic Torgeman, the developer, as an enlightened person. It was he who insisted on keeping the magnificent carob tree and thereby generated the idea of a layout based on squares. He used to come once a week to inspect the site. He also happens to be linked to the President's family.

The Vaughans too complain about window weatherproofing, but they lack the ceiling leaks of some apartments. They find the natural light quite adequate, and comment on the "softness" of indirect, reflected lighting. The cross ventilation is good. They are glad to be in a central block since the residents located on the estate's western edge suffer from winter winds and excessive afternoon sun. Other minor domestic points are raised again, like the convenience of the built-in cupboards and the need for the project to be connected to the city gas mains.

Since it is getting late, we agree on an appointment for the next morning. On our way out, I notice some works by Nja Mahdaoui, a Tunisian artist I much admire, and I learn that he happens to live almost next door. Paul Vaughan insists on taking me to meet him, and he too agrees on an appointment for the next morning.

Back in Tunis Kamran cheers up when I take him to Damascus Nights, a new restaurant just next to the International. To my great pleasure, he is delighted to experience Syrian cooking.

Before going to bed, I consider once again the Cité al-Ahmadi site plan in order to prepare tomorrow's photography session. Because of the repetitions inherent in a housing project, I finally decide on the strategy of selecting two general viewpoints, which represent the different types of space and frame different facade details.

Sunday, March 6. The weather is unexpectedly beautiful today, ideal for photography. We start with some panoramic views from the southeastern edge, which has the advantage of being elevated and surrounded by villas. One of the reasons for photographing the continuing construction along the southern end is to substitute for similar documentation that I couldn't obtain of construction elsewhere on the estate. Our task is complicated by the need to think about three different categories of photographs at once: 1) contextual ones, to illustrate the project's relationship to its environment; 2) survey ones, to be presented to the master jury, documenting every aspect of the project, including shortcomings of construction; 3) presentation ones, which will eventually be published and widely diffused if the project wins an Award.

Since Kamran's time is quite limited, we have to work especially closely. While he sets up the tripod and takes no fewer than eight shots of each view, using different formats, cameras, and films, I run ahead to select the next view and to figure out how to frame it. Kamran is the fastest architectural photographer I have ever met, and I am soon out of breath.

We hurry on from peripheral streets to internal squares and then to side decks. The driver cheerfully follows with Kamran's heavy tripod and bags in hand. He is definitely an asset. People stare from windows as we focus on cantilevered *gannarias*, pastiche windows, or stairs with enameled tiles. But this time I will not be bothered by any student *komiteh* like the one that interviewed me at length on the President of Syria's policy in Lebanon when I was in Ahvaz. I remember to look for the children playing in the gardens, as mentioned by all those I interviewed. They are not difficult to find and capture with Kamran's telephoto lens. I have mixed feelings about the project's architectural integration into the existing urban fabric, but after all, it is up to the master jury to make its own judgment from the photographs. An attempt to climb a minaret at the northern periphery of the site is unsuccessful, but the sun is in the wrong direction anyway. Some views of the northern edge with the supermarket will do.

Now we have to hurry to our appointment with Paul and Jaouida Vaughan. Everything is set up for our visit. They even seem excited at the idea that their neighborhood may receive an award. Their dwelling is not only more spacious than the first one we visited but much nicer. It is also particularly well-furnished and arranged. Everything, successively, is photogenic: the entrance, with its traditional trunk and mirror; the living room, with its *gannaria* corner; the staircase, with pottery arranged on its large side steps; the wooden window frames in the bedroom, etc. The driver learns fast: he now correctly guesses which film, camera, or device Kamran will need next.

As we leave the Vaughans' apartment, Kamran selects just two light 35-millimeter cameras to survey the additions and modifications undertaken spontaneously by the residents, while I make my way toward Nja Mahdaoui's apartment for a quick interview. Nja confirms several of the previously mentioned observations, and shows me old photographs of the palace that used to occupy the site and hosted the signing of the 1881 convention between Tunisia and France. As I start to consider acquiring one of his tempting works that hang on the walls, Kamran comes for me, having finished his own work.

After a quick lunch at the International, I take Kamran with all his luggage and equipment to the airport. He has to pay a substantial fee for excess baggage. After long bargaining with the customs officer I get a reduction for him. It is now time to part and we are both moved. We wish each other luck for the rest of the review and we hope to meet again in 1986 for the next one. I ask the driver to take me back to Tunis, and I leave him with the handsome tip that he deserves.

Later Henri Jacobi picks me up at my hotel to take me back to his apartment for dinner. He has gathered some data on construction costs in Tunisia. The rate of inflation in this sector, however, has not been officially assessed for the last six years. To estimate the actual cost of a project, which was implemented gradually during that time, is not easy. I will have to rely on a combination of personal estimates from reliable persons.

Back at the hotel after dinner I review all my information in order to identify the remaining data to be collected, for tomorrow is my last day in Tunis. I carefully prepare the last interviews.

Monday, March 7. The morning starts with a meeting on a coming seminar with Abdul Mejid Sahnoun, who introduces me to one of the directors of the Société National Immobilière de Tunisie, the public development agency that built the Hafsia. I gather additional construction estimates.

It is not easy to find a taxi to get back to the hotel. Once there, I am delighted to run into my friend Fredj Stambouli, a sociology professor and one of the former members of the Award team. All my previous efforts to get in touch with him have been unsuccessful.

After lunch, I have an appointment with Jelal Abdelkafi, who was director of the Association de Sauvegarde de la Médina when the Hafsia project was begun. He strikes me as rather brilliant. His office is just off Habib Bourguiba Avenue, conveniently close to that of Tawfic Torgeman. Torgeman's office is just above Wassim Ben Mahmoud's.

I am introduced to Torgeman at three o'clock as previously arranged by Wassim. He explains that he is in fact president and general director of the Union Internationale de Banques, of which his development company is a subsidiary (with some additional foreign participation). Torgeman also gives the background of the Dar al-Taj palace, which had fallen into disrepair after independence. Finally the state tore it down and gave its land to the municipality, which eventually sold it to him, since he had promised to create a suitable environment along its western edge for the Presidential palace.

I mention that our nomination forms include diverging estimates of the total number of dwellings in the neighborhood (150, 160, and 250). He makes a quick calculation and gives me a figure of 136. The reduction in number is due to the replacement of a housing block to the north by a new commercial center. He also gives me a set of figures concerning the site, the housing, and the commercial district, along with his total expenditure. His cost breakdown among land, infrastructure, and building, however, is only approximate. Torgeman says that all the labor was Tunisian. He gives me the names and addresses of his landscaper, decorator, and contractors, and explains his lawsuit against the first contractor.

His explanation for the project's success is that it filled a housing need for middle- and upper-middle-class families that falls between public housing and private villas.

After leaving Torgeman's office, I need only descend a few steps to Wassim Ben Mahmoud's office to collect the documents that should be ready for me now. Wassim is absent, however, and his secretary most surprised by my request. It is getting late, and I decide to visit some bookstores in search of maps and publications for the Award headquarters. An hour later a message awaits me at the hotel reception desk: the documents will be sent directly to me later on. I cautiously put the message among my papers.

My last dinner is quite solitary, and the rest of the evening is spent reviewing all my forms, notes, and interviews. Many additional comments and details will probably be forgotten unless I record them now.

Tuesday, March 8. I am in the waiting room of the Tunis airport, on my way to Istanbul. The thick Tunisian portfolios are safely locked in my suitcase, but I keep two more that are still slim in my hand luggage. Since there is no time to waste, I start getting acquainted with the next two projects to be reviewed, in Turkey.

NOTES

CONTINUITY AND CHANGE
By SHERBAN CANTACUZINO

1. A phrase used by Mohammed Arkoun in conversation. It gave Maurice Edelman the title "Espace de la Tolérance" for an article on the Aga Khan Award, *Le Monde* (Paris), Sept. 10, 1983.

2. See the statement of the master jury, p. 79.

3. Renata Holod, ed., with Darl Rastorfer, *Architecture and Community* pp. 57–58.

4. From an interview, *Günay-din*, Sept. 6, 1983.

5. From the first brochure of the Aga Khan Award for Architecture, (Philadelphia: 1980).

6. *Architecture and Community*, Contents.

7. Ibid., pp. 57–58.

8. *Middle-East Construction* (Aug. 1983), pp. 14–15.

9. Technical review for the Aga Khan Award by Samir Abdulac.

10. See p. 35.

11. *Places of Public Gathering in Islam*, pp. 81–86.

12. Renata Holod and Ahmet Evin, eds., *Modern Turkish Architecture* (Philadelphia: University of Pennsylvania Press), 1984.

13. "Islam et développement dans le Maghreb indépendant," *Arabica*, Vol. 29, Part 2, pp. 138–139.

14. "Religion et société d'après l'exemple de l'Islam," *Studia Islamica*, Part 55 (Paris: 1982), p. 44.

15. Author's translation.

16. *Architecture as Symbol and Self-Identity*, p.18 ff.

17. Ibid, p. 1 ff.

18. See p. 68.

19. *Arabica*, Vol. 19, Part 2, p. 140.

20. *Development and Urban Metamorphosis*, Vol. 1, p. 103 ff.

21. *Middle-East Construction*, Aug. 1983, pp. 14–15.

22. *Adaptive Reuse*, p. 40.

23. Doğan Kuban, "Modern versus Traditional: A False Conflict," *Mimar* 9 (1983), p. 54.

24. Behruz Çinici in "Following the Aga Khan Award for Architecture—Is It Arabesque?" *Yanki* (Istanbul), Sept. 17, 1983.

25. *Mimar* 9 (1983), p. 54.

26. *Arabica*, Vol. 19, Part 2, p. 114.

27. Ibid.

28. Ibid., p. 136.

29. Mohammed Arkoun, "Building and Meaning in the Islamic World," *Mimar* 8 (1983), p. 51.

30. *Modern Turkish Architecture*, pp. 96–97.

31. *Adaptive Reuse*, pp. 43–44.

32. Ibid., p. 110.

33. "White Elephant Graveyard." *The Times* (London), Jan. 3, 1985.

34. Brian Taylor, "ONERSOL, Niamey, Niger," *Mimar* 13 (1984), p. 66.

35. From a speech delivered by the Aga Khan at the Award ceremony, Topkapi, Istanbul, Turkey, Sept. 4, 1983.

36. *Architecture as Symbol and Self Identity*, p. 2.

37. *"Warum Denkmalpflege?"* in proceedings of First International Congress on Architectural Conservation, University of Basle, Switzerland, March 1983, p. 21 ff.

38. *Adaptive Reuse*, p. 29.

39. "Introduction to Conservation," UNESCO, 1979.

40. *Development and Urban Metamorphosis*, Vol. 1, p. 106.

41. *Adaptive Reuse*, p. 50.

42. Ibid., p. 38.

43. Ibid., p. 85.

44. Ibid., p. 94.

45. *Mimar* 9 (1983), p. 56.

46. Abdou Diouf, President of Senegal, "Opening Remarks," *Reading the Contemporary City*, p. xiii.

47. "The New Landscape," the annual discourse of the Royal Institute of British Architects, London, delivered by Charles Correa, January 15, 1985.

48. Babar Mumtaz and Emma Hooper, "Rural Development Policies: Settlements and Shelter," in *The Changing Rural Habitat*, vol. 2, pp. 11–26.

49. Zhang Ji-G, Zheng Meng-Lin, Lin Shou-Zhong, Zhao Guo-Zhi, and Li Guo-Wei, "Rural Methane Use in China," in *The Changing Rural Habitat*, vol. 1, pp. 123–130.

50. Mona Serageldin, "Planning for New Nubia 1960–1980," in *The Changing Rural Habitat*, vol. 1, pp. 59–82.

51. "Rural Development Policies: Settlements and Shelter," pp. 11–26.

52. Mohammed Arkoun, "The Socialist Village Experiment in Algeria," in *The Changing Rural Habitat*, vol. 1, pp. 45–50.

53. "Rural Development Policies: Settlement and Shelter," pp. 11–26.

54. "Planning for New Nubia 1960–1980," pp. 59–82.

55. Jim Antoniou, "The Exploding Metropolis," in *Arts and the Islamic World*, vol. 2, no.4, Winter 1984–1985. New Century Publishers, London: pp. 29–46.

56. Giancarlo De Carlo, "Gorée, Dakar, Pikine," in *Reading the Contemporary City*, pp. 73–74.

57. Ibid.

58. Book review, *Mimar* 6, 1982, published by Concept Media Pte Ltd., Singapore, p. 81.

59. John F. C. Turner, "Housing: Its Part in Another Development," in *Housing Process and Physical Form*, pp. 8–19.

60. Charles Correa, "Urban Housing in the Third World: The Role of the Architect," in *Housing Process and Physical Form*, pp. 45–49.

61. Ibid.

62. Alfred Van Hyck, "The Contribution of Housing to National Development: Can More Be Achieved?" in *Housing Process and Physical Form*, pp. 1–7.

63. His Highness the Aga Khan, "Islamic Architecture: Concerns and Directions," a speech made on the occasion of receiving the 1984 Thomas Jefferson Memorial Foundation Medal for Architecture at the University of Virginia, April 1984.

THE MOSQUE TODAY
By IHSAN FETHI

1. See the statement of the master jury, page 79.

2. Bernard Huet, "The Modernity in a Tradition," *Mimar* 10, 1983.

3. Ulya Vogt-Göknil, *Mosquées*, Paris, 1975.

4. Um al-Tubool Mosque, Airport Road, Baghdad, built in 1965, is an exact replica of an Egyptian mosque in Cairo. It was built by Egyptian masons, but this is an isolated case in Iraq. In Saudi Arabia and the Arabian Gulf states the phenomenon of Egyptianization of mosque architecture is very evident. Similarly, an Ottomanization of mosque architecture seems to be gaining popularity in Muslim countries in Africa. Examples are the Great Mosque in Kaolack, Senegal, and the Central Mosque in Ilorin, Nigeria. These regional transplants are regrettable and are not in keeping with the traditions of Islamic architecture.

5. H. Munis, *The Mosque*, Kuwait 1981 (Arabic), pp. 328–335.

6. *Madrid Islamic Cultural Centre Competition*, Union of International Architects monograph (Paris: 1980). Some eclectic/Arabian Nights examples: BF, BN, BS, CA, GA, HB (Turkey), ID (United Arab Emirates), JF, KD, OK, PS, PU, PX, QF.

7. High-tech examples are: BZ, CD (Toyokazu Watanabi, Japan), CN, CQ, EJ, FH, FI, HD, KP, MR.

8. See illustration in Venice Biennale 1982 book: *Architettura nei paesi Islamici*, seconda mostra internazionale di architettura, Venice, 1982, p. 174.

9. Madrid competition entry (CD).

10. See *Architectural Record*, Nov. 1980.

11. *State Mosque Competition, Baghdad*. Amanat al-Assima, 1983, p. 68.

12. Madrid competition entries: Triangular Musalla (DB) by Jakub Waclawek (Poland) and Circular Musalla (AI) by A. Mandizabal (Spain).

13. Architects Thariani and Company, Karachi, Pakistan.

14. Queen Aliya Mosque, architects Edward Mansfield, Halcrow Group Architectural Practice (London).

15. See illustration in Venice Biennale 1982 book, p. 92.

16. In mosque for Etimesgüt Armed Units, Ankara, Cengiz Bektaş, architect.

17. See *Architectural Design* 1/2, 1980, pp. 24–29.

18. Entry (AO) by J. Perucho (Spain).

19. Anonymous entry (BY).

20. Entry (EX) by A. S. Roguez (Spain).

21. Entry (BH) by Hoel/Elling (Norway) and entry (HY) by T. Yoshizaka and W. Sunakawa (Japan).

22. Entry (PV) by F. Venero, I. Lopez-Bero, and E. Lopez Argita (Spain).

23. Entry (GW).

BIBLIOGRAPHY

PERIODICALS AND PAMPHLETS

Conference center, hotel, and mosque in Riyadh. Trevor Dannatt and Partners, architects:
Architectural Review, vol. 151, no. 938 (Apr. 1975), pp. 194–219.
Domus, no. 595 (June 1979), pp. 22–23.
Informes de la Construccion, vol. 32, no. 325 (Nov. 1980), pp. 9–16.
Royal Institute of British Architects Journal, vol. 83, no. 6 (June 1976), pp. 251–253.

Davies, J. G. "Islamic Worship and Mosque Architecture." Article, plans, references. Research Bulletin, University of Birmingham, England, Institute for the Study and Worship and Religious Architecture, 1978, pp. 3–12.

Dressler, Fritz. "Mosques of the Island of Djerba, Tunisia." Article (German), photographs. *Bauwelt*, vol. 70, no. 45 (Dec. 1, 1979), pp. 1911–1916.

The Islamic Cultural Center in Madrid—competition. Plans, sections, elevations:
Architect (Malta, July 1980), pp. 9–19.
Architecture d'Aujourd'hui, no. 208 (Apr. 1980), p. xii.
Arquitectos, no. 31 (Jan. 1980), pp. 18–25.
Arquitecturas Bis, no. 34 (May/Dec. 1980), pp. 22/27.
Building Design, no. 494 (May 9, 1980), pp. 14–16.

"Khartoum: El-Nilein Mosque, Khartoum." Gamel Abdel Gadir, architect. Article, models. *Building Specification*, vol. 9, no. 10 (Oct. 1978), p. 50.

Morris, A. E. "Modern Mosques—Problems and Answers." Article, photographs. *Middle East Construction*, vol. 7 (July 1982), pp. 14–15.

"The Mosque" (special issue). Article (English, Arabic), references, illustrations, *Albenaa*, vol. 1, no. 1 (Feb./March 1979), pp. 28–115, 122.

Mosque, Canberra, Australia. G. and R. Block, architects. Article, plan, details, sections, photographs. *Architect and Builder* (Cape Town, March 1963), pp. 10–14.

A mosque for Rome. Paolo Portoghesi, Vittorio Gigliotti, and Sami Mousawi, architects:
Aramco World Magazine, vol. 29, no. 5 (Sept./Oct. 1978), pp. 12–13.
Architecture d'Aujourd'hui, no. 213 (Feb. 1981), pp. 57–61.
Architectural Design, vol. 50, no. 1/2 (1980), pp. 24–29.
Architectural Review, vol. 168, no. 1005 (Nov. 1980), pp. 265–266.
Art and Architecture, vol. 11, no. 47/48 (Apr./July 1979), pp. 38–53.

Consulting Engineer, vol. 43, no. 11 (Nov. 1979), pp. 35–36.

"Mosque in Etimesüt, Turkey." Cengiz Bektaş, architect. Note (Turkish), plan, section, model, photographs. *Arkitekt*, vol. 42, no. 351 (3) (Istanbul, 1973), pp. 124–125.

"Mosques in Mali." Article, photographs, maps. *Mimar*, no. 3 (Jan./March 1982), pp. 9–15.

"Mosques in Modern Style." E. Ertan, architect. Notes, elevation, perspectives. *Arkitekt*, nos. 9–12 (Istanbul, 1953), pp. 181–182.

"Mosque, University College, Ibadan, Nigeria." Fry Drew and Partners, architects. Plan, model. *Architectural Design*, May 1953, p. 173.
West African Builder and Architect, March/April 1962, pp. 24–25.

"Mosque with Adjoining Public Buildings of Medmed Ali Pasha, at Kavallu, Greece." Article (Turkish), plans, sections, elevations, photographs. *Arkitekt*, vol. 45, no. 2 (362) (Istanbul, 1976), pp. 65–69.

Picard, Denis. "Mosques in Tunisia." Article (French), photographs. *Connaissance des Arts*, no. 272 (Oct. 1974), pp. 114–123.

"A Prefabricated Mosque in Jeddah." Naim Kamel, architect. Plans, sections, photographs. *International Asbestos—Cement Review*, vol. 23, no. 2 (90) (Apr. 1978), pp. 29–30.

"Project for a Mosque in Los Angeles, USA." P. Koenig, architect. Note, plan, perspective. *Arts and Architecture* (Los Angeles, Sept. 1964), p. 33.

"Project for National Mosque, Kuala Lumpur, Malaya." Public Works Department, architects. Article, floor plan, elevation. *Hong Kong and Far East Builder*, June 1961, pp. 38–40.

"Project for One of the Largest Mosques outside the Islamic World." William Dawson, architect. Article, plans, sketches. *Architects' Journal*, vol. 168, no. 35 (Aug. 30, 1978), p. 370.

Regent's Park Mosque, London. Frederick Gibberd, Partners, architects:
Albenaa, vol. 1, no. 1 (Feb./March 1979), pp. 84–93.
Architectural Association Annual Review (1979) pp. 81–86.
Asian Building and Construction (Jan. 1979), pp. 23–24.
Concrete Quarterly, no. 115 (Oct./Dec. 1977), pp. 34–39.
Institute of Clerks of Works Journal, vol. 95, no. 1136 (Dec. 1977), pp. 184–186.
New Building Projects, vol. 19, no. 2 (Feb. 1978), pp. 3–10.

"Religious Buildings in Singapore" (special issue). Article, plans, sections, photographs. *Singapore Institute of Architects Journal*, no. 110 (Jan./Feb. 1982), pp. 2–29.

Sayari, Zeki. "Minarets—a Lost Function?" Article (Turkish), sections, photographs, references. *Arkitekt*, vol. 46, no. 4 (368) (Istanbul, 1977), pp. 154–157.

"Scotland's New Mosque Plans in Glasgow." Ian G. Lindsay and Partners, architects. *Building Design*, no. 345 (May 6, 1977), p. 4.

"Sweden's First Mosque." White Arkitekter Ab., architects. Article (Swedish), plan, sections, photographs. *Arkitektur*, vol. 77, no. 8 (Stockholm, Oct. 1977), pp. 27–28.

Zaknic, Ivan. "Of Le Corbusier's Earlier Journey—the Mosque." Article, sketches, references. *Oppositions*, no. 18 (Fall 1979), pp. 86–99.

BOOKS

Assima, Amanat al-. *State Mosque Competition, Baghdad*. Stuttgart: Reinicke International Consulting GmbH., 1983.

Barbar, Aghıl M. *The Architecture of the Mosque in Muslim North Africa*. Monticello, Ill.: Vance Bibliographies, 1979.

Doumatc, Lamia: *Mosques of the Near East*. Monticello, Ill.: Vance Bibliographies, 1979.

Grabar, Oleg: *The Case of the Mosque*. Berkeley, Calif.: University of California Press, 1969.

_____. *The Formation of Islamic Art*. New Haven, Conn., and London: Yale University Press, 1973.

Kuban, Doğan. *Muslim Religious Architecture: The Mosque and Its Earliest Development*. Part 1. Leiden, Netherlands: E. J. Brill, 1974.

Kühnel, E. *Die Moschee*. Berlin: Konieczny, 1949.

Madrid Islamic Cultural Centre Competition. Monograph. Paris: Union of International Architects, 1980.

Miranda, F. de. *The Mosque as a Work of Art and a House of Prayer*. Wassenaar, Netherlands: Mirananda, 1977.

Mu'nis, Hussain. *The Mosque Alam al-Ma'rifa, Kuwait*. Arabic, 1981.

Vogt-Göknil, Ulya. *Die Moschee*. Zurich: Artemis, 1978.

A SURVEY OF MODERN TURKISH ARCHITECTURE
By DOĞAN KUBAN

1. The Aga Khan Award for Architecture sponsored a survey of modern architecture in Turkey for the period of 1960 through 1983. Its purpose was to test the use and relevance of field research and local professional participation in the preliminary nominations of the projects, as well as to obtain contextual references for the master jury, and eventually material for the Award's documentation center at Geneva.

The survey, the first in its kind prepared for the Award, collected visual material (mainly photographs) for about 1,200 buildings from all over the country, interviewed 150 architects, and gathered a collection of written material on the modern building scene in Turkey.

Although an independent study, the information and discussions in this chapter are presented according to their relevance to the philosophy of the Award.

2. For this period see Ayda Arel, *Onsekizinci Yüzyıl İstanbul Mimarisinde Batılılaşma Süreci* (Istanbul, 1975); Pars Tuğlaci, *Osmanlı Mimarlığında Batılılaşma Dönemi ve Balyan Ailesi* (Istanbul, 1981); Serim Denel, *Batılılaşma Sürecinde İstanbul'da Tasarım ve Dış Mekanlarda Değişim ve Nedenleri* (Ankara, 1982); Afife Batur, "Les Oeuvres de Raimondo d'Aronco à Istanbul," *Atti del Congresso Internazionale di Studi su Raimondo D'Aronco e il suo Tempo* (Udine, 1981), pp. 118–134.

3. Sedat Hakki Eldem, "50 Yıllık Cumhuriyet Mimarlığı, *Mimarlık*, Nos. 11–12 (Istanbul, 1973), pp. 5–11; Süha Ozkan, "Mimar Mehmet Vedat Tek" in the same issue, pp. 45–51; Mete Tapan and Metin Sözen, *50 Yılın Türk Mimarisi* (Istanbul, 1973); Üstün Alsaç, *Türkiye'deki Mimarlık Düşüncesinin Cumhuriyet Dönemindeki Evrimi* (Trabzon, 1976); İnci Aslanoğlu, *Erken Cumhuriyet Dönemi Mimarlığı* (Ankara, 1980); Yıldırım Yavuz, *Mimar A. Kemalettin Bey ve Birinci Ulusal Mimarlık Dönemi* (Ankara, 1981).

4. Doğan Kuban, "Architecture and Ideology: The Atatürk Years," *Dimensions*, No. 1 (Ankara, 1983), pp. 3–6.

5. See special issues on architectural education in *Mimarlık*, No. 9 (1969), No. 12 (1972), No. 3 (1976), No. 2 (1978); Alsaç, *Türkiye'deki Mimarlık Düşüncesi*; Yıldız Sey and Mete Tapan, "Architectural Education in Turkey: Past and Present," *Mimar*, No. 10, (Singapore, 1983), pp. 69–75.

6. Asım Mutlu, "Yüzyıllık Mimarlık Eğitimi," *Yapı*, No. 49 (Istanbul, 1983), pp. 25–28.

7. For foreign architects, see Alsaç, pp. 120–144.

8. For the master plan, see Enis Kortan, *Le Corbusier Gözüyle Türk Mimarlık ve Şehirciliği* (Ankara, 1983).

9. For the Turkish house, in general, see Sedat Hakki Eldem, *Türk Evi Plan Tipleri* (Istanbul, 1955); Eldem, *Köşkler ve Kasırlar* (Istanbul, 1969); Doğan Kuban, "Türk Ev Geleneği Üzerine Gözlemler," *Türk ve İslam Sanatı Üzerine Denemeler* (Istanbul, 1982), pp. 195–209; Ayda Arel, *Osmanlı Konut Geleneğinde Tarihsel Sorunlar* (İzmir, 1982). For special interest, see E. Kömürcüoğlu, *Ankara Evleri* (Istanbul, 1950); L. Tomsu, *Bursa Evleri* (Istanbul, 1950); C. Berk, *Konya Evleri* (Istanbul, 1951); N. Çakiroğlu, *Kayseri Evleri* (Istanbul, 1952); L. Eser, *Kütahya Evleri* (Istanbul, 1955); Cengiz Bektaş, *Antalya* (Istanbul, 1980); R. Günay, *Geleneksel Safranbolu Evleri ve Oluşumu* (Ankara, 1981).

10. For this period, see E. Kortan, *Türkiye'de Mimarlık Hareketleri ve Eleştirisi (1950–60)* (Ankara, 1971); İlhan Tekeli, "The Social Context of the Development of Architecture in Turkey," *Contemporary Turkish Architecture*, ed. by Renata Holod and Ahmet Evin (Pennsylvania, 1983); Alsaç.

11. For this period, see also E. Kortan, *Türkiye'de Mimarlık Hareketleri ve Eleştirisi (1960–70)* (Ankara, 1974); Atilla Yücel, "Pluralism Takes Command: Turkish Architectural Scene from the Sixties to the Present," *Contemporary Turkish Architecture*.

12. For the Lav house, see *Arkitekt*, No. 322 (Istanbul, 1966), pp. 57–59.

13. See Yücel, "Pluralism Takes Command."

14. For Sheraton, see *Mimarlık*, No. 8 (Istanbul, 1967), pp. 26–27.

15. For Odakule, see *Arkitekt*, No. 362 (Istanbul, 1976), pp. 53–58.

16. For the works of Eldem, see Sedat Hakki Eldem, *Proje Uygulama—Büyük Konutlar* (Ankara, 1982); A. Yücel, "Contemporary Turkish Architecture", *Mimar*, No. 10 (Singapore, 1983), pp. 58–68.

17. The 1980 Aga Khan Award for Architecture.

18. For the work of Cansever, see the special issue of *Mimar*, No. 11 (Ankara, 1983) and also Yücel, "Contemporary Turkish Architecture."

19. For the works of Bektaş, see Cengiz Bektaş, *Mimarlık Çalışmaları* (Ankara, 1979).

20. For Çinici see Yücel, "Contemporary Turkish Architecture."

21. For the airport terminal, see *Arkitekt*, No. 356 (Istanbul, 1974), pp. 168–171.

22. For Lassa, see *Çevre*, No. 7 (Istanbul, 1980), pp. 20–25 or *Mimarlık*, No. 1 (Istanbul, 1978), pp. 61–64.

23. For ceramic factory, see *Çevre*, No. 7 (Istanbul, 1980), pp. 11–15.

24. For National Mosque at Islamabad, see *Mimarlık*, No. 11 (Istanbul, 1969).

25. For Ankara Great Mosque, see *Mimarlık*, No. 11 (1966), No. 10 (1967), and No. 1 (1976), pp. 65–73.

26. For Oküzmehmetpaşa, see *Rölöve Restorasyon Dergisi*, No. 2 (Ankara, 1975), pp. 123–129.

27. The 1980 Aga Khan Award for Architecture.

28. *Konut 82* (Ankara, 1982), p. 51.

29. İlhan Tekeli, "Türkiye'de Konut Sorununun Davranışsal Nitelikleri ve Konut Kesiminde Bunalım," *Konut 81* (Ankara, 1981), pp. 59–101.

30. For the works of Gülgönen, see *Mimar*, No. 5 (Singapore, 1982), pp. 62–80.

31. See Zeynep Çelik et al., "Konuşan Mimarlık, Dinlenen Mimarlık," *Çevre*, No. 4 (Istanbul, 1979), pp. 63–70.

32. For OR-AN, see Ş. Vanli, *Proje Uygulama* and *Mimarlık*, No. 8 (İstanbul, 1970), pp. 26–40.

33. For ME-SA housing, see *Çevre*, No. 4 (Istanbul, 1979), pp. 34–39 or *Arkitekt*, No. 374 (Istanbul, 1979), pp. 47–51.

34. See Ergun Unaran, "Yerel Yönetimlerin Toplu Konut Projeleri: İzmit ve Ankara Deneyimleri," *Mimarlık*, No. 3 (Istanbul, 1983), pp. 17–19.

35. See "İzmit Yeni Yerleşmeleri," *Mimarlık*, No. 4 (Istanbul, 1976), pp. 100–103; Tuncay Çavdar, "İzmit Yenilikçi Yerleşmeler Projesi," *Mimarlık*, No. 1 (Istanbul, 1978), pp. 55–60; "İzmit Deneyiminin Ardından," *Çevre*, No. 4 (Istanbul, 1979), pp. 53–62; Tuncay Çavdar, "Bir Katılımsal Tasarım Uygulamasının Ardından," *Mimarlık*, No. 1 (Istanbul, 1982), p. 8.

36. See E. Sayin, "Batıkent Toplu Konut Uygulaması," *Tübıtak, YAE Teknik Bülten*, No. 8 (Ankara, 1982), pp. 5–6.

37. *Konut 82*, p. 20.

38. For the law, see Ruşen Keleş, "Toplu Konut Yasa Tasarısı," *Mimarlık*, No. 2 (Istanbul, 1981), pp. 6–8; Teoman Aktüre, "Toplu Konut Yasa Tasarısı Hakkında," *Mimarlık*, No. 3 (Istanbul, 1981), pp. 18–19.

HAFSIA QUARTER
TUNIS, TUNISIA

Project Documentation. Credits, Project Timetable, and information on the origin of human and material resources listed in the Project Geography have been provided in the Award documentation by the inhabitants, by the technical reviewer, Samir Abdulac, and by the architects.

1. Project Personnel. Client: Municipality of Tunis, in many areas represented by the Association de Sauvegarde de la Médina de Tunis (A.S.M.); those who bought houses in the quarter. Planner: A.S.M., particularly its first director, Jelal Abdelkafi (1968–1973). Architects: Arno Heinz* (UNESCO), with Wassim Ben Mahmoud;** others included Saleh Younsi, Serge Santelli, and Michel Steinback. Project promotion and funding: UNESCO for its architect; municipal and international funds. Construction supervisor on site: Wassim Ben Mahmoud. Contractor: Habib el-Trabilsi. Consultant: A.S.M. Historians: Rachid Bellalouna, Jamila Binous. Sociologists: Morched Chabbi, Hedy Eckert, Melika Zamiti. Economists: Yves Farig, Jean-Paul Guislain, Gerard Maarea. Jurists: Belkacem Chebbi, Hafifa Ouertani. Developer: Société Nationale Immobilière de Tunisie (SNIT).

*Arno Heinz, an Austrian, studied architecture in Vienna and is now based in Paris and a member of the French Order of Architects. He has designed a palace for a member of the royal family of Saudi Arabia (1973), the J. Verdun Theater in Vincennes, France, and fifty-five dwellings in Rue Mouffetard and a crèche in Paris (1975–1978). He is responsible for the restoration and transformation in Algiers of the Mahieddine Villas into a cultural center and office for the Historical Monuments Service (1976). In 1977 he carried out a study in Syria aimed at listing the historical sites and monuments for the World Cultural Patrimony. Between 1977 and 1981 he was responsible for the restoration of the historical quarter of Suleimaniye and Zeyrek in Istanbul. Between 1981 and 1983 he planned 600 dwellings in Innsbruck, Austria, and a project for 200 dwellings still to be completed.

**Wassim Ben Mahmoud, a Tunisian, studied architecture at the École des Beaux-Arts in Paris and at the Massachusetts Institute of Technology, where he was a Fulbright Scholar. For his planning diploma at the Institut d'Urbanisme in Paris he wrote a thesis on the city of Tunis. He has practiced architecture in Paris and the Ivory Coast, and since 1970 in Tunisia. Since 1972 he has taught at the Technology Institute of Art and Architecture and Urban Studies in Tunis and is an architectural consultant for the municipalities of La Marsa and Mahdia. His architectural work includes many office and apartment blocks in Tunis, La Marsa, Sousse, and Mahdia; industrial buildings at Gabès, Nabeul, and Djebel Djelloud; holiday villages in Tunis and on the island of Zembra; hotels and tourist centers in Tunis, Nabeul, Monastir, Hammamet, Sidi Bou Said and Mahdia; the airport at Tabarca and the Tunisian Embassy in Riyadh, Saudi Arabia. As a planner he has been responsible for the master plan of La Marsa and Halq al-Wadi, for a large number of development plans, and for an important study that identified the areas in Tunisian towns in need of rehabilitation.

2. Project Timetable. 1970: Preliminary study undertaken. 1972–1973: Brief and design principles formulated. 1973 (May): Final project concluded. 1973 (July): Contractor commissioned. 1973–1977 (April): Construction. 1977–1978: Occupancy begun.

3. Project Geography. Tunisia: 1) architects, 2) labor, 3) consultants (historians, sociologists, jurists, and planners), 4) contractor, 5) cement, 6) timber, 7) brick, 8) terrazzo tiles.

4. Project Area. Site: Approximately 3 hectares, part of a larger mainly demolished area to the center and east of the medina. Built up: Total, 17,000 square meters (housing, 10,600 square meters; commercial, 1,700 square meters; *suq*, 4,700 square meters).

5. Climate Data. Tunis, Tunisia: latitude, 36.5° N.; longitude 10.13° E.; altitude, 66 m.

Month	Temperature (° C.)	Relative Humidity (%)	Precipitation (mm.)	Wind Direction	Global Radiation* (MJm^{-2})
J	11.0	78	70	NW	271.1
F	11.7	77	47	NW	315.8
M	13.4	75	43	NW	544.7
A	15.7	74	42	NE	641.4
M	19.1	68	23	NE	804.6
J	23.4	64	11	NE	787.7
J	25.9	62	1	NE	758.8
A	26.6	65	11	NE	694.0
S	24.6	71	37	NE	476.5
O	20.4	74	56	W	481.5
N	15.9	78	57	W	299.7
D	12.4	78	70	W	236.3

*Data indicate astronomically possible global radiation; microclimatic effects not taken into account.
Source: Temperature, relative humidity, and precipitation—World Meteorological Organization. *Climatological Normals (CLINO) for CLIMAT and CLIMAT Ship Stations for the Period 1931–1960.* Geneva: W.M.O., 1971. Global radiation—values adapted from global radiation maps in W.M.O., *Technical Note No. 172: Meteorological Aspects of the Utilization of Solar Radiation as an Energy Source;* Annex: World Maps of Relative Global Radiation. Geneva: W.M.O., 1981. (M.M.O.—No. 557); Winds—Besim Hakim. *Sidi Bou Said, Tunisia: A Study of Structure and Form.* Halifax, Nova Scotia: School of Architecture, Nova Scotia Technical College, 1978.

DARB QIRMIZ QUARTER CAIRO, EGYPT

Project Documentation. Credits, Project Timetable, and information on the origin of human and material resources listed in the Project Geography have been provided in the Award documentation by the technical reviewer, Ronald Lewcock, and by the client and restoration personnel.

1. Project Personnel. Client: Egyptian Antiquities Organization (E.A.O.), Islamic Section (director, Abd al-Tawab). Restoration: E.A.O. and German Archaeological Institute, Cairo (project leader 1973–1979, Michael Meinecke;* project leader 1979–, Philipp Speiser;** architect, Muhammad Fahmy Awad; site supervisor, A. A. Awad). Master craftsmen: S. M. al-Habbal, S. H. Muhammad, I. Abd al-Mun'im. Project funding: financial contribution from the government of the Federal Republic of Germany; expertise provided free of charge by the E.A.O. and the German Archaeological Institute. The E.A.O. also provided decorative features such as woodwork, marble columns, and capitals, etc., free of charge from old buildings and from their reserves.

*Born in Vienna, Austria, in 1941, Michael Meinecke completed his doctorate in faience decorations on Seljuk religious buildings in Anatolia, Turkey, at Hamburg University in 1968. From 1969 to 1977 he was in charge of the Islamic Section of the Cairo branch of the German Archaeological Institute and was a guest lecturer at Cairo University's Faculty of Archaeology in 1974 and 1975. In 1978 he wrote a thesis on Mamluk architecture in Egypt and Syria and since then has taught the history of Islamic art at Hamburg University's Institute for History and Culture of the Near East. In 1979 he was appointed a member of the German Archaeological Institute's Damascus branch. Meinecke's scientific projects since the mid-1960s include a survey of the medieval architecture of Turkey (1964–1968), comparative studies in Turkistan (1966), participation in the excavation of Abu Mena, near Alexandria, Egypt (1969), comparative studies in Iraq (1972, 1975) and Iran (1972), a survey of pre-Ottoman architecture in Syria and Eastern Anatolia, Turkey (1973–1975), studies in the achievements of Islamic artists (1978–1979), and an architectural survey of the Al-Salihiya quarter in Damascus, Syria, and various fieldwork projects also in Syria (1985–).

Meinecke's involvement in architectural conservation projects includes the restoration of the Madrasa of Sabiq al-Din Mitqal al-Anuki, Cairo (1973–1976), a report on the reactivation of Al-Dir'iya, Saudi Arabia (1974), restoration of the Tomb of Sheik Sinan, Cairo (1976–1978), and a survey for UNESCO of the Al-Gamaliya quarter, Cairo, aimed at its rehabilitation (1977–1978). Since 1976, Meinecke has been a consultant for restoration projects of the American Research Center in Cairo.

**Born in Bern, Switzerland, in 1951, Philipp Speiser was a student of architecture in both Zurich and London between 1971 and 1977, graduating in architecture from Zurich's Institute of Technology in 1977. Between 1977 and 1979, he was a fellow of the Swiss Institute of Archaeology, Cairo, and participated in a number of excavations. Since then he has been the project leader for the conservation of projects undertaken by the Cairo branch of the German Archaeological Institute and since 1980 a part-time lecturer in the restoration of Islamic monuments at Cairo University's Faculty of Archaeology. He is currently working on the restoration of the fourteenth-century palace of Bastak al-Nasiri in Cairo and the excavation of Islamic monuments in Busra, Syria, and he is also conducting research into the history of conservation in Cairo.

2. Project Timetable. 1973–1976: Madrasa of Sabiq al-Din Mitqal al-Anuki; Tomb of Sheik Sinan. 1979–1983: Madrasa of Tatar al-Hiǧaziya. 1979–1984: Fountain of Abd al-Rahman Kathuda. 1983–: Palace of Bastak al-Nasiri; Wakalat Bazaar; Madrasa of Gamal al-Din Yusuf al-Ustadar.

3. Project Geography. Cairo, Egypt: 1) client, 2) architect, 3) master craftsmen (masons, plasterers, carpenters), 4) stone, 5) woodwork, 6) marble, 7) glazed ceramics, 8) plaster work, 9) ashlar limestone blocks, 10) stone paving blocks, 11) gypsum, 12) glass lamps. Federal Republic of Germany: 1) architect, 2) restoration, 3) funding.

4. Project Area. Site: Madrasa of Sabiq al-Din Mitqal al-Anuki, 400 square meters; Tomb of Sheik Sinan, 50 square meters; Fountain of Abd al-Rahman Kathuda, 105 square meters; Madrasa of Tatar al-Hiǧaziya, 400 square meters.

5. Climate data. Cairo, Egypt: latitude, 30° 08' N.; longitude, 31° 34' E.; altitude, 95 m.

Month	Temperature (°C.)	Relative Humidity (%)	Precipitation (mm.)	Wind Direction	Wind Velocity (m./sec.)
J	14.0	57.0	4	NE/SW	4
F	15.0	54.0	5	NE/SW	4
M	17.5	48.5	3	N	4
A	21.0	44.5	1	N	4
M	25.5	40.5	1	N	4
J	27.5	45.5	0	N	3
J	28.5	51.5	0	N	3
A	28.5	54.5	0	N	3
S	26.0	55.0	0	NE	3
O	24.0	53.0	1	NE	3
N	20.0	58.0	1	NE	3
D	15.5	59.0	8	NE	3

Source: Temperature, precipitation, wind velocity, and wind direction—*Climates of Africa*, J. F. Griffiths, ed. Amsterdam: Elsevier Publishing Company, 1972 (World Survey of Climatology, Vol. 10). Relative humidity—*Africa, the Atlantic Ocean South of 35°N. and the Indian Ocean*, Part 4, tables of temperature, relative humidity, precipitation, and sunshine for the world, Meteorological Office, London, 1983.

SHEREFUDIN'S WHITE MOSQUE VISOKO, YUGOSLAVIA

Project Documentation. Credits, Project Timetable, and information on the origin of human and material resources listed in the Project Geography have been provided in the Award documentaton by the technical reviewer, Atilla Yücel, and by the architect.

1. Project Personnel. Client: Muslim community of Visoko. Architect: Zlatko Ugljen.* Engineer: D. Malkin. Project promotion and funding: 94 per cent voluntary contributions from the Muslim community; 4 per cent from Yugoslavs working abroad; 2 per cent from Saudi Arabia. Construction: Zvijezda, Visoko. Consultants: Institute of Architecture and Urban Planning of the University of Sarajevo. Contractor: Islamic Council of Bosnia and He.zegovina, Croatia, and Slovenia.

*Born in Mostan, Yugoslavia, in 1929, Zlatko Ugljen graduated in 1958 from the Faculty of Architecture at the University of Sarajevo, where he is currently a professor of design. He also heads a group of designers at the Institute for Architecture and Space Planning in Sarajevo. The architect of several residential and public buildings, motels, and hotels in Yugoslavia, Zlatko Ugljen has also designed the interiors of a number of nightclubs, shops, theaters, art galleries, and hotels, including the St. George Hotel in Jerusalem. He is the winner of many community and professional awards as well as of architectural competitions.

2. Project Timetable. 1967: Program development begun. 1968: Preliminary site work started. 1970–1980: Construction work carried out. 1980 (September 7): Dedication of mosque.

3. Project Geography. Yugoslavia: 1) architect, 2) labor, 3) craftsmen, 4) consultants, 5) carpet, 6) travertine tiles, 7) iron tubes, 8) cement, 9)

pine wood. Saudi Arabia: 2 per cent funding.

4. Project Area. Built up: 435 square meters.

5. Climate Data. Visoko, Yugoslavia: latitude, 43° 57' N.; longitude, 18° 11' E.; altitude, 490 m.; distance from Sarajevo, 24 km.

Month	Temperature (°C.)	Relative Humidity (%)	Precipitation (mm.)	Global Radiation (cal. cm^{-2} day^{-1})
J	−0.65	79.5	66	115.75
F	0.75	74.0	64	197.75
M	6.10	70.0	62	298.00
A	10.65	65.5	64	358.50
M	14.50	67.0	90	424.25
J	18.50	65.5	88	442.75
J	20.85	63.5	71	503.50
A	20.90	60.5	70	400.75
S	16.40	67.0	78	309.00
O	11.35	73.5	103	201.00
N	6.10	78.0	91	114.00
D	3.15	79.5	85	80.00

Source: Temperature, relative humidity, and precipitation—*Europe and the Azores*, Part 3, tables of temperature, relative humidity, precipitation, and sunshine for the world, Meteorological Office, London 1973. Solar radiation—*Solar Radiation and Radiation Balance Data: Annual Data 1974–1979*, Part 2, pub. by the U.S.S.R. State Committee for Hydrometeorology and Control of Natural Environment, Leningrad, 1983.

ANDALOUS RESIDENCE SOUSSE, TUNISIA

Project Documentation. Credits, Project Timetable, and information on the origin of human and material resources listed in the Project Geography have been provided in the Award documentation by the technical reviewer, Dorothée Vauzelles, and by the architect.

1. Project Personnel. Client: Consortium Tuniso-Kowëitien de Développement. Architects: Serge Santelli* with Cabinet GERAU, Mausour Cherif. Contractor: SOMATRA. Tile makers: SOCER. Funding: 60 per cent from the Kuwait Fund for Arab Economic Development through the Consortium Kowëitien d'Investissement Immobilier.

*French architect and planner Serge Santelli studied architecture at the École des Beaux-Arts in Paris. A Harkness Fellow at the University of Pennsylvania (1968–1970), he studied for a master's degree under Louis Kahn. Of the many architectural competitions he has taken part in, he won first prize for a housing design at Reims (now under construction) and received an honorable mention in the competition for the French national opera house at the Bastille. His many conversions in Paris have included the Tsukizi Japanese restaurant and the Tagore restaurant. During the 1970–1971 academic year he was assistant professor in the department of architecture at the College of Arts and Sciences, Pennsylvania State University, and he has also taught at the Institut Technologique d'Art, d'Architecture, et d'Urbanisme de Tunis and at the Unité Pédagogique d'Architecture No. 8 in Paris. He

has carried out research at IERAU under the direction of Bernard Huet and has himself directed an investigation into the space structure of the Arab-Islamic city, with particular reference to the three medinas of Tunis. He has written numerous articles, which have been published in *Mimar*, *Architecture d'Aujourd'hui*, *Monuments Historiques*, and other journals.

2. Project Timetable. 1977 (October): Program started. 1977 (December): Program completed and planning started. 1978 (September): Planning completed. 1979 (April): Construction started. 1980 (December): Construction completed. 1981 (June): Apartment hotel opened to the public.

3. Project Geography. Sousse, Tunisia: 1) associated architects, 2) contractor, 3) consulting engineers, 4) labor (20 per cent skilled including craftsmen, 80 per cent unskilled) 5) management staff of hotel, 6) cement, 7) cast concrete, 8) brick, 9) tiles including pink cement tiles, 10) gray marble, 11) Agglo-marble, 12) stone of the Keddel type, 13) wood. Nabeul, Tunisia: 1) traditional tiles, France: 1) architect. Kuwait: 1) 60 per cent of funding.

4. Project Area. Site: 3.3 hectares. Built up: 10,150 square meters.

5. Climate Data. Sousse, Tunisia: latitude, 35° 49' N.; longitude, 10° 38' E.; altitude, 6 m.

Month	Temperature (°C.)	Relative Humidity (%)	Precipitation (mm.)
J	11.90	72.5	31
F	13.70	69.5	17
M	16.20	71.0	22
A	19.10	74.0	32
M	21.05	75.0	14
J	27.00	73.0	4
J	28.55	72.0	1
A	28.80	74.5	17
S	26.65	76.5	18
O	21.60	75.0	48
N	17.35	71.5	36
D	13.90	73.0	42

Source: Temperature, relative humidity, precipitation—*Africa, the Atlantic Ocean South of 35 N and the Indian Ocean*, Part 4, Meteorological Office, London, 1983.

HAJJ TERMINAL KING ABDUL AZIZ INTERNATIONAL AIRPORT, JIDDA, SAUDI ARABIA

Project Documentation. Credits, Project Timetable, and information on the origin of human and material resources listed in the Project Geography have been provided in the Award documentation by the technical reviewer, H. Abdel Halim, and by the architects.

1. Project Personnel. Client: Ministry of Defense and Aviation, Saudi Arabia. Architects: Skidmore, Owings, and Merrill, New York and Chicago (partners-in-charge: R. O. Allen, Raul De Armas, G. Bunshaft, P. Gujral, Fazlur R. Khan,* G. Wildermuth, J. Winkler). General contractor: Hochtief AG Essen, Federal Republic of Germany. Contractor for fabric roof system:

Owens-Corning Saudi Company, (a joint venture between Owens-Corning and Olayan Saudi Holdings Company, Ltd.). Fabric manufacturers and roof-panel fabricators: Owens-Corning Fiberglas Corp., in association with U.R.S. Corp. Engineering consultants: Gieger-Berger Associates. Construction management: Saudi Arabian Parsons Ltd./Daniel International Ltd. (a joint venture company). Administration: General Said Y. Amin, director; Mohammad Dakhman.

'The chief structural engineer for the Sears Tower in Chicago, the world's tallest building, Fazlur R. Khan was born in Dacca, Bangladesh, and received his Bachelor of Engineering degree from the University of Dacca in 1950. In the United States he studied at the University of Illinois, Champaign-Urbana, where he received a master's degree in structural engineering and in theoretical and applied mechanics and a doctorate in structural engineering.

In 1955 he joined the Chicago office of the architectural/engineering firm of Skidmore, Owings, and Merrill, and achieved international distinction for the unique and innovative bundled-tube and long-span structural systems he designed for a wide range of award-winning buildings.

In recognition for his outstanding contribution to the profession Khan was elected a fellow by the American Society of Civil Engineers and the American Concrete Institute. He was also a member of the National Academy of Engineering and chairman of the International Council on Tall Buildings and Urban Habitat. Author of numerous scholarly papers and engineering publications, Khan received many awards from national and international professional organizations and was cited four times by *Engineering News Record* as Construction Man of the Year. He died in 1982.

2. Project Timetable. Early 1960s: Plans formulated. 1974: Design commenced. 1979: Full-sized model of one unit built and tested. 1981: Structure officially opened. 1982: Project finally completed.

3. Project Geography. Saudi Arabia: 1) client, 2) cement. United States: 1) architects, 2) Teflon-coated fiberglass roofing fabric, 3) skilled labor. Japan: 1) steel pylons. Philippines: 1) skilled labor. Pakistan: 1) unskilled labor. Federal Republic of Germany: 1) skilled labor. Great Britain: 1) skilled labor. France: 1) cables.

4. Project Area. Site: 105 square kilometers. Built up: 40.5 hectares.

5. Climate Data. Jidda, Saudi Arabia: latitude, 21° 30′ N.; longitude, 39° 12′ E.; altitude, 17 m.

Month	Temperature (°C.)	Relative Humidity (%)	Precipitation (mm.)	Wind Direction	Wind Velocity (Kts.)	Solar Radiation (Langleys)
J	23.3	66	23.6	N	9	267
F	23.9	60	11.1	N	10	296
M	25.4	58	0.4	N–NNW	8	404
A	27.4	57	7.3	N–NNW	8	483
M	29.7	57	1.5	N–NNW	8	561
J	30.7	59	T	N–NNW	8	465
J	32.0	56	0.1	NNW	7	460
A	32.0	59	T	N–NW	8	454
S	30.8	68	0.1	N	10	398
O	29.1	67	0.5	NW	5	346
N	27.1	62	15.6	N–NW	6	293
D	24.7	60	10.2	NNW	7	237

Source: Temperature, humidity, precipitation, wind direction, wind velocity, and solar radiation—Meteorology and Environmental Protection Administration (MEPA), Kingdom of Saudi Arabia, courtesy of the president of MEPA and secretary-general of the Environmental Protection Coordinating Committee, Romaih M. Al Romaih.

RAMSES WISSA WASSEF ARTS CENTER GIZA, EGYPT

Project Documentation. Credits, Project Timetable, and information on the origin of human and material resources listed in the Project Geography have been provided in the Award documentation by the technical reviewer, Piers Rodgers, and by the client.

1. Project Personnel. Client: Ramses Wissa Wassef, his family, and the community of weavers. Architects: Ramses Wissa Wassef,' Badie Habib Gorgy. Civil engineer: Ikram Nosshi.

'Born in Cairo in 1911, Ramses Wissa Wassef graduated in architecture from the École des Beaux Arts in Paris. In 1938 he was appointed lecturer in architecture and the history of art at the École des Beaux Arts in Cairo and in 1965 became head of that department. In 1969 he resigned to devote himself to research in art.

In his architecture he used such natural building materials as baked and unbaked brick, and large blocks of limestone. The style he eventually developed took into account aesthetics, climatic conditions, and economy while still maintaining a strong, living link to the past.

His best-known works include the village of New Gourna, near Luxor, Egypt, carried out in collaboration with Hassan Fathy; the French Lycée in Heliopolis; the small *lycée* in Bab el-Louk; the two churches of Zamâlik and Heliopolis; his villa at Agouza; the art center at Harraniya; the Dominican Chapel, 'Abbâsiya, Cairo; the Moukhtar Museum at Gezira, Cairo; and several villas bordering the road to Saqqara. Wissa Wassef also revived ancient craft techniques such as the Oriental windows of colored plaster and glass that won him the National Art Prize in 1961.

Concluding that the artist finds himself too late, by which time his creative energy has already been compromised by an educational system that is both abstract and dry, Wissa Wassef decided to concentrate on children and chose weaving as a means for them to express their artistic talents. As a result dozens of workshops were established in Egypt, introducing a national craft that created openings for thousands of young people.

Wissa Wassef was one of the first to give his country an original architectural style that married past and present. He aimed at the revival of the crafts of weaving, ceramics, batik, and glass, and at the reintegration of all the arts. He proved that the best way to regenerate art was to recognize the rights of all human beings to creative activity, and to give that right back to them.

2. Project Timetable. The center evolved over 20 years. 1954–1957: Ramses Wissa Wassef's house and workshop (before modification and extensions). 1955–1970: Farm buildings. 1960–1964, 1969: Children's workshops. 1964: Tapestry showrooms. 1967–1968: Habib Gorgy Museum. 1970–1971: Ceres Wissa Wassef's house. 1971–1973: Mounir Nosshi's house. 1972–1974: Seven weaver's houses.

3. Project Geography. Harraniya, Giza, Egypt:

1) architect, 2) craftsmen (including children), 3) labor (including children), 4) mud brick, 5) gypsum, 6) sand, 7) mud mortar, 8) cement, 9) lime, 10) limestone, 11) porous red brick, 12) red-brick tiles, 13) antique hand basins, 14) marble, 15) tapestry, 16) pottery.

4. Project Area. Site: 3,000 square meters.

5. Climate Data. Giza, Egypt: latitude, 29° 59′ N.; longitude, 31° 08′ E.; altitude, 19 m; distance from center of Cairo, 6.5 km.

Month	Temperature (°C.)	Relative Humidity (%)	Precipitation (mm.)	Wind Velocity (m./sec.)	Wind Direction
J	14.0	57.0	4	4	NE/SW
F	15.0	54.0	5	4	NE/SW
M	17.5	48.5	3	4	N
A	21.0	44.5	1	4	N
M	25.5	40.5	1	4	N
J	27.5	45.5	0	3	N
J	28.5	51.5	0	3	N
A	28.5	54.5	0	3	N
S	26.0	55.0	0	3	NE
O	24.0	53.0	1	3	NE
N	20.0	58.0	1	3	NE
D	15.5	59.0	8	3	NE

Source: Temperature, precipitation, wind velocity, and wind direction—*Climates of Africa*, J. F. Griffiths, ed., Amsterdam: Elsevier Publishing Company, 1972 (World Survey of Climatology, Vol. 10). Relative humidity—*Africa, the Atlantic Ocean South of 35° N and the Indian Ocean*, Part 4, tables of temperature, relative humidity, precipitation, and sunshine for the world, Meteorological Office, London, 1983.

TANJONG JARA BEACH HOTEL AND RANTAU ABANG VISITOR'S CENTER TRENGGANU, MALAYSIA

Project Documentation. Credits, Project Timetable, and information on the origin of human and material resources listed in the Project Geography have been provided in the Award documentaton by the technical reviewer, Syed Zaigham Jaffery, and by the architects.

1. Project Personnel. Client: Tourist Development Corporation (T.D.C.) of Malaysia/Pempena Consult (from T.D.C.: Tan Sri Philip Kuok, chairman; Dato Baharuddin bin-Musa, formerly director general, now retired; Mohammed Ikbal bin-Mohammed Hamzah, deputy director general; Azizan bin-Mustafa, director—from Pempena Consult: Terry Kenaston, formerly director, Project Management, now director, Development PATA Head Office; Madeline Regis, formerly operations manager, now sales manager, Kuala Lumpur Regent Hotel; Sulaiman Rahmat, sales manager). Architects: Wimberly, Whisenand, Allison, Tong, and Goo, Honolulu (Pete Wimberly, Gerald Allison); Arkitek Bersikutu Malaysia (Daud Joyce, Ong Guan Teck). Landscape architects: Bert, Collins, and Associates, Honolulu (Raymond F. Cain); Master craftsmen: Abdul Latif, wood carver; Nik Rahman, tilemaker. Interior design: Juru Haisan Consult of Malaysia

(Alan Loke). Consultants: Stantly Consultants (for electrical and mechanical services).

2. *Project Timetable.* 1960: First proposal to construct tourist accommodations consisting of a ten-room motel at the Rantau Abang site. The proposal fell through because of disagreement on the architectural design. 1971: Design concept for the Tanjong Jara Beach Hotel and Rantau Abang Visitor's Center first proposed in a tourism study commissioned by T.D.C. of Malaysia. 1973: Local firm of architects "Team Three" asked by T.D.C. to prepare a design for a resort complex. 1975: Groundbreaking for the design presented by Team Three begun. Original design concept abandoned and new study commissioned resulting in the construction of two separate tourist facilities—one a 100-room beach hotel, the other a museum/crafts/bazaar/visitor's center, at two separate sites 10 kilometers apart. 1977: Construction on beach hotel and visitors' center begun. 1980 (June): Visitors' center opened to the public. 1980 (November): Beach hotel opened to the public.

3. *Project Geography.* Malaysia: 1) architects, 2) craftsmen, 3) labor, 4) contractors and subcontractors, 5) tiles, 6) hardwoods: *chengol, balan, kapor, nyatoh,* 7) softwoods, 8) lampshades, 9) carved panels, 10) construction technology, 11) soap dishes (halved coconut shells), 12) wicker chairs, 13) woven mats. United States: 1) architects.

4. *Project Areas.* Located on the east coast of Malaysia, 65 and 55 kilometers south of Kuala Trengganu respectively, the hotel site covers 31.6 hectares and the visitors'-center site 6.07 hectares.

5. *Climate Data.* Kuala Trengganu, Malaysia: latitude, 5° 20′ N.; longitude, 103° 08′ E.; altitude, 35.1 m.

Month	Temperature (°C.)	Relative Humidity (%)	Precipitation (mm.)	Wind Velocity (m./sec.)	Wind Direction	Global Radiation (mWHr cm⁻²)
J	25.0	84.0	174.4	3.2	N/E	486.7
F	25.6	83.7	99.7	3.1	N/E	532.2
M	26.3	83.5	109.3	2.7	N/E	592.7
A	27.0	84.4	101.6	2.5	S/W	582.0
M	27.3	84.7	103.2	2.5	S/W	553.3
J	26.9	85.3	108.4	2.3	S/W	485.8
J	26.5	85.3	110.0	2.3	S/W	488.0
A	26.5	85.7	141.8	2.3	S/W	492.7
S	26.3	86.2	184.2	2.3	S/W	500.9
O	26.1	87.6	266.4	2.3	S/W	457.0
N	25.4	89.7	643.0	2.5	N/E	369.4
D	25.3	87.2	559.8	3.5	N/E	354.1

Source: Temperature, relative humidity, precipitation, wind velocity, wind direction, and global radiation from the records of the Climatological Division of the Malaysian Meterological Service, courtesy of the director-general, Abraham David.

GREAT MOSQUE OF NIONO NIONO, MALI

Project Documentation. Credits, Project Timetable, and information on the origin of human and material resources listed in the Project Geography have been provided in the Award documentation by the technical reviewer, Raoul Snelder, and by the master mason.

1. *Project Personnel.* Client: Muslim community of Niono. Designer/master mason: Lassiné Minta.* Project promotion and funding: local Muslim community of Niono.

*Lassiné Minta is originally from Djenné, Mali, and came to Niono in 1940 after having worked on the construction of the dam at Markala.

2. *Project Timetable.* 1948: Original mosque completed. 1955, 1969: Design. 1955–1956 and 1960–1963: Main building enlarged. 1969–1973: Main building further enlarged and new sections added. 1973: Main body of work completed. 1983: Caretaker's room converted into sepulcher for first imam.

3. *Project Geography.* Niono, Mali: 1) designer/master mason, 2) labor, 3) craftsmen, 4) sun-dried clay bricks, 5) timber/palmyra sticks, 6) rendering made of clay and hardened rice bran, 7) clay mortar. Ivory Coast: 1) wood. France: 1) galvanized laminated steel, 2) metal sections.

4. *Project Area.* Site: 1,980 square meters (33 x 60 meters). Built up: main building, 726 square meters; women's room, 140 square meters; annexes, 230 square meters; veranda, 230 square meters.

5. *Climate Data.* Niono, Mali: latitude, 14° 17′ N.; longitude, 5° 08′ W.; altitude, 277 m.; distance from Mopti, 294 miles.

Month	Temperature (°C.)	Relative Humidity (%)	Precipitation (mm.)	Wind Direction	Wind Velocity (m./sec.)	Global Radiation (calculated in Angstrom units)
J	22.2	36	0.1	NE	2.6	497
F	24.5	32	0.0	NE	2.9	545
M	28.1	29	1.3	NE	3.0	581
A	31.1	33	8.3	NE	2.5	582
M	31.9	47	33.2	SW	2.3	577
J	30.6	58	71.1	SW	2.5	569
J	28.1	68	129.0	SW	2.5	562
A	27.1	75	170.6	SW	1.9	552
S	27.5	74	60.9	SW	1.7	550
O	28.1	62	14.7	W	1.3	542
N	25.2	46	1.0	E	1.8	497
D	22.0	43	0.0	NE	2.2	461

Source: Courtesy of the Meterological Office, Ministry of Transport and Public Works, Republic of Mali.

NAIL ÇAKIRHAN HOUSE AKYAKA, TURKEY

Project Documentation. Credits, Project Timetable, and information on the origin of human and material resources listed in the Project Geography have been provided in the Award documentaion by the technical reviewer, Samir Abdulac, and by the architect.

1. *Project Personnel.* Client: Nail and Halet Çakirhan. Architect/contractor/construction/construction supervision/project promotion and funding: Nail, Çakirhan.* Carpenters: Ali Duru; Cafer Karaca.

*Born in Ula, Turkey, in 1910, Nail Çakirhan decided to become a poet and journalist after a short spell at both the medical and law schools of the University of Istanbul. His architectural career began fortuitously in the early 1950s when no architect could be found to complete an open-air museum for archaeological finds in the remote ancient Turkish village of Karatepe. Çakirhan, accompanying his archaeologist wife on this mission, became part of a team that took over and completed the project. It was his first acquaintance with concrete construction. Since then Nail Çakirhan has been involved in a number of projects, including a program to build five primary schools; workshops and lodgings for teachers; a building for the Turkish Historical Society; the restoration of a timber house on the Bosporus belonging to his parents-in-law; and the contract for a German school in Ankara. To date he has designed eighteen houses in Akyaka, a house in Marmaris, a motel and seaside restaurant in the town of Datça, a house in Bodrum, and several other houses. His restoration works include two houses in Bodrum, one house in Ula, and the 400-year-old tower of Mustafa Pasha in Musbegi.

2. *Project Timetable.* 1970 (September): Design laid out on site; foundations, framework, walls, and roof completed in forty-five days. 1971 (June): Woodwork completed within twenty-one days; built-in furniture and finishes completed within fifteen days. 1972: Landscaping undertaken.

3. *Project Geography.* Akyaka, Turkey: 1) architect, 2) client, 3) carpenters, 4) masons, 5) timber, 6) brick, 7) furnishings, 8) *alaturka* tiles, 9) cement mortar.

4. *Project Area.* Site: 2,000 square meters. Built up: house, 147 square meters; caretaker's lodge, 48 square meters.

5. *Climate Data.* Akyaka/Marmaris Region, Muğla Province, Turkey: latitude, 36° 56′ N.; longitude, 28° 49′ E.; altitude, 200 m.

Month	Temperature (°C.)	Relative Humidity (%)	Precipitation (mm.)	Wind Direction 1st and 2nd	Wind Velocity (m./sec.)	Solar Radiation* (cal/cm²/min)
J	12.25	76	226.2	N–NW N	3.4	146.15
F	12.95	75	145.0	N–NW N	3.3	197.33
M	15.05	74	93.0	N–NW N	3.0	287.67
A	17.95	74	41.9	N N–NW	2.7	367.09
M	22.35	70	23.2	N N–NW	2.5	443.58
J	27.15	62	2.8	W–NW N–NW	2.8	495.11
J	29.25	62	0.7	W–NW NW/N–NW	3.1	503.30
A	29.60	63	0.3	W–NW NW/N–NW	3.0	473.22
S	26.45	66	41.7	N–NW N	2.6	373.58
O	22.25	72	90.6	N N–NW	2.3	268.10
N	18.10	77	141.1	N–NW N	2.3	173.70
D	14.15	81	301.1	N N–NW	3.5	122.38

Source: "Meteoroloji Bulteni, Ortalama ve Ekstreem Kiymetler" ("Meteorological Bulletin—Average and Extreme Figures"), Turkish State Meteorological Institute, 1974.

*General values for Muğla Province.

AZEM PALACE
DAMASCUS, SYRIA

Project Documentation. Credits, Project Timetable, and information on the origin of human and material resources listed in the Project Geography have been provided in the Award documentation by the technical reviewer, Ronald Lewcock, and by Shafiq al-Imam.

1. *Project Personnel.* Client: General Directorate of Antiquities and Museums, Syria. Architects: Lucien Cavaro (deceased); Michel Ecochard (before 1951); Shafiq al-Imam (since 1951); Zaki al-Emir (before 1946), director of the workshop when the restoration was under the French.

2. *Project Timetable.* 1925: Restoration work begun. 1946: Work begun again after a gap. 1954: National folk museum consisting only of *haremlik* opened to the public. Early 1960s: Restoration work on *salemlik* begun.

3. *Project Geography.* Damascus, Syria: 1) client, 2) conservator, 3) supervisors, 4) labor, 5) craftsmen, 6) marble, 7) stone, 8) wood, 9) lime, 10) gypsum, 11) earth clay, 12) cement, 13) limestone.

4. *Project Area.* Site: 6,400 square meters. Built up: 3,000 square meters.

5. *Climate Data.* Damascus, Syrian Arab Republic: latitude, 33° 29′ N.; longitude, 36° 14′ E.; altitude, 729 m.

Month	Temperature (°C.)	Relative Humidity (%)	Precipitation (mm.)	Wind Direction	Wind Velocity (m./sec.)	Solar Radiation (cal/cm²)
J	7.1	71	50.6	W	2.7	247
F	8.6	65	36.0	W	3.3	349
M	11.8	55	26.5	W	4.0	455
A	16.2	46	16.1	WNW	4.3	542
M	21.0	38	6.5	WNW	4.1	638
J	25.1	34	0.1	NW	4.1	712
J	26.8	36	T	WNW	4.9	611
A	26.9	38	T	WNW	4.2	635
S	24.1	41	0.2	WNW	3.0	539
O	20.0	45	8.3	E	2.5	412
N	13.8	58	28.2	E	2.1	311
D	8.6	71	48.4	W	2.2	255

Source: Temperature, relative humidity, precipitation, wind direction, wind speed, and solar radiation from the Meteorological Department, Ministry of Defence, Syrian Arab Republic, courtesy of the director-general, A. W. Kabakibo.

TOMB OF
SHAH RUKN-I-'ALAM
MULTAN, PAKISTAN

Project Documentation. Credits, Project Timetable, and information on the origin of human and material resources listed in the Project Geography have been provided in the Award documentation by the technical reviewer, Ronald Lewcock, and by the conservators.

1. *Project Personnel.* Client: Government of Punjab, Pakistan. Conservators: Awqaf Department of the Punjab under the direction of the project supervisor Muhammad Wali Ullah Khan.* Site supervisor: Talib Hussain. Subengineer:

Bushir Ahmed. Master tilemaker: K. Allah Divaya. Assistant tilemaker: Kashigai Nazar Hussain. Woodcarver: Abdul Wahid. Mason: Haji Rahim Bukhsh (deceased). Draughtsman/photographer: Imtiaz Ahmed.

*Trained as an engineer, Muhammad Wali Ullah Khan spent fifty-two years in the preservation of ancient and archaeological monuments in Pakistan. His contribution won him the Tamgha-i-Imtiaz (Medal of Distinction) from the Pakistani government in 1962 and the Tamgha-i-Pakistan in 1971. In 1981 he organized an exhibition in Islamabad of twenty-four mason crafts used in Pakistan's Islamic architecture.

2. *Project Timetable.* 1971: Restoration work begun. 1977: Restoration work completed.

3. *Project Geography.* Pakistan: 1) client, 2) project supervisor/conservator, 3) craftsmen, 4) site supervisor, 5) subengineer, 6) tiles, 7) baked brick, 8) timber/wood, 9) carved woodwork, 10) stone, 11) electrical materials, 12) cement.

4. *Project Area.* Site: 6,303 square meters. Built up: 600 square meters.

5. *Climate Data.* Multan, Pakistan: latitude, 30° 12′ N.; longitude, 71° 26′ E.; altitude, 123 m.

Month	Temperature (°C.)	Relative Humidity (%)	Precipitation (mm.)	Wind Direction 0300	Wind Direction 1200	Wind Velocity km./hr.	Global Radiation (cal/cm²) 1975
J	12.3	64.0	10.7	NNE	N	2.76	298
F	15.9	61.5	7.6	NNE	N	3.86	397
M	21.5	56.0	22.6	NNE	NNW	4.60	497
A	27.5	44.0	10.4	NNE	NNW	5.15	565
M	32.2	39.0	12.7	NE	SW	6.26	610
J	36.1	44.0	5.8	S	SSW	10.30	588
J	34.1	76.5	33.8	S	SW	9.40	552
A	33.3	84.0	32.0	S	SSW	9.00	514
S	31.7	68.0	22.9	S	S	6.80	545
O	26.1	50.0	1.0	SSE	SSW	3.86	391
N	19.1	43.0	7.4	NE	NNW	2.00	364
D	14.1	52.0	13.5	NNE	N	2.56	278

Source: Temperature, relative humidity, precipitation, wind direction, and wind velocity Pakistan Meteorological Department, courtesy of senior meteorologist for the director general of Meteorological Services Arshad Noor Khan, and also Kamil Khan Mumtaz, B.K.M. Associates, Lahore, Pakistan.

SELECTED
BIBLIOGRAPHY

This bibliography is limited to the book *Architecture and Community*, published to commemorate the first Aga Khan Award (1980); the proceedings of eight seminars held under the auspices of the Aga Khan Award for Architecture; and the proceedings of four seminars offered by the Continuing Education Program of the Massachusetts Institute of Technology Laboratory of Architecture and Planning and the Harvard Graduate School of Design in collaboration with the Aga Khan Program for Islamic Architecture at Harvard and M.I.T. Each of these publications has its own extensive bibliography.

Holod, Renata, ed., with Darl Rastorfer. *Architecture and Community: Building in the Islamic World Today.* Millerton, N.Y.: Aperture, 1983.

Toward an Architecture in the Spirit of Islam. Proceedings of Seminar 1, Architectural Transformations in the Islamic World, held at Aiglemont, Gouvieux, France, April 1978. Aga Khan Award, 1978.

Conservation as Cultural Survival. Proceedings of Seminar 2, Architectural Transformations in the Islamic World, held at Istanbul, Turkey, Sept. 26–28, 1978. Aga Khan Award, 1980.

Housing Process and Physical Form. Proceedings of Seminar 3, Architectural Transformations in the Islamic World, held at Jakarta, Indonesia, March 26–29, 1979. Aga Khan Award, 1980.

Architecture as Symbol and Self-Identity. Proceedings of Seminar 4, Architectural Transformations in the Islamic World, held at Fez, Morocco, Oct. 9–12, 1979. Aga Khan Award, 1980.

Places of Public Gathering in Islam. Proceedings of Seminar 5, Architectural Transformations in the Islamic World, held at Amman, Jordan, May 4–7, 1980. Aga Khan Award, 1980.

The Changing Rural Habitat: Case Studies. Vol. 1. Proceedings of Seminar 6, Architectural Transformations in the Islamic World, held at Beijing, People's Republic of China, Oct. 19–22, 1981. Aga Khan Award, 1982.

The Changing Rural Habitat: Background Papers. Vol. 2. Proceedings of Seminar 6, Architectural Transformations in the Islamic World, held at Beijing, People's Republic of China, Oct. 19–22, 1981. Aga Khan Award, 1982.

Reading the Contemporary African City. Proceedings of Seminar 7, Architectural Transformations in the Islamic World, held at Dakar, Senegal, Nov. 2–5, 1982. Aga Khan Award, 1983.

Development and Urban Metamorphosis: Yemen at the Crossroads. Vol. 1. Proceedings of Seminar 8, Architectural Transformations in the Islamic World, held at San'a, Yemen Arab Republic, May 25–30, 1983. Aga Khan Award, 1983.

Development and Urban Metamorphosis: Yemen Background Papers. Vol. 2. Proceedings of Seminar 8, Architectural Transformations in the Islamic World, held at San'a, Yemen Arab Republic, May 25–30, 1983. Aga Khan Award, 1984.

Higher-Education Facilities. Proceedings of Seminar 1, Designing in Islamic Cultures, held at Cambridge, Mass., Aug. 18–22. 1980. Cambridge, Mass.: Aga Khan Program for Islamic Architecture, 1982.

Urban Housing. Proceedings of Seminar 2, Designing in Islamic Cultures, held at Cambridge, Mass., Aug. 17–21, 1981. Aga Khan Program for Islamic Architecture, 1982.

Adaptive Reuse: Integrating Traditional Areas into the Modern Urban Fabric. Proceedings of Seminar 3, Designing in Islamic Cultures, held at Cambridge, Mass., Aug. 16–20, 1982. Aga Khan Program for Islamic Architecture, 1983.

Continuity and Change: Design Strategies for Large-Scale Urban Development. Proceedings of Seminar 4, Designing in Islamic Cultures, held at Cambridge, Mass., Aug. 15–19, 1983. Aga Khan Program for Islamic Architecture, 1984.

Overleaf: Ramses Wissa Wassef Arts Center. Young weavers turn out their famous tapestries.